gail.of wind

A HARD WALK INTO REALITY

A memoir by
GAIL DUGUAY

To: Judy
Two feet + a heart beat!
Gail Duguay
2018

LOCOMOTIVE
PRESS

This book is dedicated
in loving memory of Cory, and to you Jaycee,
for mere words cannot describe
the laughter and joy you have given me.

EDITOR
Nan Jeffrey

COPY EDITOR
Lindy Coggeshall

BOOK DESIGN
Ryan Hutchinson

Locomotive Press
locomotivepress@gmail.com

Gail of Wind - A Hard Walk Into Reality. A memoir by Gail Duguay.
ISBN: 978-1-55383-229-4

First Canadian edition published 2009.

Printed in Canada on chlorine-free paper made with 100% post-consumer
waste which saved the following resources: 26 fully grown trees, 9,494
gallons of water, 1,107 pounds of solid waste, and 2,099 pounds of
greenhouse gases. Calculations based on research by Environmental
Defense and the Paper Task Force. Manufactured at Friesens Corporation.

Mixed Sources
Cert no. SW-COC-001271
© 1996 FSC
FSC

ACKNOWLEDGEMENTS

It is a privilege to thank those who have made this book a reality. To my editor Nan Jeffrey, you were brave to take this work on. With all its spelling and grammatical errors, you went above and beyond. To all the dear friends who took the time to read it, when it was nothing but a far-off dream: Jeff Wood, Diana Wood, Nathan Wiley, Alice Guergis, Natalie Guergis, Ed Guergis Sr., Laura Lee, Shaniza Sakoor, Cathy Lenihan, Nancy Quinn. To those who have steered me in the right direction, opened all the right doors and held them as I walked through: Maida Rogerson, Yvette Doucette, Susan Rodgers, Jana Laiz.

Shawn Duguay and Rita King for taking time out of your vacation to wander through such ruins, and at great risk, to get me the wallpaper, and taking pictures of Memere and Pepere's crumbling home.

Ryan Hutchinson for the design of my book, you took something so tattered and torn and turned it into a work of beauty.

To The Children's Wish Foundation, you have given more than you will ever know—a life worth living.

To John, mere words cannot express my thanks for your love and understanding. While I relived all the pain, as I typed away endlessly for hours and days through the tear-stained pages, you held your heart in my hand and gave me the strength to keep going. My undying love I give to you.

To my dear son, Jaycee, for the knowledge and wisdom you have given me. You taught me things I never could have imagined. I love you more than words can envelop.

CHAPTER ONE

Cradled in the Foothills

Cradled in the foothills of New Brunswick, lies the sleepy little logging town of Campbellton. Across from it is the border of Quebec, the two provinces are joined together by a bridge over the Restigouche River. The salmon ran wild here, and the view is breathtaking, with mountains rising on both sides of the river. But in those days, the town was not a prosperous one, for it was a place of unemployment, a place where some were more fortunate than others. The fortunate ones worked at the Mill, or on the roads or railway. People relied on fishing and hunting to keep their families fed. Most worked hard for their bread and butter. The time was August 1958, and on a warm, sunny day, a little dark-haired girl was born; part French, part Native Indian and part Irish. Who could have known that the sunny days for this child would be few and far between, that as the eldest of four children, three girls and a boy, there would be more rain than sun, more pain than joy? I was that little girl.

My very first memory was that of my mother. We were at my grandmother's house. I was perhaps three years old at the time, yet I still recall this vivid vision trying to peer past my rotund grandmother. As she stood there in the washroom doorway, she was purposely trying to block my view of my mother, whom was bent over the wash basin spewing bright red blood from her mouth; my grandmother was desperately trying to push me away, and telling me my mother had eaten something bad. I stood there with eyes wide open and frightened bearing witness to it all. The sight of blood frightened me, even as a child; I could sense that what was happening was more serious than my grandmother was admitting too. Little did I know that this was just the beginning of a life filled with constant suicide attempts by my mother.

By the time my mother was twenty-one, she was already saddled with three little girls. My father was not working, but still somehow found the money to drink and party, going on binges that lasted for days, weeks, and even months. My poor mother would work cleaning houses for the doctors and lawyers in town, while we children were bounced from one set of grandparents to the other. Coming home from work, she would find strange buttons in her bed and know they were from the young girls my dad was sleeping with. To this day I thank God for my grandparents, for without them, I would never have known what stability and love and family meant.

We children spent many of our early years at my father's parents' house. We called them Memere and Pepere, which was French for grandma and grandpa. Pepere had served in the war, then come home to work on the roads while Memere raised their six children and one adopted child, Memere's sister's daughter. All the children were grown up now except Lanie, the youngest, who was born when Memere had her life change. Lanie was only two years older than I was.

When their children grew up, Memere and Pepere had more trouble with them than when they were raising them, for they all developed a problem with alcohol and the violent behaviour that comes with it. Nor was this just a problem with my uncles, for my aunts also drank too much and became violent. Only Lanie escaped the curse of alcohol, for she would become educated and well adjusted, never causing my grandparents any grief or trouble.

Much of the grief in our lives, and those around us, was caused by the lack of education, poverty and low self-esteem as we were taught to hide our Native Indian heritage, as if it was a shameful thing. We would have to refer to ourselves as French and Irish or else we would be treated as second-class citizens, denied things like entrance to many of the stores and businesses. Later in life we would find that such a denial came at a price for us children and our children's children. We would be denied our Native Indian Status, stripped of our rights and dignities forever, never to be regained. Even after the laws changed, Dad was unable to show proof of being Native which would have guaranteed us many new rights. Instead, we continued to carry the heritage of a lost people which had devastated us for as long back as I can remember. It was a heritage of poverty and depression, of alcoholism and abuse, of violence and loneliness. Only Memere ever seemed to be able to rise above it, to show us children what life could be like, had we been born into a different set of circumstances.

Sometimes when I lie in bed, I can still envision the small little house where the strokes of love were painted deep within me. The house was white with a green trim and Pepere took great pride in it. Every year, I would sit and watch him climb up his tall ladder then dip his brush in the paint can that he had tied to the side of the ladder. And as he applied each and every stroke of paint to the little white house, I felt it was the new coat of paint that was the secret that sealed in all that love and kept it there. Pepere never told me that secret I just felt it. It had a nice screened porch on one side and the closed in one on the other.

Only the train tracks and a gravel road separated us from the mountain. The train tracks were about thirty feet from the back of the house and every time a train went by it would shake the house, as there was no foundation. Then the dishes would rattle in the cupboard and we children would shriek with laughter and do a little dance swaying back and forth to accompany the movement of the house because we thought it was such fun. Sometimes we would sit on the old wooden swing outside and Lanie would read us comic books out loud. I never really knew if she was reading them or just looking at the pictures and making it up, but to us younger ones she always seemed very intelligent. And I loved her dearly.

In front of the house would be the road, and then the bank of the river. I sometimes wonder why none of us ever got hurt living there, for we were surrounded by dangers. My grandparents' dogs were constantly getting killed by a train, or hit by a car on the road. We children would just get attached to a dog and then it would be gone.

Even now, after all these years, I can still catch a glimpse of Memere's milky white skin, and feel the soft gentle touch of her hands as she lifted me up to put me on the old wooden chair that was backless and splattered with paint. Then she would wash my face and hands and I would feel the love radiate from her, as she sang in her operatic voice, for I knew this wasn't a chore, but done from the heart. It was a magical place for a little child to be. Sometimes we would get into Memere's old wooden trunks full of wonderful dresses, and furs, and hats and we would play dress up. Memere's sister from Boston owned a dry cleaners and would send her many pretty things that the customers never came back for.

Then at night the three of us, my aunt Lanie, my sister Marilyn and me would crawl into bed with her but it would be some time before we would fall asleep. We girls would all take turns snuggling and cuddling up to Memere while she told us funny stories but we would always clamor for at least one scary story. My other sister Jody wasn't with us because she was only a baby. We would laugh and giggle until Pepere yelled at us from the other room to get to sleep. He never slept with Memere, which was just fine with us.

The walls of Memere's house were paper-thin. Actually, they were paper. We would help Memere make glue out of flour and water, then cut pretty pictures from old newspapers and catalogues and paste them to the walls. Of course, we had more fun putting our hands in the glue and making a mess than anything else. Memere would constantly be baking, and because she always encouraged us to participate in everything she did, we would bake with her. Sometimes we would pick blueberries, wild strawberries and raspberries for the pies, or go up the bluff in early fall and pick hazelnuts. They had prickly green fuzz on the outside and we would fill old burlap potato bags, then take them home and peel the green fuzz off. Our little fingers would be raw by the time we were all done, but there's nothing like the taste of eating a fresh nut. Then we would stand on the side of the road and sell them in a juice glass for ten cents. Most parents wouldn't let their children do that today, but life was much more innocent back then.

One nice, warm July day, Memere's kitchen was filled with the aroma of freshly baked buns and wild strawberry rhubarb pie. We helped her get the cold roast beef and potato salad out of the fridge, then packed everything in a big basket, along with some cold drinks, and were off to the beach for a picnic.

We loaded up into the car and Pepere was driving with Memere beside him in the front and all three of us in the back seat and out of nowhere came the most beautiful singing you ever heard. I remember thinking it was the radio, but it was my Memere singing opera like an angel.

We all sat back and enjoyed the ride. We went to the beach often in the summer. Memere would sit under a big blue and white striped umbrella because she was so pale, just like a porcelain doll. Her hair was always in pin curls and rags with a kerchief on her head, and we would laugh at her because she was so white and we were all so dark. Pepere was Native Indian and French, so I guess that's where our dark skin came from.

I hated it when the time came for us to go home to our mother and father. Our house was not like Pepere's. It had no paint, it had only old weather-beaten shingles that were rather grey and unloved just like the people inside. Dad didn't know the secret that if he just painted the house we would all feel the love. At home, there was always a party and drinking going on. Everywhere you looked there were Indians with long braids. I would hide behind the old wood stove and feel frightened most of the time. The only person who could talk me into coming out from behind the stove was my dad's friend Bernard. He would sing and play on his guitar, "There's a little white duck swimming in the water," acting out all the motions as he sang. He knew I loved that song, so I would come out and sit on Dad's lap to listen. When it was time for my sister Marilyn and me to go to bed, we would go upstairs and peek down through the grate in the floor to watch the fights and craziness that always took place. Dad's older brother, Zeb, was a scrapper and known for miles around as the guy to try and beat. Dad and Zeb would get drunk and start to fight with each other, and anyone else who happened to cross their path. Then they would cry like two babies and console each other. As young as I was, this seemed like odd behaviour. Where was Dr. Phil when you needed him?

Sometimes our lives seemed normal. Dad would take me fishing in his canoe, or he would go hunting and come home with pheasants, partridge and rabbits. I would hold the feet of the rabbits while Dad skinned them. I guess it didn't bother me to do that as I knew it meant we were going to eat well. I did not see the rabbit as Peter Cottontail, as Mom never read to us and it wasn't a priority in our home. I loved the times when Dad was sober. In the winter he would put me on his shoulders and ski down the mountain, over the train tracks, across the road and straight down into the river. My mother would be in a better frame of mind and everyone would be happy.

When I was only two years old, my mother put barrettes in my hair. One day while I was running, I fell and hit my head on an old-fashioned floor model radio, right where the barrette was. It caused a huge cyst to form which got gradually bigger over the years. By the time I was five the doctor decided it should be removed. All my black hair, which was curly and long past my bottom, was cut off. No one explained a thing to me. I remember they just put a black mask over my face and the horrible smell it gave off and I was put under in seconds. When I awoke the next morning in the hospital, the doctor had me look in the mirror, and there was my head all covered in a big white bandage which was bloody. To say the sight of it terrified me would be putting it mildly. It turned out I had had my tonsils and adenoids removed as well, yet no one ever told me anything about what was happening to me.

It was a very lonely time as it seemed like I was in the hospital forever. I would gaze out the window and wonder where I was and how far away home was. I knew when it was getting close to bedtime because I would hear the music introduction for the seven o'clock evening news with Irv Einstein, and see the nurse in her stark white uniform coming down the hospital corridor with that cold-looking, sterile, stainless steel food cart to give me apple juice and two bland social tea cookies. If I didn't eat them I knew that would be all until morning. The odd time I hear that music introduction it takes me back to the loneliness I felt so long ago. I have recollections of seeing Memere and Pepere and Lanie coming to visit me, as well as my other grandmother, but no one else. My dad must have been drunk most of the time and Mom only came on the last day to pick me up and take me home. We went straight to her mother's house, which I never liked to go to. The only thing anyone did there was play cards and speak in French the whole time. We kids were always being told to be quiet because our great-grandmother was old and didn't like noise. I could have told her that if there was any noise, it was coming from the grown-ups. We kids always felt like a burden and not wanted when we were there. Great-grandmother would just sit in her rocking chair with her rosary beads and pray in a way that sounded like mumbling to us small children. I often thought there was something not quite right about her. She always wore an apron with big pockets full of candy, but she never gave us even so much as a smell of the wrapper. We would play little games without her knowing, pretending she was a witch.

By now I was getting close to six years old and had started school with the nuns. They scared me to death with their long black dresses and never a smile. I've often wondered why people who take a vow to serve God seem so miserable and strict, as though God put it on the application form as one of the requirements for the job. At the school, everyone was in one room, with all the different classes together. I was in the same school as Lanie, which meant I had one familiar face in school.

One day there was a horrible pungent smell wafting in the air next to me. The nun asked me if I had dirtied my pants, and I said "No," it wasn't me. As she assumed I was lying, she took me outside and beat me with a leather strap until I cried my heart out. Later, on the bus ride home that night, Lanie tried to console me. I found out the next day that it was the girl sitting right behind me, but the nun never apologized and I hated her after that. She had humiliated me in front of the whole class.

Times were getting harder now. Dad still couldn't find steady work, and the little bit of money my mom was bringing in wasn't enough. Mom and Dad started talking about moving to Toronto where one of Dad's brothers, Mikey, and his family lived. Uncle Mikey had phoned Dad and told him the steel industry was booming, so there would be a job available for him. Before we knew what was happening, Dad was leaving for Toronto without us. The only way he could console us kids was to cut three curls from his curly black hair and give one to each of us, with each curl wrapped in wax paper together with a quarter. He said he would send for us once he found a place for us to live, and if we still had the curl and the quarter when we arrived in Toronto, he would give us each a dollar.

When the day came for him to leave, we all went to the train station to see him off. After we said our goodbyes and I saw the train start to pull away from the platform with him waving out the window, I started to cry uncontrollable tears. I was sure I would never see him again. When you are small, you can't comprehend distance or time; it all feels like an eternity. Even as an adult today, whenever I see a train as it passes by or hear the whistle blow, it gives me a little jolt of sadness.

After Dad left, Mom took us back to stay with Memere and Pepere. That night, when we went upstairs to bed, I asked Lanie to tell me about Toronto. What a mistake that was. As we sat in bed she told me there were lots of bad men who break into houses, so we would have to live with our windows and doors locked all the time. It would be like a prison, with no more being able to play outside. Scared out of my wits by what she had told us, I began to cry. When Memere learned what had happened, she asked Lanie why she would say such things. Lanie told her she didn't want us to move because it made her sad. She thought that maybe if we kids refused to go, then our dad would have to come back. After that, Memere sat me down and told me that Toronto was an interesting place to live with lots of fun things to do, and Dad would have a good job and we would live in a nice house and meet lots of friends so I felt reassured.

After a few months had gone by, Dad finally found us an apartment in a brownstone complex. As we still had a mortgage on our house in New Brunswick, Mom made arrangements to rent it. The house had originally been purchased for five hundred dollars, which was a big debt back then. We also had a dog, a white collie named Timmy which had belonged to a businessman who kept him fenced in as a guard dog. Timmy kept on breaking out and showing up at our house until the owner finally gave up and let us keep the dog. Now Timmy would have to be left behind for a while and sent to us later, but being so young, I couldn't understand why he wasn't coming with us now. At first I was excited about seeing my father again, but then I realized that Memere and Pepere and Lanie and the dog were going to be staying behind. I would be losing all their love and stability, and the family that I felt I really belonged to.

Once again we were at the train station, reliving all the sadness of saying goodbye. Everyone hugged and cried, and Memere said not to worry because they would come up to see us in Toronto and we would be back for visits. This time it was us on the train waving out the window as we pulled out of the station, and I felt as though my heart was in my throat. Fortunately, I was young and it didn't take long for my mood to change. It was interesting and fun on the train, with the scenery flying past like nothing I had ever seen before, and the train rocking back and forth from side to side. It felt like I was back in Memere and Pepere's house swaying back and forth again. Our first sight of Toronto was overwhelming; the huge buildings, all the traffic, the different coloured people, and everything lit up just like Christmas. Where on earth did all the people come from I wondered. I had never seen such a sight, for the most colourful people I had ever seen were Native Indians. The only reason I thought the Native Indians were different was because I would overhear it during the adult conversations. The whole experience was eye-popping for a child coming from such a small town. Only later would we realize that we had left heaven to come here. Why? Because of the poverty we lived in. We left a comparative paradise to find the proverbial pot of gold. In the end, like so many before and after us, we would end up in a rat race, longing for what we had left behind in the first place. But that was still all ahead of us, and now when we finally arrived, there was nothing but excitement.

Mom's older sister Lizzy was at the station to pick us up because Dad was working and couldn't be there. She was married to Dad's older brother Mikey, and they had two children, Conner and Laci, who were our double first cousins. Although we had never met them before, we all became instant friends. When Dad came home from work with Uncle Mikey, we were so excited we started to jump all over him. He was excited to see us, too, and the first thing he asked was whether we still had the lock of hair and the quarter. I still had mine because I had slept with it every night. Dad was thrilled when we showed them to him and gave us each five dollars instead of one. After all, Dad was making big money now—a hundred and fifty dollars a week.

It was getting late, so Uncle Mikey drove us to our new apartment, a nice little place which Aunt Lizzy had helped decorate, including toys and dolls and everything else a child could want. It didn't take long for us to become spoiled little girls, and there's nothing worse than a spoiled little girl. She grows up to be a spoiled big girl. Dad would give us the moon, and Mom would be the frugal one. Having worked like a slave for twelve dollars a week, Mom knew the real value of a dollar. She also came from a family of seven girls and three boys, with a father who had popped in once in a while to get his wife pregnant. Then he would go back to Toronto supposedly to work, but he never gave so much as a dime to his wife and kids. Mom told me later that they only had one skirt between all seven girls. At the time, however, we kids were too young to understand Mom's reasoning for being what we thought was cheap and mean. Dad was always our hero. If we asked for a quarter, he would give us a dollar. If we asked Mom, she would give us a nickel. We figured her out fast and soon learned to ask for double the money we wanted, knowing we would only get half.

School was about to begin, so we were all given new clothes. Didn't I think I was dressed in style with my frilly white blouse, green mini-skirt, white belt and white go-go boots? I was happy to be sent to St. Raymond's School because there wasn't a nun in sight. Or so I thought. They were there, just not in their traditional garb. St. Raymond's School would end up being the one door we could count on as we would eventually move so many times in our lives and go through so much uncertainty. It was our one stability. They pushed me ahead to grade two, although no one seemed sure whether my New Brunswick education had prepared me well enough.

The day finally came when Timmy was sent to us on the train. At the station, he went wild when he saw us, jumping and licking us until he almost knocked us to the ground in all the excitement. After that, he would walk us to school each morning and be back to pick us up at three-thirty. I don't know how that dog could keep time, but there he was, just like clockwork every afternoon.

It seemed like life couldn't be better at that time when we first lived in Toronto. On Christmas morning there was an amazing amount of dolls, clothes, tricycles and skates, everything a young child could want. Dad was friends with the superintendent of our apartment, so he let us make a skating rink in front of the building where all the neighbourhood children came to skate. We should have known that this was all too good to last. The first sign that our hard times weren't over was when the drinking and partying started up again on weekends. Mom would do the cooking and cleaning while Dad did the drinking, partying and fighting. It must have been the Irish in him, but the blood would fly as he continually tried to prove his manhood, thinking that strength in fighting was proof of what he needed. I don't know what dictionary he was looking in when he tried to find a definition of manhood. Of course he was illiterate, with a grade two education, so that probably explained it. But it didn't excuse it. Although Dad never cared who he fought, usually it was his brother Mikey. They had had a love-hate relationship since childhood which they never really outgrew.

It was now summertime, and every weekend we would all go to Innis Lake for the day. Dad and Uncle Mikey would be sober when we went, then drink and get into a fight, finally driving home in a drunken state. There were times when Dad was so drunk he would fall asleep at the wheel of the car and Mom would have to steer with him sleeping, his foot on the gas and a bottle of beer in his hand. If you tried to remove the beer, he would wake up. When I think about it now, it seems amazing that we were put in such a predicament, along with the other families on the road. I'm not sure how we all survived, but we did.

None of the women ever drove, or were permitted to, although my aunts would eventually learn, but not my mother. I guess it was probably for the best, as her mental capacity might not have been able to handle the responsibility. At times Mom seemed very intelligent and quite normal, despite her illness which was later revealed to be bipolar disorder. We kids could never fully depend on her when we were young and soon came to accept her illness as normal. Only later when I was an adult did our roles reverse and I found myself feeling like a mother towards her. But as a child, I could never lean on her to give me what most loving mothers gave their children, a sense of stability and support. Nothing about my mother's life had prepared her for the responsibility of parenting, for how could she give us parental support when she never received any herself? Even in her childhood she was the one who was always picked on by her older sisters and other kids. Everyone knew she was different. She had stayed in grade seven four years in a row. As a mother she could never help us with our schoolwork or any other problems we encountered as we grew up. Then, while still a teenager, she entered into a relationship with a man who never showed her any kind of love and support, a man whose idea of a relationship was strictly about sexual pleasure for him and nothing more. When the inevitable happened and Mom got pregnant, her own very stern and strict mother stood at the back of the church with a shotgun aimed straight at my dad's head. Recognizing that marriage and fatherhood was not the road my dad wanted to walk along, Grandma wasn't going to give him a choice in the matter. By age twenty-one, Mom was the mother of three young children herself and the wife of an alcoholic womanizer. That she would eventually become emotionally unstable was almost inevitable.

Before long we were moving again. This time it was a nice basement apartment, clean and a little bigger than our last place, and located right beside the school, with Christie Pitts Park across the street. Beyond the park was the Elizabeth Recreation Center which Mom immediately used as a baby-sitter for Marilyn and me.

Soon after we moved in, the landlord came downstairs to our apartment one day while Mom was in the shower and tried to attack her. When Dad got home from work and heard about it, he was so enraged; he rushed upstairs and beat the landlord senseless. No one ever reported it to the police. Instead, we just moved the next day. Luckily, there was a small house for rent just around the corner and down the street, a block away from our first apartment. At first, the place was quite a shock, for it was painted inside like a psychedelic shack. The kitchen had fire engine red walls and a black ceiling, and the sun porch was puke green with a yellow ceiling. After that, I don't remember what the rest of the rooms looked like, but Mom and her sister went right to work painting everything to cover up the mess. Once it was finished, it looked quite nice. Dad was making two hundred and fifty dollars a week now, while Mom was hired at Cutler Brands LTD, a glass and dishes factory just around the corner. The employees could buy the defects for next to nothing, so we had an abundance of dishes and stemware falling out of the cupboards.

Life wasn't too bad for us kids, but I started to notice that Dad and Mom were fighting a lot more now. Dad worked out of town, and when he came home on weekends, I would hear Mom accuse him of cheating on her. He would have phone numbers in his pockets with a name like Roland on it, but when Mom called the number, it would be a Rhonda who answered. Dad thought he was pretty slick, but Mom was always one step ahead of him. She should have kicked him out at this point, and maybe she would have except there were three kids to care for and she never had a drop of self-esteem. Dad was never any good at hiding his affairs, and the whole thing must have been emotional torture for her. When Dad got drunk he would start to smash all the nice pictures and furniture in the house instead of hitting Mom, for he knew how much it hurt her to break the nice things she had. Then he would buy them all over again when he got sober and felt guilty. What he never realized was how it was affecting us. It made us believe everything was replaceable, and that all would be forgiven no matter how badly you behaved.

When I was eight years old we had a party on Christmas Eve. The house was full of relatives and we kids were sent upstairs to bed, including all our cousins. Not that we could sleep with the racket going on. We were looking outside the window for Santa's sleigh when—bang—a car hit my uncle's brand-new Volkswagen Beetle so it flew up on the neighbour's lawn. I ran downstairs screaming the news and then everyone went nuts, running outside to see the car. I started to look around through the smoke-filled dining room at all the toys that were under the tree. There were so many you couldn't even see the tree; walking dolls as big as me, a cradle, a stove and sink set, a typewriter. How did everything get there, I wondered? We kids ended up staying up and opening all the presents because we were still wide-awake. It was the most enchanting moment of my childhood. Later that night, when he got drunk, Dad told us the truth about Santa Claus, that he was really Santa. It was never the same for me after that, for it took the joy of Christmas right away. I felt betrayed. Whenever he was drunk Dad would cry uncontrollable tears and hug us and say how much he truly loved his little babies. I would look forward to that state of drunkenness, for it was the only time I ever felt love from my parents. But Mom would soon take what little love and security I would get from him away, saying that our father only said those things because he was drunk, that it was just crocodile tears. This would leave me confused and hurt, for who was I to trust—my mom who beat me and never said she loved me, or my dad who was in tears, and looked and felt genuine when he spoke the words? That was the only time he ever showed us any emotion, just before he would turn belligerent and get into a fight with whoever crossed his path. Now, years later, I know my mother was right in a way, but we children needed to believe in that love, for it was all we had.

It was after that Christmas that Dad quit drinking. He got the basement all fixed up as a playroom that was a little girl's dream come true, with a blackboard and classroom area, so we decided we were going to teach Dad how to read. Every time Dad didn't get the answer right, we would hit him across the fingers with a yardstick, so it wasn't long before he quit and went upstairs to tell Mom we were beating the fingers right off him. He said if that was what it took to learn to read, then he would rather be illiterate. We begged Dad to give it another try, but after one more attempt, he quit once and for all, calling us little savages. We just about died laughing; we thought it was so funny.

Why were we so nasty and rebellious to the person we loved the most? What was the trigger? All the secrets Mom was flavouring within her must have been starting to manifest themselves, secrets we only learned about later, but which we paid the price for even at this early stage. All the lying and cheating that Dad did caused Mom so much pain that she had to take it out on us kids, especially as she knew that in a way we liked Dad better because he always spoiled us. When Dad was gone from home for weeks on end to work, Mom would beat us for the least little thing. Because we bore the brunt for every pain and insecurity she felt, it started to reflect in our own aggressive behaviour. None of us wanted to get on her bad side, so we treated Dad in a way we knew she would like. To this day, it affects the way I act, for I find myself always going out of my way to keep the peace and hold my tongue.

That summer, Memere, Pepere, Lanie and Dad's other sister, Mary-June, came for a visit. They arrived with a shoe box filled with hazelnuts and gifts, and it was just like old times with lots of cooking and drinking. Mary-June was quite a hot pants when it came to men. She taught us some interesting values, like how to dance and put on makeup and wear trashy clothes, even how to smoke cigarettes stolen from the adults. She stood about five foot two and had long black hair which was all teased. I guess she thought she was a showgirl, with her tons of makeup, her mini skirts and low cut blouses, and her two bowlegs which she liked to show off so much. She would take us to Christie Pitts Park, saying we were going to play, but she really went there to pick up all the men. When it came to men, Mary-June was just like a kid in a candy store. She couldn't get enough and she liked them of all different nationalities. Compared to her small hometown where she was related to most of the men who lived there, Toronto must have seemed wonderful. We kids never really understood her antics, but Memere and Pepere would look at her like she was from outer space.

We had great fun while they were visiting. One afternoon, Pepere was sitting on the verandah when he noticed a black man walking by with a limp and a cane. Leaping off the verandah, he rushed over to talk to him, and the next thing we knew, they were hugging and crying. They had been in the war together, and the other man had always thought my grandfather had died because he was shot and taken prisoner. Pepere invited him in for a beer and they talked for hours. After that, the man visited every day during Pepere's stay in Toronto, so they could relive their war memories. You would have thought they were long lost brothers. I sure was glad that was why Pepere had jumped off the verandah that first time because I was worried he might be prejudiced like my dad. Dad always had something negative to say about people of other races, warning us that when we got older he'd better not catch us with anyone of a different race. I hated it when he spoke like that because at school I played with kids of all races. To me they all seemed the same. I don't know where my father got his prejudice from, for his mom and dad weren't like that at all.

Finally the visit was over and it was time for Memere and Pepere to go home. Once again we were back at the train station, only this train was a whole lot bigger than the one we had taken from New Brunswick. Each time we said goodbye, it seemed harder than the last, as though it was somehow more final. Looking back, I realized we had experienced some good things over the summer, and some not so good. Pepere had found his war buddy, while Memere had been glad to see we had a roof over our heads and food in our bellies. Lanie had told us jokes, read to us, and made us laugh, and I guess you could say that Mary-June was our teacher of sorts. It was definitely a summer to remember.

Then it was time to go back to school and I was nine years old, going into grade four. At that age, I was old enough to attend the Friday night school dances. After the education I had received over the summer from Mary-June, I was now armed and dangerous, even at that young age. The boys were suddenly more noticeable to me, and being the spoiled girl I had become, I was always complaining that the laundry wasn't done and I needed new clothes for the dance. Dad would hand over the money so I could run down the street to buy new clothes every second Friday. After a while Dad started asking Mom why she was so busy that the laundry was never done and a fight would break out between the two of them. Well, my mother soon got smart and decided to show me how to use the old ringer washer. I was already familiar with it in a different sort of way, for it offered an escape on a rainy day, with my body huddled up to its warmth, and the hum and vibration of the motor drifting me off to sleep. Now I discovered that the innocent-seeming machine involved a scary chore as well. Before I knew what had happened, I had my arm going right through the ringer and I was screaming and yelling. Mom came running and pulled the plug out of the wall so the machine stopped, but I was in agony. When he heard about the accident that night, Dad got mad, calling Mom a lazy bitch and saying I was never to do the clothes again. After Dad went back out of town to work, Mom got quite wild, calling me a little bitch and insisting I was going to learn to clean the house and do laundry. Once she thought about it, Mom realized that she now had three girls who were old enough to do all the chores. She made a list and put it on the fridge and on Saturdays we were her little maids. When she said "clean", she meant clean the house from top to bottom, including washing the floors, ironing clothes, changing the beds, and cleaning the stove and fridge. Then she would come and inspect to make sure everything was done thoroughly. Instead of going to the pool, we now learned to dread Saturdays when it would be late afternoon before we were finished. While we worked, Mom would lounge around drinking Pepsi with peanuts thrown inside. It's funny she never choked on that concoction.

One of the worst jobs for me was doing the dishes. I hated when it was my turn because every time I turned the taps on, I felt like I needed to pee. Mom thought it was just a stall tactic and would beat me until I ended up peeing in my pants. I finally got smart and developed the habit of peeing just before I had to do the dishes, a habit I still retain to this day, but it wasn't until years later that Mom realized I had not been lying. She was always like that when we were growing up, expecting the worst of us kids and punishing us for it.

While Mom was working, she managed to save five hundred dollars for the down-payment on a brand new 1968 Skylark Buick. Before that, all we had was the old, blue Bell Telephone van that Dad used to haul scrap steel in. We were ecstatic over that two-tone green, shiny new car. At Christmas time, Mom and Dad decided we would drive all the way to New Brunswick in the new car for the holidays. It was a fourteen-hour drive in the middle of winter and Dad drank and drove the whole way. He would sing along with Johnny Cash playing over and over again on the eight-track tape deck, but at least we knew he was still awake at the steering wheel.

When we arrived, we stayed at Memere and Pepere's house. Mom and Dad stayed with Uncle Zeb and his girlfriend Jan, but their only child Candy, who was four years younger than me, stayed with us. Jan was a real winner. She had bleached blond hair, probably weighed about ninety pounds, and was drunk most of the time, with a cigarette dangling from her lower lip. Jan would fight and argue with Zeb every chance she got until Zeb beat her black and blue, but somehow that darned old cigarette always stayed in place. Sometimes I thought it must be glued there. I had seen pictures of Jan when she was young and gorgeous, but alcohol and beatings had taken their toll on her.

One night we girls managed to sneak out and walk along the train tracks to Zeb and Jan's place. We wanted a peek at what the grown-ups were doing. When we reached the house, we took turns standing on each other's backs to get a look in the window. At first they were singing dirty songs in French while they were drinking and dancing. Then the inevitable fighting started. I remember that Jan was wearing white pants that were soon all covered in blood from Zeb beating her. She came running out of the house and down the train tracks before slipping on a pile of snow and ice. Down she went, yelling and screaming dirty names at Zeb even though he wasn't even there. My mother had followed, and she stooped to help pick her up. They never even saw us kids, but we were so scared we ran all the way back to Memere's house. When Memere heard what had happened, she told us very firmly never to go there again. That was no place for children to be, she said. After that, our vacation was finally over, thank God. Although I was going to miss my grandparents and Lanie and our cousin Candy, I didn't think I could take much more of that grown-up foolishness.

Soon after we reached home, I could see Mom was falling into a depression. She would stay in her housecoat all day, with her hair uncombed. Usually she had such pretty blond hair all done up in a beehive, which was the style at that time. Mom had always kept herself looking nice, but not any more. Dad would come home and yell at her for not being dressed or doing her hair. By now I was ten years old and a little more aware of the changes that were happening around me, but I still wasn't old enough to understand why things were happening. I now realize that Mom's depression began when her sister Yvette had a sister-in-law come to live in Toronto. Her name was Belinda, and she came from Sudbury, Ontario with her four children, Jake, Marie, Gaylord and Liam. As Marie was only three years older than I was, she soon became our friend and baby-sitter. She had long blond hair that she brushed every five minutes, high cheekbones, blue eyes, and to quote my mother, she was thin and lanky. Marie was also a bit ahead of her time when it came to boys. As she was the oldest of us girls, she liked to be in control of things. She had us form a club with her as president and my sister Marilyn as treasurer, but Marilyn and she were always in conflict with one another, while I would just sit back and take it all in. Marie taught us how to do the cancan, putting on little dance skits. She slept over at our house a lot, playing records, dancing and talking about boys. Mom, I guess, was already seeing things that we kids weren't, things like the fact that Marie always wanted to sit in the front seat of the car when we went for ice cream with Dad. Marilyn would fight with her, saying she couldn't sit in the middle next to our dad. After a while, Mom said she didn't want us hanging around with Marie any longer, insisting she was too old and knew too much about boys. Mom was right about that, for Marie had some boys come over to her house one day when her mother wasn't home. She put a bra on me and made me stuff it with tissue, although I didn't really know why she wanted me to do that. The boys were older and not very nice, so I got upset and pulled all the stuffing out, insisting I wanted to go home. Marie was furious, calling me a baby, and saying I had ruined everything for her. It was all very confusing for me, as I really didn't know what it was that I had ruined. My gut feeling was that it was dirty and wrong. Why was it all a secret that we were meeting these boys? Was it because they were older? I played with boys all the time and it never felt wrong, nor was there any need to stuff my bra for them. I was uncomfortable with the pressure she had placed on me to try and act older than I was.

By now, Mom knew that Marie had a crush on my dad. She also knew what a pig Dad could be when it came to females of any age. Marie was only thirteen, and Dad was twenty-nine, but that didn't stop them. Any time Dad went over to play cards with the uncles at her mother's place, Marie would run up and kiss him goodbye when he left. The others all figured it was innocent enough, but Mom knew there was nothing innocent about it, telling us what a little slut Marie was and that she didn't want us hanging around with her any more. After that, when Dad took us for a drive without Mom, we would get him to pick up Marie on the way. We were still too young to understand what was going on; why Mom didn't like her or what Marie and Dad were really up to. In a way, it was like living in a three-ring circus.

I was now eleven years old and we were moving to a new place just around the corner on Hallam Street. It was a very nice three-bedroom house, with a verandah on the front and another off the bedroom in the back. For the first time in our lives, we were living in a really nice home. Things should have been wonderful, for Mom was now expecting a baby and everything in our lives seemed great. As it turned out, things couldn't have been worse and our lives were just about to take a downward spiral that would lead each one of us on a path of nothing but destruction, pain and misery. Dad was really upset about the baby, and wanted her to abort it, but Mom wouldn't hear of it. This was her chance to finally give him a son, she said. In her mind, this must have been the one thing she felt could save their marriage. She couldn't have been more wrong. Dad was now having sex with Marie, a teenage girl who was barely fourteen years old and our best friend, baby-sitter and playmate. Viewed nowadays, it would be considered child molesting.

Every night after work, Dad would shower, shave and leave. To the best of our knowledge, he was at the Lansdowne boxing ring just a few blocks away, supposedly boxing. It turned out he was boxing, all right, but with a different kind of sparring partner, and in a different kind of box. As we kids had no knowledge of what was actually going on, we couldn't understand our mother's weird behaviour. By this time, she had become a super sleuth, dragging us along on her escapades. I remember one evening when Mom's sister Yvette came over to pick us up in her little blue Volkswagen Beetle and we all piled in the back to go on a mission to catch Dad and Marie in action. First we went to the boxing club to see if his car was there, then on to Marie's apartment above a restaurant just five minutes from our house. It must have been hard for Yvette, for here was her sister's husband running around with her niece. What a crossfire she was in. I remember sitting in a huge parking lot across the street from where Marie lived. It was an industrial area surrounded mostly by factories and train tracks. They lived above a Chinese restaurant and from where we were parked right across the street with the car lights off, we could see perfectly into her living room. There they both were, sitting in the room drinking what looked like a cup of coffee or tea. I was curious as to why we were hiding and not going in to visit. Finally, I started to catch on somewhat to the conversation Mom and Yvette were having in French so we kids would not know what they were talking about. Although I could understand very well what they were saying, I knew nothing about sex and therefore did not see what all the fuss was about. There was no way I could understand the pain my mother was feeling as we drove away with her crying her eyes out. Aunt Yvette kept telling her not to cry, and that he was not worth it, but just a dirty bastard. At this point, Mom was a pregnant woman with three young children, knowing she was about to lose her husband and her lifestyle. It must have been one hell of a jolt to her self-esteem. She had been through so many of his flings, but I guess she kept hanging on because of us kids. Kids or no kids, for her own sanity she should have left him right then.

That night after Yvette dropped us off at home, Mom was so distraught she kept crying uncontrollably. I felt so sorry for her, but none of us knew what to say or do for her. She wasn't saying anything to us kids, so we were left in the dark not understanding the full impact of what was going on. When Dad finally came home, they had a terrific battle and Dad ended up sleeping downstairs on the sofa. That night marked the beginning of a new stage in our lives.

A few months passed and everything about our lives felt different. With the exception of Marilyn and me, each of us seemed suddenly alone, as though we were all going off in different directions. Despite the fact we were all living under the same roof, we still seemed miles apart. I was lucky to have my sister Marilyn, for we were very close and continued to do everything together.

One day, when Mom was just about ready to give birth, she took the notion to walk over to Marie's place. Opening the door with the intention of going upstairs to the apartment, she ran smack into Dad and Marie embracing and kissing on the staircase. Dad immediately punched Mom right in the face, hurling her against the wall so she fell stunned to the floor. Managing to escape, she walked aimlessly and lost, finally making it to Aunt Yvette's house where she stayed for three days before finally coming home. We kids had no idea what had happened to her, as Dad did not say a word while we stayed alone in his care. I would only learn about this incident years later when Mom told me how she had seen stars when he hit her. When I asked her why she went there in the first place, she said that up until then, she had not been sure whether he was having the affair with Marie, or Marie's mother Belinda. She wanted to see for herself.

The next week, Mom gave birth to our baby brother Shane. We kids were all tremendously excited, but Dad never even went to see Mom or the baby in the hospital. The day they were coming home, Marilyn, our friend Magi, and I decided to skip school so we could stay home to clean the house and bake goodies. Well, I think we would have been better off going to school. My baking specialty was sugar pie and Marilyn's was peanut butter cookies, but this time we got brave and decided to bake a chocolate cake as well. Magi was helping, and before we knew what had happened, she had pulled the beaters out of the cake mixture and was spitting chocolate batter all over the kitchen table, walls, curtains and floors. What a mess we had gotten ourselves into. To make matters worse, while I rushed over to yank the plug out of the wall, Marilyn got mad and started throwing cookie dough at Magi. Finally I yelled that they had better stop and start cleaning up. We must have looked like The Three Stooges in drag as we tackled the mess, splashing buckets of water all over the floor. Suddenly, time ran out and here came Yvette's husband Gerry bringing Mom and the baby home. Did we have some explaining to do? At first, Mom was angry at us for being home from school, not to mention making a mess of the kitchen. When we finally got a chance to explain how we had wanted to surprise her by having everything nice and clean, she wasn't impressed, but at least she understood. After that, we cleaned up the kitchen and hugged and kissed our new baby brother. That night, when Dad came home from work, he didn't even look at the baby or Mom. He just did his same routine of shaving and showering, and then went out the door. Nothing had changed.

In spring, when Shane was a few months old, Mom went to New Brunswick with the younger kids to visit her mother, leaving Marilyn and me with Dad. One morning when we arrived home early after spending the night at Magi's house Marilyn and I heard strange moaning sounds coming from our bedroom. Tiptoeing upstairs, we flung open the door and found Dad naked with Marie in the middle of a sexual act. Dad started screaming and cursing at us and we started screaming and cursing right back at him between all our hysterical sobbing and tears. We told them they were two fucking pigs and to get the hell out of our bedroom. Then we started throwing things and hitting the two of them as they huddled in bed under the blankets, yelling at our dad that we hated him. In the end, we cried all the way down the street, ending up on the doorstep of a friend of Mom and Dad's. We could not really understand what we had witnessed that day. All we could think about was that our dad did not love Mom or us anymore.

The next morning, the people we were staying with called Aunt Yvette and told her what had happened. Yvette went straight to Belinda's house where she told her to get her daughter Marie out of our house this minute. So Belinda hauled her daughter home, gave her the worst beating of her life, then got a peace bond against Dad so he could not come near her daughter, thinking that would put an end to the nightmare. When Marilyn and I finally went home the next day, Dad was sober and nothing was ever said about his dirty little romp.

Marilyn and I did not want to sleep in our room any more, so while Mom was in New Brunswick we switched to Jody's bedroom. It was smaller, but it had bunk beds, so we could still fit. Just the thought of sleeping in the other room made us feel sick. A few days later, Dad came into our room and announced that there were going to be some new rules for us to follow, like a curfew for when we had to be home. As he stood in the doorway telling us, we started to grab all the shoes from the shoe rack hanging on the closet door and whipped them at him, yelling at him to go to hell because we were going to come home whenever we felt like it. After what we had seen, we sure didn't feel much like listening to him.

Someone phoned Mom in New Brunswick and told her about Marilyn and me finding our dad in bed with Marie. I always thought it was too bad they did not wait until she had finished her visit, for Mom packed right up and came back early. By the time she arrived with Jody and Shane, she was a complete basket case. She immediately started drilling into our heads how bad our father was, saying he didn't love us kids any more. Feeling completely lost and alone, and not old enough to differentiate between love for a child and sexual lust, we could not understand why he would love Marie more than us.

Like Dad, Mom tried to maintain some level of control over us, but by now, Marilyn and I were just coming and going as we pleased, in no mood to obey the very people who were making our lives so miserable. We went to Christie Pitts Park most of the time, playing sports like softball, volleyball, track and field, or swimming. One night Dad came looking for us at around ten at night and discovered us engaged in a sport of a different kind. There were his three daughters and our friend Magi lying in the grass, each locked in the arms of a young boy. All this romping in the grass with boys was new and exciting to us, but where was it coming from? We had certainly never been exposed to this kind of behaviour at home where there was never much love and intimacy shown between Mom and Dad, just aggression, swearing and yelling vile words at each other. It had really started the summer Mary-June came to visit, for this was what she did in the park with all the men. We must have been paying more attention than any of us knew. Now, at the first holler from Dad, the boys jumped up and scattered like cockroaches every which way, while if we girls were not excited from all the kissing and touching, we sure got excited from the shock of seeing my dad standing there.

When we got back home with Dad in the car, we sent Magi into the house first, as Mom was a "hit now and ask questions later" kind of mother. Well, she sure hit Magi, whacking her with a shoe and laying into her while the rest of us ran past them and up the stairs. We all looked the same with our long hair and long coats, so Magi got quite a beating before Mom noticed who she was. I think Mom must have been taking all the frustration in her life out on us, she was so furious.

A week after Mom got home, her grandmother "the witch" died and she had to go back for the funeral. It was while she was gone that Dad totally lost what little bit of control he still had over us. He just did his thing and we did ours, both of us largely ignoring the other. By the time Mom came home, our home had turned into a hell, with Marilyn and me sneaking out late at night when everyone was asleep, skipping school and smoking cigarettes. There was no stopping us. Rebellion had become our only defense against a life we had come to hate.

The day finally came when we were told Dad was leaving for good. Even knowing everything we knew, I cannot tell you how hurt we felt at the news. At the time, I was twelve, Marilyn eleven, Jody nine and Shane nine months. Marilyn and I decided we wanted to live with Dad, but he had no intention of taking us. Why would he want to, he was moving in with Marie, our fifteen-year-old baby-sitter? We could not comprehend whether she was going to be his wife or his new daughter. He already had a wife and daughters, so what was wrong with us that he did not love or want us any more? The whole situation was completely beyond our comprehension.

Dad said he was leaving a week after telling us, but he should have gone immediately because Mom decided to put us up to some pretty nasty tricks. She wanted revenge on Dad so badly that she filled our heads with terrible things so we would help her get back at him. One evening while he was in the shower after work, Mom went to the kitchen drawer and grabbed a butcher knife. Taking it outside, she stabbed all the tires of Dad's car, the very car she had worked overtime to help buy. Next, she made us take all his eight-track tapes and put them in a pile about a foot high so she could set fire to them. We did not want to help her, but she was so wild we did not dare refuse. When Dad finally came downstairs and saw his damaged car, he rushed back inside and threw Mom against the kitchen cupboards while we kids screamed and kicked him on the legs, telling him it was us who did the damage. We told him we had done it because we did not want him to move out. At that, Dad called us a bunch of retarded bastards, phoned a tow truck, and left when they came to pick up the car. Nothing was going to stop him going out that night that was for sure. The next evening, when he was pulling out of the driveway to leave, Marilyn and I stood on the verandah and threw eggs at the windshield. It was such a scorcher outside that the eggs started to fry right then and there and we could not stop laughing at the sight of his face. He had even just finished washing the car, but he never even stopped; he just drove away and left us.

On his last night home, Dad packed all his things up in preparation for leaving. He was going to walk away from his family, the one he had helped create, and just cast us away like rejects that were no longer useful to him. Late at night, after everyone was asleep, Marilyn and I snuck downstairs with all our clothes and stuffed them underneath Dad's clothes in his suitcase. We finally fell asleep on the floor beside the suitcases thinking we were going to go with him. When we woke in the morning, the suitcases and Dad were gone, but our clothes were still there piled on the sofa. It was a terrible moment of realization, for it made us feel deserted and worthless. As bad as we were acting towards Dad, I always felt closer to him than to mom. Now all we could do was cry. After Dad left, Mom had nothing good to say about him. I will never understand why parents who have separated or divorced put their children in the middle and use them as a means of punishment. The only thing they accomplish is grief and suffering for the children they supposedly love.

Months went by and things started to get tough for my mother. We were living on the welfare that Dad was giving her, but it wasn't much money each week. Pretty soon the landlord wanted us out because we did not have enough money to pay the rent on our big house. Then Mom started to sell off most of our furniture until we got down to the bare necessities. By the time it was close to Christmas, Marilyn and I had no coats to wear and Mom did not know what she was going to do about it. In the end, she sold the upright freezer for seventy-five dollars to buy us each a coat. Jody was fine because she always got our hand-me-downs. I guess the freezer was the most logical thing to go because we would never be able to fill it up again. We were going to be lucky if we had enough to fill our stomachs on a daily basis. When we finally had to move, we all crammed into a bachelor apartment. It was such a nightmare after the way we had been living, and none of us children really understood why we were living this way.

By now, Mom was in total depression. You might as well say we lost both our parents at that time, for she never talked or did much of anything after Dad left. I was trying to go to school, but had lost interest and was now just going through the motions. We stayed in our new place two months before moving again, this time to an apartment above a store, with an entrance in the back of a lane way. It was a bit bigger, with a kitchen downstairs, a living room, and one bedroom upstairs. It was then that Bob Shaw came into our lives.

A few days after we moved into our new apartment, Mom locked herself out by accident. We kids were all asleep upstairs and didn't hear her knocking to get in. What finally woke us was the noise of someone coming into the apartment from out of nowhere. He was a thin man, with his pants half falling off, straight black hair, startling blue eyes, and craters all over his face. He was also drunk. We started screaming at him until Mom appeared in the door, saying he was a friend of hers and not to worry because he had helped her get in. It was then that I got a good look at Mom and realized she was drunk too. All I could think was when the hell did she start drinking, and who was this man. I guess it was a nervous reaction, but Marilyn and I looked at each other and started to laugh. Mom told us his name was Bob Shaw, which made us laugh even harder because Shaw in French means cat and at that particular moment, he looked exactly like a stray alley cat. Naturally, all our laughing made Mom quite mad as she yelled at us to go to bed. By the time Marilyn and I got upstairs, we were laughing hysterically. Little did we know it at the time, but Bob Shaw was going to play a big role in our lives. Good or bad, he was here to stay.

It wasn't long before Marilyn and I started doing some detective work. First, we went down the lane way to Lidia and Cheyenne's apartment. They were brother and sister the same age as us, and a whole lot more educated in the world of adults than we were. We had met them at the Elizabeth Recreation Center a year or so earlier and became friends. I remember feeling so sorry for them when we first met, seeing the way they lived in a filthy apartment with just one bedroom for four children and two adults, along with every stray alcoholic on Bloor Street. Their mom and dad were always drunk.

When we arrived that day, they let us in and took us to their bedroom. There were piles of clothes lying all over the place and we had to move some just to find a place to sit down. Lidia and Cheyenne told us that Bob Shaw was one of their uncles, but in that home, everyone that walked through the front door with a case of beer was called an uncle. Then Lidia said she had heard that we were about to move again into the same building that they lived in. We were to be downstairs right next door to them. By now, I was starting to feel like we were gypsies and wondering when the moving was ever going to stop. Marilyn and I sure didn't want to move there. It was a dump. People were drunk every day at Cheyenne and Lidia's, most of them just walking in from the street right through the living room window instead of the front door. Then they would step down onto the couch, and most of the time, someone would pass out on it. As if that wasn't bad enough, there were two guinea pigs for pets that ran loose everywhere in the apartment and you never knew when you might step in their droppings. By now, Mom had started being at their apartment getting drunk every night along with everyone else.

The time had come for us to move again, this time into that dump of an apartment building. Each time we had moved had been a steady downhill course, but this was the worst imaginable. When we opened the front door into the living room, the smell of old musty carpets made you want to vomit. The slant of the floor had at least a six inch drop in the front of the house to about a foot at the back door. While we were moving in what few possessions we had left, someone had the nerve to steal our little brother's highchair and some other things right off the truck in the parking lot while Bob and his friends were having a beer break. That shows you what kind of neighbourhood it was.

Our little brother was a year old now and we girls were fast becoming his moms. Food was at an all time low and diapers were few and far between. When we ran out of diapers, which happened often, we would use dish towels with a plastic supermarket bag pinned to his bottom. He was with us most of the time, because Mom pretty much lived with the rest of the drunks next-door. Sometime after we moved in, when Dad came to pick up Jody and Shane for the weekend, he said he didn't like the way we were living now. Why wasn't there ever any food, he asked? Once he realized what was going on, he said he wasn't going to give Mom any more money for booze; he would take us grocery shopping himself instead. It was then that I realized we were now living the life just like the kids I had felt so sorry for the year before, for here we were living in the same squalor and filth, with parents who were drunk most of the time. When we first met Lidia and Cheyenne what we didn't know it had been a glimpse of what our future was to become.

After we had lived there for three months, we moved upstairs to a two-bedroom apartment which was much bigger. Bob Shaw was now officially living with us. He worked as a house painter, but I really don't know how he did it, because he was drunk most of the time. He drove a white '56 Chevy Impala, and Mom would phone Marilyn and me to come to the bar down the street and drive the car home because he was too drunk to do it himself. At twelve years old, Marilyn would do the driving, sitting on pillows so she could see out the windshield. Most of the time we could barely get Bob in the car, but somehow we always managed it. Off we would drive, right down Bloor Street in broad daylight.

As Marilyn and I always had a soft spot for someone in trouble, we soon befriended two girls in Christie Pitts Park who had run away from Ohio. They would climb up to our second story balcony at night to get in, so we could feed them whatever we could find and let them sleep under our beds. Finally, Mom caught them one night as they were climbing up, and nearly fell off the balcony trying to push them back down again. She said she never wanted to see us near them again, so we had to come up with a new plan to help them. There was a small building next-door on a vacant used car lot which was never in use. We broke into the building, found an old mattress, and set it up so they could sleep there. Next, we stole an abandoned car from the lane way, pushed it next to the building, covered it with graffiti and different-coloured paint, and used it as a hangout. We were now skipping school every chance we got, and had even started to drink, but our parents didn't care what we were doing, as long as we were out of their way.

Marilyn and Lidia eventually got the brainstorm to run away. I don't know how they got there in one piece, but they hitchhiked all the way to Montreal. When they finally arrived and discovered everything was in French, they found it wasn't as exciting as they had thought it would be. Scared and alone, they phoned home collect, crying over the telephone and saying they didn't know where they were and didn't have any money. Bob talked to Marilyn and told her to break a window, and then wait for the police to arrive. After the police picked them up, Bob and Lidia's dad Blackie borrowed the money for their train fare home, along with a police escort. When they made it back home, it was not a nice scene, ending in both girls being grounded for a couple of weeks. It was a miserable time for me as well, because they wouldn't let me tag along any more, saying I was chicken for not having run away with them. As unstable as our life was, we still had a roof over our heads and that's where I intended to stay.

I guess being grounded for two weeks wasn't enough to stop Marilyn, or I for we arranged to have two boys named Gilbert and Sydney come over. They both had blond wavy hair and blue eyes, and their mother drank and partied with our mother, so that's how we knew them. As they were older than us and could get into the liquor store, they arrived one evening with a forty-ounce bottle of vodka. After Mom and Bob left for a party, I went into the kitchen to mix some frozen orange juice. Gilbert and Sydney were on the balcony, so no one noticed what Marilyn was doing as she took the bottle of vodka and downed most of it. Marilyn was always more aggressive than I was, craving attention and wanting to put on a hard, tough exterior as her way of hiding her fear. I always felt she wanted to be the older sister, the one in charge, and would often let her play that role to keep the peace between us. Now, in her attempt to impress us all, she had finally gone too far. Before anyone knew what was happening, she was going into a convulsion. Fortunately, Bob and Mom had forgotten something and arrived back home just as Marilyn started vomiting and sweating. Mom began screaming "What did she take?" At first none of us knew until we noticed the half empty vodka bottle on the counter. When he saw the bottle, Bob grabbed Marilyn and threw her into a freezing cold bath of water; clothes and all, then kicked the boys out, telling them never to come back again. After about an hour in the tub, when Marilyn finally seemed to be regaining some of her senses, Mom and I took her wet clothes off. She was kicking and screaming, but we still managed to wrap her in blankets and put her to bed where she lay trembling. When Mom and Bob left, they said they would be right downstairs and I was to come get them if there was a problem. How they thought they would be able to help, I had no idea, for by the end of the night, they would be in the same shape as my drunken sister.

I was asleep on the couch at four in the morning when I heard Bob and Mom come in. They were both drunk and out of their minds, so I pretended that I was still sleeping. The next thing I knew, Mom was shouting that she had found the washroom, and Bob was pissing in the corner of the living room. When I got up in the morning, Mom was passed out in the hall where someone had shit right in the corner. When I checked on Marilyn, she was still sick and her body was vibrating, but she would recover, never to remember much of what happened.

After this whole episode, we must not have learned much, for we really started getting in serious trouble. As we lived right across the street from Christie Pitts Park, we started climbing over the huge fence to the pool at night and going swimming. The pool was built into a hill, with one side on ground level and the other so high you needed a ladder to see in. We would make so much noise that the police would come, and we'd hide on the side of the pool where they couldn't see us, even when they shone their flashlights around. This went on for a week until one evening the police got smart and waited for us, hidden in darkness in the pool office. After we were caught, they took us home, but Mom wouldn't answer the door so they took our names and gave us a warning. When we finally let ourselves into the apartment, we found Mom on the floor of her room in quite a state. Her eyes looked really strange and glassy and kept rolling from side to side with a vacant look. We had no idea what had happened, but we knew she had never looked like this before when she was drunk. Marilyn and I picked her up and put her on the couch, but when I went to call for help, she staggered up and ripped the phone out of the wall. After that, we went outside to a phone booth and called an ambulance. The next day when she came home from the hospital, she said we were nothing but little bitches and she should break our necks for calling the ambulance. The doctors at the hospital didn't know her history of depression and suicide attempts, so they released her, believing her story that it was an accident and she had forgotten how many pills she had taken.

One day, after the laundry had been piling up for some time, Mom and

Bob drove Marilyn and me to the Laundromat where we were supposed to stay and do the laundry while they walked to the bar down the street. The minute they were gone, Marilyn got the bright idea to take the keys which Bob had left in the car, and go for a drive. We were only twelve and eleven, and the whole idea seemed wildly exciting. Before I knew it, we were driving along Bloor Street with Marilyn barely able to see where she was going because we didn't have the pillows with us. Next, we made a left turn on Dufferin and drove all the way to just pass St. Clair Avenue where we turned into the driveway of my boyfriend Thornton's house. As we pulled in the narrow driveway, the car actually scraped the side of the house. You could hear the metal grinding along the building. As if that wasn't bad enough, we then hit the garage and smashed the driver's side headlight. Thornton and his older brother Clyde thought we were nuts, and weren't too happy about the damage to the house and garage which was bound to get them in trouble with their parents. By the time we got back to the Laundromat, I could see Mom and Bob looking around frantically. Bob ran to the driver's side and yanked Marilyn out of the car by her hair, punching her in the face so she hit the ground. I jumped out the other door to avoid Bob, but there was Mom ready to clock me as well, so I too got knocked to the ground. By now, Bob was yelling that we were little whores and trying to get another hit in, so we both jumped up and ran like hell all the way to Christie Pitts Park where we stayed until dark. We were terrified to go home, but by the time we finally went, Bob had cooled down and just grounded us for a week with no allowance. You would have thought the experience and punishment would make a difference, but they didn't in the long run.

That was the year I finished grade eight and headed for high school. It was amazing that despite all the moves we did over the years, we never had to change schools, and were always within walking distance from home. That was the one stable thing in our lives. Now it was time to go and get acquainted with a new school for the first time. I decided to attend Central Tech because they had the best art program in Toronto and I had already discovered that I could really lose myself when I did art. It was the only time I was truly happy. Besides, I was making money at it, making posters which I would sell to Bob's acid-head friends for two dollars apiece. I used the school's supplies, so it never cost me a cent for materials. I never did any of the other subjects at school, but the teacher knew that if I was there working on my art, at least I wasn't getting in trouble or out on the streets skipping school. He even suggested I take the art course at Central Tech.

When I first arrived at high school I was excited and apprehensive at the same time, for this was a big change from my only stability in life. First I went to pick up my school supplies; reveling in the idea that now I would be a real art student. It sounded so nice to my ears. As I came back out the front doors, a black guy walked right up to me, pulled a huge knife out of his knee-high platform boot and stuck it to my throat. Then he grabbed me by the hair and said I was going to be his bitch and work the street for him. I felt nothing but sheer terror as the tears started to stream down my cheeks. Next, he asked if I was a virgin. At first I couldn't say a thing, I was so stunned, but when he dug the knife a little more into me, I said yes. He said, "Well, first I'll have your ass, bitch—you're coming with me." Just then, Thornton's brother Clyde came running up the stairs and saw what was happening. He told the black guy to let me go or he'd kill him, and that I was his brother's girlfriend so he'd better never so much as see him looking in my direction again. Clyde was a boxer and everyone on the streets knew of him because he had a reputation for being a tough guy. Clyde and Thornton were also black and we'd known them for about five years, ever since we met at the Elizabeth Recreation Center.

That incident changed school for me forever. I had wanted to study art ever since second grade when I painted a squirrel and the teacher praised me and said she was so proud of me and hung it up on the wall. But that art student would never come to be. When the school year began, the art school was separate from the main building, so I skipped all the classes in the main building. I never wanted to go into that part of the school again, I was so terrified I'd run into the same guy in the hallways. Any time I had to go anywhere near it, I'd always look around feeling uneasy. Finally, all that skipping classes caught up with me and the principal called me into his office. When he asked why I never went into any other classes except art, I was afraid to tell him the truth. All I could think of to say was that I didn't like the other subjects. He told me I needed all my classes in order to pass, so now I knew that unless I went into the other building, I would fail. That's when I stopped going to school all together. The only escape I had from reality was now taken away from me.

I started hanging around the local restaurant near the school where all the kids playing hooky stayed during the day. Whenever a teacher would come near the place, we kids would hide in the basement with the owner's consent. Eventually the truant officer caught up with me and off to court I went, where the judge informed me if I didn't start going to school, I would be sent to reform school. I can still remember how I was half leaning over the bench as he spoke, until he told me to stand up straight and address him as Your Honour. All I could think of to say was that reform school was probably a lot better than the life I had at home. The judge just told me to shut my mouth and he didn't want to see me in his courtroom again. I was only thirteen at the time.

Once again we were on the move, this time to a brownstone on a corner lot just down the street from where Marie's mother lived. It was a main floor and basement, so it felt more like a real house, but it would never feel like a home to us. Mom was now drinking from morning until night. Combined with the nerve pills she was taking, it must have been quite a cocktail. Things were hitting rock-bottom fast. One morning I was on the bus heading for school when I looked out the window and saw my mother walking down the street. It was snowing, a wet clingy kind of snow and she had on a pair of old tattered shoes with the back heels half walked off and no socks. Her pant legs were too short and she had a flimsy little sweater on that didn't fit her. It was the dead of winter and the snow was up to her shins. I couldn't help but weep for her. I didn't know it at the time, but she was on her way to the liquor store to get her first pint of the day. I was suddenly looking at my mother in a different light, but there was no light at all coming from within her. All I could see was the emotionally broken and battered woman my mother had become.

CHAPTER TWO

Abandoned

When I was thirteen and a half years old and my sister Marilyn was twelve and a half, our mother had a nervous breakdown. She took our younger sister Jody, and Shane, our little brother, on a train to New Brunswick and left Marilyn and me behind. For a long time afterwards I really didn't understand how a woman in her condition with two little children could even manage to find her way there if she was so sick. Years later, I learned that her mother had come to Toronto herself and taken the three of them back with her to New Brunswick. I have to wonder if there was not something wrong with my grandmother's head that enabled her to willingly help a mother abandon two young girls like a couple of stray dogs. My mother claims that her reasoning was she didn't want to see us go to the children's aid. I can forgive my mother, for she was emotionally sick and had an excuse. But I will never understand the rest of her family for not knowing better. Even if we were bad and rebellious, there must have been a more appropriate way to go about this than pretending we didn't exist. Among all her brothers and sisters living in Toronto at the time, there should have been someone willing to get help for her in Toronto, thus also providing for us. Instead, they just let her go, for that way they wouldn't have the burden of taking responsibility for her or her children.

When Mom arrived in New Brunswick, her mother had her committed to a mental institution. Bob followed Mom to New Brunswick three months later and moved in with my grandmother, although Mom was still in the hospital. She would remain there for a year. Before long, Bob had found a job painting houses, and tried to help out with the kids between bouts of drinking.

In the meantime, Marilyn and I were totally unaware of how our lives were about to change. At first, neither of us realized that we had been left totally alone in the city of Toronto. We thought our mother was just visiting family or friends since it was not unusual for her to be gone for overnight stays. Finally, a month went by and the landlord came looking for his rent. We told him our mother was visiting family, but the truth was that by then we had no idea where she was. It was now summertime, and we were having a hell of a good time having fun. We could now come and go as we pleased, or invite friends over to listen to music. Prior to my mother leaving, I had fixed up the old basement by putting crumpled tin foil on the walls, then painting old record albums different colours and stapling them to the beams on the ceiling. I found some old draperies and used them to partition off the laundry area from our party room, and then put in a stereo, couch, strobe lights, and a bed held up with paint cans. It had an outside entrance so we could sneak our friends in anytime without our mother knowing, but now we were alone, we didn't have to sneak them in any longer.

After a while, the neighbours started to complain about all the noise and carrying on, the cars coming and going at all hours, and the endless round of parties. The police came and asked what was going on around there, telling us they had received complaints from people in the neighbourhood and were told there didn't seem to be any adult supervision present. When they asked where our mother and stepfather were, we lied and said they were working nights. Then they came inside and looked around at everything upstairs in the apartment, which we had managed to keep clean and ordinary looking. What they didn't know was that all the partying happened downstairs in the basement where they never even looked. At the time, we had about fifteen kids downstairs, including a runaway. I told them I was sixteen, soon to be seventeen, which wasn't hard for them to believe because I had large breasts, makeup on and looked much older than my real age. After looking around and asking questions, the police left, telling us to calm down and go to bed. Neither Marilyn nor I felt bad about lying to them. We figured we were saving our necks, and besides, we were having too much fun to worry about it. Lying and cheating to adults, even the police, was hardly something new for us. By now we had quite a history of it.

In the midst of all this frantic partying, the feeling of rejection and abandonment was very intense. Although Marilyn and I were close, I knew I couldn't talk to her about my feelings because she always seemed to be more aloof and self-contained. And besides, I was the older sister and supposed to show no sign of fear or weakness. We were terrified that if we told the truth, the children's aid would take us away and separate us. Just the thought of being separated was unbearable because we were all each other had. Having grown up on the streets of Toronto, we had friends who lived in foster homes, and we had heard the horror stories about what went on. Lying to the police seemed a small price to pay for escaping a similar fate.

By now, the situation was starting to get really bad since the cupboards were almost bare. There hadn't been much food to begin with, only canned soup, Kraft dinner, peanut butter, jam, some frozen bread and spices. Once the peanut butter and jam were gone there was still the spices and bread which we thought was "good dam good" because we had never had cinnamon toast before. But with the food almost gone, we now found ourselves with no money and no way to buy any more. What pop bottles or beer bottles we could find had long since been returned for a little extra cash. Fortunately, the guys we were hanging around with at the time were older and knew the streets better than we did. They told us that if we went to the big stores early in the morning before they opened we could get all the food we needed. Because of the early morning delivery, the food was left outside the back doors until the first employees arrived. With no watchmen in sight, it was easy to take as much as we wanted, things like bread, milk, baked goods and frozen foods. The milk was best of all because you got not only the milk, but a jug that was worth a forty-cent deposit. "Wow, a cash cow!" So Marilyn and her boyfriend Bill took us early in the morning to the stores where we loaded up on goods, especially milk. Back home, we emptied the jugs so we could get the money, then took them to all the different stores so none of the owners would catch on to our scheme. I hated to pour the milk out, but we needed money for laundry, soap, toilet paper and things for personal hygiene. Stealing those things wasn't nearly as easy as taking the food.

We had a runaway girl named Karen living with us who we'd known since moving to Toronto when I was six years old. She was a tall thin girl with red wavy hair and pale freckled skin who went to our school. It was just like having a maid around, because Karen would do anything to be one of the crowd. We never had to ask her to do anything, she would just volunteer. You could talk Karen into anything, even stealing records, tapes or clothes. One time she even stole a pair of stylish platform shoes and left hers behind in the store. It was pretty funny watching her walk out of the store in those shoes, two sizes too small and four inches high. How the store staff didn't catch on is beyond me. After that, Karen walked around all summer with no shoes on her feet, which I guess was her choice. If she'd wanted new shoes, she could have stolen a pair for herself. Karen wasn't one for appearances as she never put makeup on, or had any style. She was just a plain Jane, and more of a tomboy than the rest of us.

Six weeks after we were abandoned, Dad showed up to give Mom some money. In the beginning he had come every week, but that soon became too much for him as he worked out of town, so he had started to come once a month. It wasn't much, but at least he was helping support us. When he found us alone he asked where Mom was and we said she'd gone out. Deciding not to leave the money with us, he said he would be back when she got home. Next time he would phone first before coming. He called up the next day and the next, and then he got a brainstorm and phoned friends of the family. Everyone told him we had been alone for quite a while. It's amazing to realize that all our friends and family knew we were alone, yet did nothing about it. My mother's family thought of us as little hell-raisers who had probably contributed to her breakdown. I'm sure we didn't help matters, but no one took the time to sit down with us and explain what was going on around us. We might not have fully understood, but at least we wouldn't have felt so left out. Our mother had always been a sick person from early on in her life and we didn't have much of a role model or any guidance to follow in our childhood. No wonder we were such hell-raisers. We'd been born into circumstances that were destined to fail us since our parents were mismatched from the start. They played with fire and we all got burnt.

At just about this time, the landlord came back with an eviction notice and Dad decided to play the hero by moving himself and his fifteen-year-old girlfriend in with us. We couldn't believe it. She was our baby-sitter and playmate and now she was going to play mother. As far as we knew, she was the problem in the first place because Mom had drilled into our heads that she was a tramp and home wrecker, and that our father was a child molester. Mom would say he might as well have raped his own daughters as there was only a three-year age difference between Marie and me. Actually, Marie wasn't a bad person, just a kid that had grown up without a father figure and now had a childish crush on an older man. She had no idea what kind of life she was actually getting into. And Dad took advantage of the situation by playing Don Juan instead of a father role.

Before moving in, Dad hired Marie's teenage brother and friend to throw out everything in the house—furniture, mementos, all our memories gone in one swoop. I didn't know until later in life how much that would affect me, watching the past just be erased before my eyes. At least if it had been a fire there would have been an excuse, but this was just plain stupidity. The only thing that they kept was our cedar bunk beds, which I still have to this day. Marie took all our clothes to the Laundromat and told the whole neighbourhood that she filled nineteen washers. I will never forget that number because it made us sound like a bunch of pigs, which was unfair. Marilyn and I had always kept our clothes clean. Most of the things Marie washed must have belonged to Mom.

Once we were all living together, Dad tried to set rules about things like curfews. What a joke that was. He had never spanked or disciplined us in his life, so how was he going to start now. That we would finally have to pay the price for such defiant behaviour was inevitable, for we were far too young and too rebellious to keep ourselves from getting hurt. In the end, all our wild behaviour finally caught up with us the night Marilyn and I decided to go with some guys to our friend Linda's place in Mississauga. Marilyn and I were in Bill's car, a blue Thunderbird, and Gilbert went in Sidney's car, a black convertible. The cars needed gas, so first we went to a gas station where Bill's friend worked. Normally, Bill would give him two dollars and his friend would fill the car up, but this time he wasn't working. Bill didn't have enough money to pay for gas, so Sidney said he'd give him some if Bill could talk me into going in Sidney's car. When they heard that, Bill and Marilyn more or less kicked me out for a tank of gas. I didn't really know what was going on. I just thought they wanted to be alone, so I got into Sidney's car and went with him and Gilbert. Right away they insisted I sit in the front between them, threatening that I would have to walk home if I didn't. They were both drinking beer the whole time.

When we got to Linda's, her parents were away, so we played music and had some more beer. After a while, the guys and girls went into the bedroom to smoke grass, but I didn't want to. As it was now getting late, we decided to leave soon afterwards. By now Sidney and Gilbert were pretty loaded and high, but drinking and driving wasn't considered the great crime it is today. A slap on the wrist was about all you would receive if you got caught. Once again, I had to go in Sidney's car, only this time Bill and he decided to have a drag race. Before I knew what was happening, we were flying down the street just as the lights up ahead turned red. Bill wasn't as drunk and stopped for the light, but Sidney went right through, hitting a station wagon full of people just as it was pulling out of a driveway. We hit them dead on the passenger's side, then spun out of control and hit a cement light pole. Sidney and Gilbert quickly jumped out, but I was stuck under the dashboard where the corner of the hood had driven right through my forehead. I could hear my sister screaming for me as Gilbert grabbed me and pulled me out of the car moments before it caught fire and blew up.

By some miracle, I was the only one hurt in either car. There was a nurse in the other vehicle that came to help me until the police and ambulance arrived. I was losing a lot of blood, but I never passed out. I remember Marilyn kicking and screaming at the police because she wanted to see me and they kept restraining her. When we arrived at the hospital the nurse cleaned my head, taking out the shattered glass. She had a Scottish accent and when the doctor came I heard her say that I was full of glass. I thought the nurse said I was full of *grass* and I started to yell out that I didn't smoke grass like the others did. The doctor calmed me down and said it was glass, not grass, in my head. By the time I was stitched up, it was morning and my dad was there to pick me up. All I could think about was how much trouble I was going to be in because I was wearing Marie's new sweater without permission. I had no idea what terrible shape my face was in, with a six-inch gash from my eyebrow into my hairline, a badly broken nose, and black and blue marks all over me. All I worried about was that sweater.

As immature as I was at that time in my thinking, I didn't realize the impact of what had just happened to me, almost losing my life at the hands of a couple of drunken boys. Looking back, I recognize now that much of

Marilyn's and my rebellion had to do with our fear of being deserted again. As far as we knew, first our dad had gotten fed up and left us for Marie, and then our mom had abandoned us for some reason we couldn't even understand, other than what we were told by family and friends. We were always allowed to believe it was our fault that had led to all that abandonment. With this fear constantly lurking in the back of our minds, we were continually getting into trouble. Perhaps it was to get attention, for any attention seemed better than none. Or did we do it because of lack of guidance, or for the sheer thrill of it all? Whatever the underlying reason, our actions came at an emotional cost to our lives, as we constantly sought love and attention and received it in the most harmful ways, never learning to just believe in ourselves first. Marilyn and I would take the same icy, stormy, curve in the road, the one that leads to emotional devastation. We were two kids lost in a blizzard of self-destruction, unable to find our way to a full and worthwhile life, a life of inner peace and love.

A few months after the accident, Dad moved us to Jane and Sheppard Avenue, to a brand-new building. We had all new furniture and everything nice inside, but for me the place felt cold and empty. Dad and Marie had just had a baby boy named Bradley, and I felt like I didn't fit in. Marilyn and I had a curfew which I followed because if we came in five minutes late we would have to be in an hour earlier the next night. I was afraid that if I didn't obey Dad's rules, I would end up being sent to a foster home. Marilyn never bothered, though, because she was now spending most of her time at Bill's parents' house. As I wasn't going to school any longer, I would go down to visit Marilyn, but it wasn't the same any more. I had lost her as well. With Bill such a big part of her life now, there just wasn't room for me.

The apartment we lived in had a gym and pool, so I spent a lot of my time down there. That's where Dad was most of the time, too, so we were often together. Dad finally found me a job at a furniture factory near where he was working on a new building, so he would drive me to work and pick me up. I now had money of my own, which sure felt good. After a while, Dad had to work somewhere else, so I would take the bus and then walk a mile to get to work. There was a bridge on the way where the trains went under. One day, after weeks of just walking over that bridge with no real thoughts one way or another, I found myself glued there, just staring at the train tracks. I was thinking about my mother and how much I missed her.

When I got home that evening I phoned New Brunswick to see how she was doing and my sister Jody answered. I could immediately tell from her voice how happy she was to hear from me. Jody didn't like living with our grandmother, and besides, she said that Mom was slicing her wrists, taking overdoses of pills, even lying on the train tracks in her attempts to commit suicide. I found out that the day the police found her on the tracks was at the very same time I had been standing on the bridge thinking about her. I started to cry because I missed her so much. It may seem strange, seeing as how terrible she had often been to me, but she was my mother and I loved her and worried about her. Whatever kind of care she was getting, it sure didn't seem to be working.

Marilyn popped in one day out of the blue, saying she had come to get the rest of her things. By now, she was thirteen and I was fourteen. She said she was leaving for good and wanted me to break the news to Dad that she was pregnant. When I told Dad, he went crazy, calling her a little whore and a slut while she yelled abuses back at him. What the hell was he talking about, she shouted, when he was a pig living with that teenage bitch and having a baby. Marilyn rushed over and called Bill to come pick her up, then turned and told Dad she was never coming back.

This was all confusing for me because I was pretty naive about sex. I had fooled around with boys, but I was afraid of doing more and was still a virgin. I knew that Marilyn had been living there for a while with her twenty-year-old boyfriend, and I knew they had been sleeping together, but now she was pregnant. I was also worried about her. Bill's parents were nice people, but they were alcoholics and so was Bill.

Now that Marilyn was pregnant and living with Bill, she was alone much of time while Bill worked nights, so I started spending a lot of time with her. They were living upstairs in Bill's bedroom, which was really big, but rather dark and gloomy. I don't remember if there were any windows, but if so, they weren't very big. There was a double bed, two dressers, a couple of chairs, a table and a TV. Marilyn was trying to make room for the baby's crib and dresser. I don't know if she realized it, but it was almost as if she was in some kind of prison. She was expecting a baby and I think that must have clouded everything for her. By now, she was fourteen, living with an alcoholic boyfriend who abused and beat her. His parents never tried to interfere because I think in a way they were afraid of him.

When Marilyn reached her ninth month, I stayed with her every evening in case she went into labour. I had never liked Bill much, but I loved my sister. When he would get back from work at midnight, I would leave and go home. It was a fair hike from their house in an industrial area to the nearest bus stop, a route that took me under a dark and dimly lit bridge by the train tracks. One night I left and caught the bus as usual. We hadn't gone three stops when I saw Bill running behind it signaling for the driver to stop. "Gail," he was out of breath when he had jumped on, "you have to come fast because Marilyn is in labour." We both got off the bus and started to hurry back to his house. "Slow down," he said, "I'm out of breath." When we were pretty close, he said we couldn't go in the front where his mother was sleeping, but had to go around to the back lane. This all sounded kind of strange to me. What had he done, I asked, left Marilyn alone? Bill said he didn't want to wake his mother because she had to work in the morning.

When we got to the lane way, it was so dark and scary. Just when we arrived in the back of his place, he grabbed me and started to beat me, throwing me on the ground and ripping at my clothes. I was in such a shock. I started kicking and screaming and biting him while he kept on hitting me and fighting back. My dad was a boxer and had taught me how to give an upper cut to the jaw, so bang, I nailed him. Bill let out a terrific scream and let me go long enough for me to jump up and start running I did not even look back. My clothes were all ripped and I was crying hysterically. That's how Bill's dad found me on his way home from work. I had just reached the bridge and he could see I was crying and shaken, with my clothes half torn. He stopped and asked if something was wrong at the house, but I couldn't tell him what had happened because Bill's brother Garth was a cop and Bill had told me I'd better keep my mouth shut. It's amazing how terrified we can be when we are young, always making the wrong decision out of fear, and never seeking help when we need it. So I just told Bill's dad that I was fine and was going to hail a cab to take me home. After he walked off I really didn't know what I was going to do. The last bus had gone and I had no money to pay for a taxi. I was standing there crying and bewildered when I saw a cab go by, and then another with someone in it. Without even thinking what I was doing, I hailed the next one that came along, not having a clue how I was going to pay for it. By the time we reached the apartment building where I lived, the fare was eighteen dollars. I told the driver I lived on the eighteenth floor and would be right back with the money. Then I ran inside and got in the elevator. The building really only had fifteen floors in it and we lived on the eighth. Once inside our apartment, I took a deep breath, I was so glad to get home. It made me feel so safe to be there. Then I went into my room and cried. It was a terrible moment of feeling alone, for there was no one I could tell. I certainly couldn't tell my sister or it might send her into labour. If I told my dad he would kill Bill, and I didn't want to upset what had finally developed into a closer relationship between Dad and me. There was no one I could tell, but I knew that I would have to think of some excuse for not staying so late in the evening with Marilyn any more. After a few days I started going back again, always arriving after Bill had gone to work, and leaving well before he came home.

Just about the time Marilyn had her baby, a little boy she named Brandon, I met Domino. He had a slim build, curly blond hair, blue eyes, and worked at a gas station I walked past every day on my way to the bus stop. A few months after we began dating, Domino started pressuring me to have sex with him. If you are a female, you're probably familiar with the line. It goes something like how he really loves you, but has his needs too and if you don't have sex with him, he'll look for it somewhere else. Although I didn't really want to do this, I was a young fifteen-year-old longing for love, and figured this was the only way I was going to get it. All I could think was that my sister wasn't a virgin anymore and she was having sex, so it must be okay. Her boyfriend was still with her, so it couldn't be that bad.

We started having sex, and the next thing I knew I was pregnant. Immediately, I realized I wasn't crazy in love for this boy and I sure didn't want his baby. Besides, I could see how tied down Marilyn had become. Domino's mother convinced me to have an abortion, not to spare her son, but because I believe she really cared about me. Her son had been in and out of reform school, and she said he would end up a good-for-nothing alcoholic just like his dad. She told me she didn't want to see me go through the same thing she had been through with her husband. Unfortunately, the only way I could have the abortion was with a parent's consent, and as there was no way I was going to tell dad, I had no choice except to call my mother and get her to sign the required form. I really didn't want Dad to find out and treat me the way her had treated Marilyn when she told him she was pregnant.

Mom was still in New Brunswick, so I called her and asked if she would sign the papers giving me permission to have an abortion. She said she would have to think about it, but I told her she'd have to think fast because I only had two weeks left before it would be too late. Then she wanted to know why Dad wouldn't sign, so I had to tell her I couldn't let Dad know or he would kick me out. Actually, this was only part of the truth. I really loved my dad and didn't want him to hate me. Both he and Marie thought I was a virgin still, so why rock the boat, was the way I looked at it. I had had so little security and stability and love in my life since we moved to Toronto, I didn't want to lose what small amount I had finally gained.

Mom called back a day later after she had talked it over with Bob and said she would sign the papers. Of course, the doctors asked why my mother was signing instead of my father who I lived with, so I was honest for once and told them he didn't know and wouldn't understand. One of the questions on the papers was whether the parent signing had ever been hospitalized for mental illness. Fortunately, Bob had filled it out and said no. Years later, Bob told me he always felt bad about talking my mother into signing the papers, but he knew it was the best thing for me, including lying about Mom's health.

With everything signed, I was finally able to have the abortion. Dad and Marie came to visit me in the hospital, wondering why I was in the maternity ward and what I was there for, so I told them it was stomach pains and they were doing tests. I also asked the nurse to lie to them and say there was no room anywhere else in the hospital to put me. When I was released, Marilyn insisted I stay with her for the night so she could help me if anything went wrong. I still didn't feel that comfortable going there, but Bill was working, and besides, Marilyn had always had a way of talking me into things. Rather than fight about something, or argue, I always wanted to keep the peace.

That night, I was sleeping next door to the washroom when I awoke and could sense that someone else was in the room with me. Suddenly, Bill pounced on me, and putting his hand over my mouth, started trying to rape me again. Here I was, straight from having an abortion, being attacked by my sister's boyfriend. Bill must have been incredibly stupid, because the house was old and the floors creaked, so Marilyn woke up and caught him in the act. He tried to get out of it by saying he was looking for the washroom, but Marilyn wasn't that stupid. Now I realized what happens when you don't tell anyone about a rape attempt. The person figures they can try again because you won't tell on them.

Marilyn and I never talked about what happened that night; I just didn't go visit her as often. By now I had a new job doing packing at a catalog company a short distance from Domino's mother's apartment, so I often slept there. I'd gotten smart by this time and was now on the pill. There was no way I wanted to get pregnant again.

As Christmas approached, I began really missing my mother, so I decided to go to New Brunswick to see her and Bob and my brother and sister. When I called Jody to tell her I was planning to surprise Mom by showing up, she said Mom would be getting out of the hospital for two weeks at Christmas, so I booked a train ticket and went to see them. When I arrived, Jody was alone at the station to meet me, because she was the only one who knew I was coming. I was so glad to see her. She seemed to have grown up tremendously.

As Mom was still in the hospital, we went straight there in a cab. I'll never forget my first sight of her because it took everything I had in me not to cry. She looked so happy to see me. First I gave her a locket and watch, and then we sat and talked a while. Suddenly, Mom said I shouldn't have come because the whole family was going to Toronto tomorrow for her two weeks out of the hospital. Jody didn't know anything about it, which was why she hadn't let me know. We both just sat there stunned. Was I going to be stuck in New Brunswick all by myself for Christmas? Mom suggested we try to change my ticket so I could go back with them, but the whole thing suddenly seemed so different from what I had planned. When Jody and I finally left, I hated leaving Mom there alone. It seemed like such a prison.

Next, we went to my grandmother's house where Bob was shocked to see me. After talking a bit, he agreed that we should try to change my ticket at the station and explain what had happened. Last of all, I went to Memere and Pepere's house, the only truly stable, loving home I had ever known. The happiest times of my life had been spent there. When I arrived, everyone was so excited; it made the whole trip worth it. Memere and Pepere and my aunt Lanie just couldn't stop laughing and hugging and kissing me. I felt so loved for that brief moment in time. Memere and Lanie and I giggled and laughed all night long, just like old times. It almost felt like I had never left. The only sad thing was that it was such a short visit. The next morning I got up late and Memere made the same wonderful pancakes I always remembered, with lots of molasses. When it was time to leave, it was so cold outside that she gave me her muskrat coat. I had always loved that coat. Then Pepere took me to my other grandmother's house and it was time to leave and go back to Toronto. Pepere and Memere had always called me "The Gail of Wind", a nickname which suited me well. This time my visit had truly passed like a gale.

Once back in Toronto, it was nice to be with my family again. I had fun with Shane; he was such a funny little kid. We had a terrific Christmas that year. Mom and Bob stayed at her brother's place, while Jody and Shane stayed with us at Dad's. They had gifts galore, which must have been marvelous for the two of them. Then it was time for them to go back to New Brunswick and plans were made for another visit at Easter when Mom would again be let out of the hospital. When they arrived in Toronto that Easter in 1974, Bob announced he had no intention of going back to New Brunswick. To put it mildly, Mom had escaped from the hospital. Bob soon found work and an apartment where the rent was cheap, in the same building as his friends Blackie and Vera, Lydia and Cheyenne's parents. Blackie and Vera's lives hadn't changed from the days of living on Bloor Street. Their apartment was still a hangout for drunks and drug addicts.

Although I could go visit them often, I finally decided to move in with mom and Bob and the kids. Why I would want to leave a nice, clean apartment for that dump with no furniture, I'm not really sure, but by now I had drifted apart from Domino and enjoyed spending time with my sister and brother. We'd go to the park and play, and do what kids should be doing instead of dating and acting like grown-ups.

Sometimes I would go up to Vera's place to see Lydia. There was always something going on there, guitars playing, music and people coming and going. Wherever Vera moved to, the party followed, including dirty old men. One of them was a man named Paul. He had long, black hair that he combed over to one side and held in place with hair spray to cover up the scars on his forehead from a car accident. He was a scary looking man and it was no wonder he didn't have a real girlfriend. All he did was drink all day and look like a psycho. When he got mad, he would flip back his hair and reveal the scars which would frighten you to death. Always part of the entertainment scene, he would play the harmonica and guitar, singing religious songs like "Why Me, Lord". He was also a bastard who raped and beat young girls. It wasn't long before I was caught in his web.

One night I was leaving Vera's place quite late when Paul said he was leaving too and would walk me down to my apartment. I said no, that was fine, I could go myself. I left quickly, but as I turned a corner, he appeared out of nowhere, grabbing me and asking why I had made him look like a fool in front of everyone. Why wouldn't I let him walk me home? I asked him to please let me go and he yanked my hair and said, "No, you little tramp, you're coming with me." I started to kick and bite, but he was stronger, and pulling me by the hair, he dragged me into an empty apartment. There on the floor he beat me and raped me, saying I was a slut and a whore and if I said one word to anyone he would hurt my little brother and sister. I lay there bleeding and in pain and crying, believing every word he said. When he finally left, I put my clothes on and went home to take a bath, all the time sobbing uncontrollably. I wondered why this was happening to me. In the future I would try to stay clear of where he was, but it would happen several more times before it all came to a vicious end.

I started to hang around the corner pool hall with my new friends, Keria and Tanya. Keria was a tall blonde girl with a baby boy, while Tanya was blonde and short. One day as I was leaving my apartment to take Shane to a restaurant for something to eat, there was Paul right behind us. He grabbed hold of my arm, but because Shane was with me, I had to pretend everything was all right. A little way down the street, at the corner of Dundas and Ossington, I first set eyes on John, standing with his friend in front of the bank. Something drew me like a magnet to John. It was like love at first sight. I was smiling from ear to ear and kept looking back at him while he kept smiling at me. I was barely sixteen, but I knew what I was feeling. It was total love. That idiot Paul never even noticed what was happening. John was Portuguese and had a slim build, with curly black hair, big brown eyes and olive skin. It didn't take me long to find out who he was.

After Paul left us at the liquor store, and Shane and I had eaten, I went upstairs to Tanya's place above the restaurant. I knew she would know who this guy was because she was always hanging around the pool hall and knew everyone. Tanya threw a party so John and I could finally meet, and like most teenage parties, everyone ended up paired off and in the bedrooms. John and I found ourselves kissing together in her mother's bed, but even though I was in serious la-la land, I didn't let him have sex with me. I felt sure that if I gave in right away, he would have gotten what he wanted and the whole thing would be over. Most young guys I knew were like that, so why would he be any different? I thought I'd just see how much he liked me, and did he like me enough to wait for what he wanted.

John and I started seeing each other every night after that. It took him a month before I gave in. He thought I was a virgin. He never asked, just assumed I was because I made him wait longer than most girls he had been with. The whole thing was bliss for me, it didn't matter what else I was going to have to face in life. John was now part of my reality and I was happy.

CHAPTER THREE
The Fall

It was a warm and sunny morning and I was still asleep. I had no idea yet just how cold it was going to get before the day would end so cold and out of control. The chill was going to come from the pain I would experience. Very soon, my whole life would go topsy-turvy.

I was lying in bed, but as I awoke, I could feel a presence standing beside me. It was the police. Opening my eyes, I rubbed them, trying to get focused on what it was that I was seeing. Was it real or not? Then the police asked, "Are you Gail?"

"Yes, I'm Gail," I answered, trying to wake up.

"We'd like you to come with us and identify your mother," they said. "She's had a fall."

Looking over at the clock, I saw it was only 7:00 A.M. What was my mother doing up so early? She never got up early if she could help it, preferring to get up around lunch time. Maybe it was a mistake and it wasn't my mother; it didn't make sense. I asked if they could wait while I got dressed, but they said no, I had to come right away. I told them my little brother Shane was still asleep, but they said it was fine to leave him there. Shane was only four years old and I didn't want to leave him. If he woke up and discovered he was alone, he would be frightened.

Following the police, I walked with one in front of me and one behind. I'm sure they must have been at least six feet tall, maybe taller. I was only fifteen years old, and the hair on my arms started to rise in fear. Where were they taking me? What was I going to see? Was she dead? *Identify, identify.* The words were clanging in my head like the sound of cymbals banging. The noise was getting louder and louder as we walked out of the bedroom into the hall. Then we were in the kitchen. We lived in a place they called the ghetto, an old U-shaped brownstone with six fire escapes that led to the courtyard below. Then we were at the back door. The police officer in front opened the door to the fire escape. Some of the old wooden boards had rotted away and were missing so if there ever were a fire you would break your neck long before you got out. Either that, or the fire escape would ignite first from being as dry as kindling wood. Looking over the side, I could see people everywhere, some looking up at me and some looking down. I stopped in my tracks, wondering what they were staring at, and feeling like I was lost somewhere in time. I didn't want to take the first step down those stairs; down to whatever it was they were looking at in the courtyard. The look on their faces was cold and frightening, for these were faces I knew, faces that usually had a smile or a warm hello. Even though it was a booze and drug-infested place, everyone knew each other and felt a kinship to one another. Now their faces were just like stone, mouths gaping, eyes wide open. Everyone was silent and still. I felt like I was going to the gallows to be hung. Step by step I got closer until I was in the courtyard, still walking between the two officers. Feeling them tower over me, I wasn't sure which I feared more, the police who sandwiched me between them, or what I was about to see.

We walked towards the south side of the courtyard, to the next fire escape on my right. There, lying in a pool of blood at the bottom of the cement stairs, was my mother. Her head looked like a bomb had just gone off. How did anyone know this was my mother? Had she fallen? Did she lose her balance? The fire escape was in such bad shape that must have been it. No! How about pushed, was she pushed? That is what everyone must have been thinking, but only I knew the truth of what had happened. I wasn't going to say anything to anyone. Let them think what they wanted. No wonder the police used the word *identify*. My mother's hair was blonde, but I could only see a few blonde strands because the rest was drenched in blood. I didn't know the human body had that much blood. She lay there lifeless. I started to look down to the rest of her body, looking for any sign to be able to say, no, this is not my mother. But I couldn't, because I recognized her clothes. What little I could see of them that weren't soaked in blood. A pair of brown and tan stretch pants. Yeah, it was my mother, all right. I felt frozen, and began thinking I must be dead. Someone was holding me, but I was in shock. I didn't even see their face. I could now hear the ambulance siren in the background, one of the most haunting sounds in the world. I had heard that sound so many times in my life. Then the paramedics were looking for signs of life as they placed her on a back board, then on a stretcher and into the ambulance. Oh God, my little brother Shane was standing beside me. How did he get there? How long had he been there, what had he seen? He was sleeping when we left the apartment, now he was dressed, with his little yellow and blue jacket zipped up. Shane was only four years old; he didn't know how to zip up his jacket. Someone must have woken him and dressed him. Why would anyone do this, it was so cruel. Now he had seen our mother and all that blood while he just stood there silent. His little brown eyes were just staring. What was this whole tragic picture going to do to him? I picked him up and held on for dear life, not saying anything. Staring up at the fire escape, I could see where Mom must have hit the handrails at least three times before she reached the ground, because they were broken off in three different places. The ambulance was ready to leave, although the paramedics hadn't told us if she was alive or not. The police said they needed to question me, and would drive me to the hospital afterwards.

Jenna and Tim, the superintendents of the building, took Shane into their apartment. Shane knew them well, for they had five children of their own who he often played with. Tim was an overweight alcoholic and Jenna was about an eighty-pound bundle of nerves, addicted to Coca-Cola and cigarettes, but I knew they would be kind to my little brother.

The police took me back upstairs to our apartment for questioning. As we climbed the fire escape stairs, I could hear the people's voices go from a whisper, and then louder and louder, the further away we went. Once inside, the police started to ask questions. Does your mother drink, do drugs, have any enemies? Does your stepfather drink, does he beat her? I felt like a zombie and just sat there until they stopped. They could see that I wasn't

51

going to be of any help to them. So instead, they searched the place, starting with Mom's bedroom where they found some of her pills and bagged them for evidence. There were little drops of blood on her mattress, then more on the hardwood floor, just kind of sprinkled there. But that's where the blood stopped, in her bedroom. It didn't go into the hall or anywhere else. The officer said that was strange, very strange. The whole time they searched, my mind was racing a mile a minute. All my thoughts were jumbled so I couldn't think straight. Even my tears, if I had any, were frozen like icicles deep down inside me.

After what felt like a whole day, but was actually only about an hour and a half, the police said it was time to go to the hospital. I got up from the old orange davenport sofa that Mom had found in the garbage. The material was as rough as sandpaper, so when you got up from sitting on it, your legs looked like a cat had just gotten to you. I locked the apartment and we started to leave, this time through the front door. Going down the front stairs usually wasn't much better than the back ones, as they reeked from the smell of urine, human feces, vomit and garbage. As we walked down, I saw the people standing there, looking and staring. The news reporter had arrived as well, snapping pictures and asking questions. Didn't they have any compassion? I guess they had a job to do, so there was no time for compassion. They were just like vultures swooping down on their prey. I got into the police car and we started to drive away slowly. All the time I was still silent, sitting there as we got closer and closer to the hospital, wondering if my mother was dead or alive.

When we arrived, we went straight to emergency where we were told to go to the intensive care unit. That was a good sign because it led me to believe she wasn't dead. At intensive care, a doctor and nurse asked to speak to me first, to prepare me for what I was going to have to face. They informed me that she was in grave condition and I could only see her for five minutes. I took a deep breath and went in, while the nurses kept a firm grip on me. And no wonder. She looked like a mummy, all bandaged from head to toe. All I could see were her eyes, which were closed tightly. They had her in a neck brace and body cast, with tubes and bags hanging from everywhere. It was a horrifying sight for a fifteen-year-old child to experience. I was only allowed five minutes, and now I knew why. Those five minutes felt like hours.

Mom's sister Yvette arrived, followed soon by the rest of her brothers and sisters. Everyone was asking questions all at once. Where did it happen? How did it happen? And the big one—*why* did it happen? They weren't stupid, they knew the answer. They just wanted confirmation, and I knew it wouldn't be long before the *why* was answered.

Yvette and I finally left the hospital and went back to the apartment building. My aunt wanted to see where Mom had fallen from, so we went into the courtyard where there were still people hovering around. Yvette couldn't believe it was possible that Mom was still alive. Everything had a cold and eerie feeling as we walked up the fire escape to the top, from where my mother had fallen. There was nothing except an overwhelming feeling of loneliness and despair, the feeling of a woman on the edge with no one to turn to. Standing there, I imagined the hurt and desperation she must have been feeling. After that, we went into the apartment and sat and talked until my stepfather Bob arrived home from work. Yvette told him what had happened and he just couldn't believe what he was hearing. Bob was an alcoholic, but he treated Mom pretty well and loved her in his way.

After Yvette left, Bob and I went into Mom's bedroom and started to look around. Bob knew her ways more than I did, as he had been through this many times before, if this was what we thought it was. Lifting the mattress, he found our answer, a white envelope with "THIS HIS MY LAST WORDS" written on the front. Mom was French, so instead of the *is* she had used the word *his*. No matter how she spelled it, I knew exactly what it meant. Suddenly, those icicles that were frozen inside me started to melt and the tears came as it finally hit home what had really happened. There it was written in ink, confirming my worst fears and what deep down inside I already knew. She must have thought long and hard, for it was five pages. Together, sitting in her room, Bob and I read it.

Bob was distraught, feeling guilty about taking her out of the mental institution in New Brunswick on his own without the doctors' permission. I tried to console him and said it didn't matter, that it was going to happen sooner or later, one way or another. It was just a matter of time and opportunity. I don't know if it helped, but it was the best I could do. At the same time, I was trying to come to grips with all this myself, and at fifteen it was a hard lesson in reality. Before Bob left for the hospital, he warned me not to tell a soul about the letter, especially the police. Then he opened the back of the TV and hid the letter inside. I didn't understand at the time why he didn't want the police to know about the suicide letter, but later he said if the police found out, they would have her committed to a mental institution. Poor Bob, he was so confused in his thinking about Mom. In one breath he felt guilty for helping her escape the mental institution, and in another breath he didn't want her to go back. I think he was in some sort of denial when it came to my mother's mental capacity, and the alcohol he drank didn't help him in his thought process. I know how he felt, for even though I didn't drink, my mom could lead me to believe she was fine one moment, and then totally incapacitated the next. It kept us so unstable and always on our guard. In the end, she could have us questioning our own sanity.

After Bob left, I thought about what my mother had done. She had been suicidal most of her life, but how could she inflict so much pain on herself? She had jumped three floors down, landing on cement basement stairs. Didn't she love us any more? She had always tried to drill into our heads that our father had left because he didn't love us. When you hear things like that from your mother for long enough, you finally start believing it yourself. Then Mom had abandoned Marilyn and me two years ago, taking Jody and Shane with her and just leaving us to fend for ourselves. Was this the final exit? How much rejection did she think we could take?

Marilyn came and picked up Shane and Jody so they could stay with her for a day or so until we found a more permanent place for them. At only fourteen, Marilyn was a mother herself, living with her boyfriend Bill and his parents. Her baby Brandon was now six months old. Jody had been staying at her boyfriend Wilfred's parents' place when this all happened. She was only twelve years old at the time. When I look back, I am amazed at how involved we three young girls were in such sexual relationships. With no love or comfort at home, we must have been trying to find it the only way we knew how. We were children thrown into an adult world with no real understanding of what it was all about.

Seeking to escape from everything I'd had to deal with that day, I went to see some of my friends at the local hangout, a small diner on the corner of Dundas and Ossington. I can still remember the song that was billowing out of the jukebox when I arrived—Elton John's "Don't Let The Sun Go Down On Me". How appropriate, as it fit the exact frame of mind I was in. As my friends Tanya and Keria sat and talked with me about what had happened, someone in the diner kept playing that same song over and over. Finally we left, heading over to Sam's Pool Hall just around the corner. And what do you know; the same song was playing there as well. It may have been coincidence, but somehow I felt it was being played for me. To this very day, whenever I hear that song it takes me back to that very lonely and painful time.

Not long after we arrived, John showed up at the pool hall. I was so glad to see him. He'd heard what had happened and had already looked for me at the apartment. As we hugged and kissed, I knew that he was all I would ever want, that this was an attraction that would last a lifetime. He was to be my first and last love. We hung around the pool hall until one o'clock in the morning, and then John took me back to the apartment, asking if I would be all right there by myself. I said yes, I'd be fine. Then he kissed me like I'd never been kissed before and left. As I unlocked the door and let myself in, I could feel the emptiness inside as though it was tangible thing, reflecting the sadness and pain that had filled our lives as a family. Even without the tragedy that had beset us, it was an empty, cold, sparsely furnished place, like our lives. There was the old orange davenport sofa, a budgie bird on a stand, and a TV under the drafty window, but little else. My mother's room had an old brown metal bed with a reading light attached to it. Was the light for reading, I wondered, or for writing suicide letters? As I had never so much as seen Mom pick up a book or newspaper, I didn't think it was for reading.

Most of our furnishings came from the Salvation Army, or empty apartments, things that people would leave behind when they moved away. Our kitchen was just a small pass-through, with an old chrome table and three chairs. We had never even once eaten at that table all together. Not many meals were made in our home. We kids mostly had to fend for ourselves with cereal, sandwiches, or whatever we could find. With most of the money going for booze, there wasn't much left over for food.

Going into the bedroom that I shared with Shane and Jody, I lay down and tried to go to sleep, but my mind was racing too much. Getting up again, I went and took the letter out of the back of the television and started to read it, trying to understand what had driven my mother to do such a desperate thing. "THIS HIS MY LAST WORDS" would come to haunt me for the rest of my life. Everything else in the letter would eventually become a blur, but never those words. They would stay etched in my heart forever.

That night I hardly slept much, if at all. Was my mother going to pull through, I wondered. If she did, would she be little more than a vegetable? If that were the case, maybe it would be better to let her go. She was causing herself so much pain, not to mention what she was doing to the rest of us. You just never knew when she was going to try to end her life and how. It was always a different way; pills, slicing her wrist, standing in front of a train, a plastic bag over her head, or drowning. The emotional abuse was like a roller coaster ride from hell, one we never seemed to be able to get off.

By the next morning, I could hardly wait to leave the apartment and go to the hospital. I just couldn't stand it there alone any longer. As I had no money for the street car, I had to walk. Some of my mother's family was already there when I arrived, and again we were allowed only five minutes with Mom since she was still in a coma with the same laboured breathing as yesterday. It was nerve-wracking standing there listening to her, realizing there was no sign of improvement. I stayed at the hospital most of the day, and then my Aunt Yvette took me home. That's when I told her about the letter and she asked to see it herself. After reading it, she asked if she could take it with her, so I told her what Bob had said about not telling anyone, especially the police. Yvette assured me she would talk to him, so I finally gave in and let her take it.

In the letter, Mom had said she wanted her brother Phil and his wife Betty to take care of Shane and raise him. I guess the rest of us were supposed to be Dad's responsibility. A couple of days later Yvette must have decided to put Mom's wishes into action because Uncle Phil came to get Shane. It was really the best place for him as he would at least be fed and looked after. It broke my heart as I packed his clothes, for he was so small, he didn't understand. With my mother in the hospital and Shane and Jody leaving my life again, the feeling of abandonment crept back into my mind. Only my stepfather was still living with me in the apartment. I could have gone back to live at Dad's, but I wanted to be close to the hospital to be with Mom, even if she didn't know I was there. There was no way of knowing how much longer she would be on this earth. I still wanted to have a mother who loved me as much as I loved her, or was my love only a form of pity for her? Whatever my feelings were, I knew I needed to be close to her just to feel some connection to the woman with the title *mother*. No matter what kind of mother she was, she was still the person who had given me life. Despite the pain it had brought us both, there was a bond between us.

As it turned out, she was in intensive care for six weeks. What she didn't know was that she had created a void within me, a feeling of helplessness. Her pain and suffering had a snowball effect that had wounded all of us kids and the family around her. I wondered if she knew, or even cared, about what damage she had done, or was she so lost herself that she had no idea?

During the three and a half months that she was in the hospital, my life was a living hell. Bob spent almost all his time either working or upstairs at Vera's place where the parties went on every night, with the booze and drugs flowing like a river. In the meantime, I befriended a homeless girl named Melanie and took her in, glad to have the company in the empty apartment. She was a dark-haired French girl who had run away from her home in New Brunswick. I couldn't imagine wanting to leave home, when all I wanted was to have a home and a stable life. We both started to look for work, but at first we were so desperate for money that I went back to my old ways of stealing milk from the stores early in the morning and cashing the jugs in. It wasn't long before I found a job in a little coffee shop on Dundas Street. I had to lie about my age to get the job, which wasn't difficult as I had always looked older than I was. By now I looked about twenty-one and was getting into bars. There were times when I would hitchhike and the police would drop my friends and me right off at the bar. As trained as they were, even they couldn't tell my true age.

Now that I had a job, it was nice having some money of my own, but nighttime was a terror when I had to walk home alone. Paul would be waiting for me, always in a different place so I never knew where he would be. Just when I would think I had made it home, he would jump out and grab me. If he saw me standing at the corner waiting for the lights to change, he would drag me right through the red light into a lane way, or empty apartment. Most times it was the furnace room in our own apartment building where he knew no one could hear me scream. There, in the damp and dark and cold, I would hear and feel mice and rats running around as he raped me. One time he wanted me to have oral sex with him, so I bit his penis as hard as I could. I regretted it afterwards because he drove my head into the concrete floor and just kept on smashing it until I was bleeding. Always, he would force me to have violent sex with him.

Another time he took me to the apartment that he shared with his uncle Pat and Pat's wife Nora. When he dragged me into the bathroom, I saw with horror that the bathtub was filled with about two inches of blood. It was Nora's blood from Pat having beaten her black and blue. She worked at the restaurant next door and you never saw her without her sunglasses on. Now I knew why. I found out later that Nora died from choking on a chicken bone, but the story is that Pat hit her while she was eating and that's what caused her to choke. It wasn't long after her death that Pat skipped out of town and got away with it.

Paul told me that if I didn't do what he said, my blood would be in that bathtub too. He was a terrifying person, with one eye that turned in, and those dreadful scars on his forehead. He looked like a monster. Sometimes I felt like this nightmare would go on forever, which must be why I finally got so desperate that I did what I did. One day, my day off from work, Paul came pounding and kicking on the front door of the apartment, insisting that I let him in. I didn't want to, but I knew I'd be punished later for locking him out, so I opened the door. Immediately, he started to hit me and rip off my clothes. All of a sudden, something inside me snapped and I knew what I was going to do. Trying to avoid his blows, I backed slowly into the kitchen until I had Paul just where I wanted him. There was a aluminum glass door there, and before I lost my nerve, I pushed him right through it. All the glass shattered and he was in shock at what I had done. The look on his face was fearful as he gazed at his hand that was all gouged, with the blood squirting everywhere. The cuts were so deep you could see the tendons and veins just gushing all over. I kept on pushing until I got him out the back door, then I slammed the door and locked it. Standing there terrified, I could hear him outside yelling, "I'm going to kill you, whore! Just wait! You're dead, slut!" Running to the front door, I locked that too and sat there silent, trembling all over and in tears, hoping he would just go away. Finally I heard his footsteps leaving, going down the fire escape, and the whole time he was yelling, "You're dead! You're dead! You're dead!" All I could think to myself was, "Oh no, what have you done? You're going to get killed." The truth was, at fifteen years old, I just couldn't take the emotional and sexual abuse any longer from this brutal monster.

It wasn't long before I heard a knock at the front door. Oh God, I thought, he's back. Sitting there paralyzed with fear, I was completely silent, terrified that he was about to come through the door and kill me. The knock sounded two more times, and then I heard footsteps leaving. A sigh of relief came over me, while my heart continued to pound. After a while, I finally went and opened the door to peer out. The lady living next-door came out of her apartment when she heard me and said John had come to find me. I had been so scared when I heard the knocking that it had never occurred to me it might be someone like John. Now it was too late and he was gone. Feeling bereft, I went back into the apartment and started to cry, wanting to be with John, but too afraid to leave and go find him in case Paul was hiding somewhere. What I didn't know yet was how much damage I had actually done to Paul's arm when I pushed him through the door. I had never even told John, or anyone else about Paul, because I was afraid if I told him he would get his buddies and give Paul a good beating. Then I would have put John in danger as Paul and his uncle were lunatics and hated the Portuguese. Instead, I wanted to take care of the problem myself so I could protect this one person who had given me so much love.

For a while there was peace for me. Paul was in the same hospital as Mom, so I found out that he was now crippled in one arm and would be that way for the rest of his life. Finally safe from him, I soon learned that he had been doing the same abusive thing to another girl in the building. Like me, she was only fifteen, and had been too afraid to tell anyone what was going on. I was so glad that I had put a stop to that sexual deviant who preyed on young girls. It was painful enough just trying to deal with my mother's crisis.

After three and a half months in the hospital, my mother came home. Bob had decided to move us to a basement apartment so Mom wouldn't come back to the same place she had lived in before. His logic was that there would be too many memories, and she would be safer in the basement. This meant that now we would be right next to Paul, but I wasn't afraid of him any more. He was a cripple and could no longer hurt anyone. Besides, I had seen enough blood in the last three months to last a lifetime. No one, I decided, was ever going to hurt or scare me again.

CHAPTER FOUR
Motherhood

We were all now settled in the basement apartment. It had a large living room, two bedrooms, a kitchen, and a door off the back to the fire exit. Classified as a three-bedroom, it also had a small room just off the kitchen that was more like a pantry, but served as my bedroom. I soon had it furnished with a bed, dresser, my stereo and whatever decorating I could do considering the limitations of what I had to work with.

Mom returned from the hospital in a cast and crutches. She was still in really bad shape, so the social workers arranged for a hospital bed. The health nurses came daily to wash and clean her, but Bob and I still had our hands full trying to look after her. When Bob was home he would cook us meals like stews and spaghetti, always a one-pot meal with every spice in the cupboard thrown in. He wasn't a bad cook, for the food was always tasty and it was definitely better than no meal at all. We never actually sat down together as a family to eat, just helped ourselves from the pot when we wanted it. In our family, it was always a case of everyone fending for himself.

When the cast finally came off and Mom started getting around on her own, Bob went back to spending most of his time upstairs at Vera's. One day I sat down with Mom to talk about what had happened and why she would do such a thing to herself. She explained that she had lost her balance

and fallen. That was all. I debated with myself whether to mention the letter, then finally decided to leave well enough alone. Instead, everything was
allowed to slip back into the same familiar pattern, the pattern of life in the
ghetto, where food is the last priority and drugs and booze come first on
every parent's list. It was a place where you can look out and see the kids
eating out of the garbage cans, a place where lives are lived in desperation
and denial. My mother didn't want to admit what had happened and I was
too young to help her. Instead, like I had done all my life, I tried to find
stability by ignoring what was bad.

As soon as she could negotiate the stairs, Mom started going back to Vera's, right on the same floor she had jumped from. I didn't like the thought
of her going up the rotten fire escape stairs because her balance was still
off and there were always drunks and drug addicts as well as kids running
up and down. Sometimes it seemed more like a highway; the traffic was so
heavy on those derelict stairs. I still recall one night when my mother was
in the hospital and Paul had just raped me in the furnace room. As I came
running into the courtyard with Paul right behind me, I heard arguing going
on between a man and his girlfriend who were both drunk. Paul grabbed
me by the hair to stop me, told me to shut my mouth and not say a word,
and then held me behind a large pillar. As I waited in fear, I saw the woman
get thrown down and killed by her boyfriend. I didn't know she was dead
at the time, but I found out the next day. The talk was that she had lost her
footing and fallen, breaking her neck, but I knew better.

There was no way I could convince Mom not to go up those stairs. One
thing you could never give my mother was advice. It was like all those times
we would ask her for money and she would give us half what we asked for,
only in this case if you gave her advice, she would double what you didn't
want. Like a child she would go to the opposite extreme just to get under
your skin. It was a form of control for her.

Things moved back into the same familiar pattern for us kids as well.
Jody went back to school, Shane was with Mom where ever she went, and
I went back to hanging around the corner with my friends Keria, Tanya,
Sally and Melanie. Mostly we went to the movie theater on Dundas and
Bathurst, where the only thing showing always seemed to be Bruce Lee or
another kung fu movie with subtitles. We girls weren't crazy about those
movies, but we sure liked the cuddling and smooching that would eventu-

ally take place. It was just a hangout for us, as all of our boyfriends would meet us there, including John.

By now I was feeling really in love with John, just like all the other love-sick teenagers I was hanging out with. Desperate for affection, I was thinking more and more of marriage and babies while John was only thinking of fun and sex. One by one, we girls all started getting pregnant. First there was Tanya, who decided to give her baby up for adoption, then Melanie who had a little girl and decided to keep it. Next, Sally had a girl and kept hers as well. Finally, it was my turn and there I was thinking it was fantastic being pregnant and that John was going to feel the same. Well, I was wrong. Someone told John before I had a chance to, and the minute he showed up that evening I could tell he wasn't happy about it at all. He told me the best thing would be to have an abortion. It wasn't that he didn't love or care for me, he just figured we were too young for a big responsibility and that I had no idea what we'd be up against. He said we just didn't need this right now because it wasn't all fun and games raising a child.

Well, he was talking to the wrong girl as there was no way I was going to give this child up. I loved John so much, but even if he wasn't going to be there to help me, it didn't change anything. I was willing to go it alone, with or without him. Of course, at seventeen you think you know it all. You have a job making one hundred and twenty dollars a week; you're living at home and know nothing about paying for things like rent, food, bills, baby-sitters or education. You're too busy buying clothes and going out to eat in restaurants, or to the movies, and just having fun with your friends.

Once John realized I was going to have the baby, he kept coming around to see me, but our nights together started to slowly get further and further apart. John began going downtown to different bars and after-hours clubs where the rest of us didn't hang out. In the meantime, I went to the bars on Queen Street and to the Portuguese dances on Sundays where I soon met an Italian guy named Regan. He had long black hair and wore shaded glasses all the time to cover up the fact that he had one blue eye and one brown. Before long we started meeting each other on weekends at the club until he finally came to my apartment for the first time. We were listening to music and talking in my room when there was a knock on the door. I didn't hear it, but Jody answered and it was John. When I heard John's voice I jumped up and hid Regan behind my bedroom door, but in that tiny room there wasn't much chance that he wouldn't be discovered. After John found him, I asked Regan to leave, seeing as we were only friends and not sexually involved, but I could clearly see the hurt in John's eyes, and in the end they both left. I had no idea they already knew each other. What a way to find out. I guess John thought I would always be there for him because I loved him so much, but I didn't feel like just sitting around and waiting. I was too young and having too much fun for that, especially as John was continuing to go out on his own.

By November 1975, when I was ready to have my baby, we were again moving to a new apartment above a store on Queen Street. I had managed to find things like a dresser and small crib in the second hand stores and was busy stripping and painting them. The night before the move, when everything was already packed up in boxes, Jody didn't come home. By the time it was past midnight, Mom had worked herself into a panic and phoned Jody's boyfriend Wilfred, but he said she wasn't there either. At one o'clock in the morning, Mom said, "Gail, come on and get dressed. We're going to Wilfred's place because I don't believe him." It was snowing and cold outside and I didn't want to go, but I couldn't let her go alone. We walked along Dundas, up Ossington, and on to Foxley Avenue. Normally, this would be a five-minute walk, but it was snowing hard and I was ready to deliver my baby any time. Finally arriving at the house, I stood on the sidewalk while mom rang the bell, then yelled that she had just seen someone run from the kitchen, so she knew Jody was there. I said, "Are you sure?" and Mom said, "Yes, I can see her sweater hanging on the chair." Mom kept ringing the doorbell until Mrs. Foxley, as Mom referred to her, opened the door. She was totally drunk or half asleep and standing there with no clothes on. Mom yelled at her, "You fucking whore, go get dressed." Leaving us standing there, she went and pulled a housecoat on, then came back and said Jody wasn't there. Mom just pushed her forcibly out of way and ran down the hall through the kitchen to the back porch where she found Jody hiding. Grabbing my sister by the hair and picking up the sweater, she left the house in a fury that didn't abate all the way home. She had a few choice words for Jody along the way, and they didn't include any Hail Marys. When we got home, Mom shoved Jody into the apartment so she fell in between some of the boxes and onto the couch, then started punching and hitting her. First I yelled at Mom to stop, then I tried to pry her off Jody, but she was so furious that she just kept clouting her everywhere, hitting her with those huge gaudy rings she liked to wear on her fingers. She was so angry, I thought she might clobber me too, pregnant or not. I just kept crying and yanking at my mother until she finally snapped out of it.

After everything calmed down and Mom went to bed, I snuck into Jody and Shane's bedroom. I sat on her bottom bunk-bed and held her in my arms. She was still sobbing and I asked her why she had tried to run away. She said she hated our mother, that she felt like Mom's slave; always having to look after Shane and cater to Mom's every whim of "Get me this and get me that." At her boyfriend Wilfred's house, she didn't feel like that, because they were nice to her there. They ate supper together, the father went to work every day, and it seemed normal in that house compared to ours. Until she met that family she didn't know the life we were living was not normal. Now that she knew what a real family was like, that was how she wanted to live, instead being used like a baby-sitter and beaten like a slave day in and day out.

"I hate her, Gail," she said. "When I get old enough, I'm leaving this hell."

I felt her pain because I had experienced it all through my life, but I was also older and knew something of our mother's emotional instability and pill-popping habits. Being older, I felt more pity for mom than hate. I could never find it in me to hate her, yet I understood Jody's desperate longing to live a normal life.

Tucking Jody in, I went to my room and lay down. No matter ho hard I tried to go to sleep, however, my mind would not rest. How could it? I was just about to become a mother myself and now I found myself wondering what kind of a mother I was going to be; a loving one or one, like my mother, who never seemed to have anything but hate for her children? In my heart and mind, all I could think of was the love I felt for this child I had inside of me, and the love it would also have for me. But now I was a bit frightened. If all we were shown was hate and abuse, maybe we would go on and on inflicting that same hate and abuse until it became our family trait, something inherited and passed on like a bad gene. I could only hope that it wasn't in me to be like that. I had spent so much of my early years with my dear Memere and Pepere. Perhaps the love they had given me was like a gift, something that would last a lifetime and become ingrained in me to be passed on down to my child. I could only hope that all that love and compassion would overcome the hate and abuse we had endured as children, until it was tossed out like yesterday's trash, never to be passed on. Lying there in bed, feeling my child move in me, I didn't know where the abuse had started in our family, whether it was just our mother, or a part of her own upbringing as well. Wherever it started, I was determined it wasn't going to continue, so our own children wouldn't feel the need to run away in order to find the love and stability they craved.

The next morning we moved, thank God. There was no way I wanted to raise my child in that ghetto. Our new apartment was much bigger, with an entrance in the back off a lane way. First, you had to walk through the garage into a backyard, and then into the massive kitchen. Upstairs was a huge living room and three really nice bedrooms which we decorated with the second hand furniture Mom and I had found together. Between the welfare money I was receiving, Mom's mothers allowance, and Bob's salary, things were finally starting to get better. Now that we were living a little farther from the ghetto, the money was also being put to better use than just alcohol and drugs. It took more effort to get back to the ghetto, so Bob often came home with a twelve pack of beer that would last him the whole week. Plus Mom had stayed sober ever since her fall, and even though she still took pills, she was not as out to lunch as she used to be. When she went out to the bars down the street, she would just sit there listening to the local bands, drinking her inevitable Pepsi with peanuts thrown in. I liked the area we were now living in, because you could walk everywhere. All my friends lived close by and when you are young, your friends are your whole world. Nor could I go back to Dad's to live even if I had wanted to. That door was now firmly closed. Dad didn't want anyone knowing he had kids as old as his girlfriend and was actually a grandfather. Because he felt and acted like he was twenty, he didn't want to be reminded of his real age. Whenever we went out together, I always had to say I was his sister.

On a cold and snowing day when I was three weeks overdue, I went to the doctor for an appointment. He checked me out, assured me that everything was fine, but said the baby wasn't quite ready to be born yet. I was really disappointed and felt quite teary-eyed, for I was so sure the doctor was going to put me in the hospital since I was overdue. Instead, he just told me to go home and wait. My friend Sally, who had just given birth a month ago, had told me how she took castor oil to bring on the labour. Now I kept thinking about what she had done and how her baby seemed healthy, and how I wouldn't have to wait any longer if I just took some as well. Finally, I went down the street to the drugstore and bought some, then took it home and went into the bathroom. I remember standing there thinking about what I was about to do, then pouring two tablespoons full. It was thick and hard to swallow, so I gagged a few times, but finally it was done and I felt a sigh of relief come over me. Sally had told me that exactly four hours later I would go into labour. I never said a word to my mother until six-thirty when she said she was going out to the bar down the street.

"Well, I can't go with you. I'll be going into labour at eight o'clock," I told her. Mom looked at me like I had lost my mind.

"What are you talking about? Who knows when they're going to go into labour?"

"Well, I do because I took some castor oil."

"Gail, what the hell did you do that for?" she exclaimed.

"I can't wait," I told her. "I'm overdue and I want my baby."

After Mom left, I phoned my sister Marilyn to come over and wait with me. Sure enough, at eight o'clock my stomach started to move from side to side. By the time we went to the hospital around midnight, the pain was getting stronger. The next thing I knew, the nurse was giving me an enema and I didn't dare tell her that was the last thing I needed. I think Sally must have purposefully omitted that detail. Then on December 6, 1975 at 9:55 on a Saturday morning, my beautiful son was born, weighing seven pounds fourteen ounces, with dark hair and almond eyes. I named him John Cory. It was such a thrill looking at this new life that John and I had created together. Now I would always have a part of him with me no matter what happened in my life. I loved Cory the minute I saw him, for he was mine to love. I knew right then that I would live my life for this child because he brought purpose and joy to my bleak existence. I was desperately longing for something to love and now I was sure that this was it. Having created it myself, I finally had the love I craved. For me, this was the ultimate love, the love of a mother for her child.

After Cory was born, I started thinking about John, wondering if I should phone him to tell him he was now a father. No, I finally decided, someone else would have to tell him. Even his father and mother didn't know I existed. Sitting there by the window, I wished he was there sharing the joy of this birth with me. Suddenly reality started to set in and I began feeling guilty and selfish. What had I done bringing this child into the world knowing full well he would be raised without a father. I was already denying him his first basic right, the very thing that I too had lost as a child. Suddenly I faced the reality that all the love in the world doesn't feed or clothe you either. At seventeen, I was so sure I already knew what life was about, having been to the school of hard knocks most of my short life. I thought I had already graduated from that one, but I was soon to find out that I had a few more lessons to learn, that what I already knew and what I thought I knew were two different things.

Mom came to visit me once, but she didn't stay long, saying she had just come to see the baby, not me. She fussed and mussed over Cory, then stole the blanket right off my bed, plus anything else that wasn't nailed down. Dad and Marie also came, which was a lot nicer than Mom's visit. Despite having already given me a baby shower, they now brought an abundance of gifts for both Cory and me. I was really grateful for the visit and gifts. It made me feel loved.

When it was time to leave the hospital, I discovered I couldn't fit right back into my old clothes now that the baby was born. How unrealistic I was, thinking I could gain sixty-five pounds and it would just disappear. I had to phone Mom to bring my maternity clothes, then she and Jody came to pick Cory and me up. I'll never forget those clothes because Jody had a doctor's appointment and had to bring a urine sample that she packed in with my clothes. Well, it spilled all over them and I had to go home feeling wet and smelly.

For the first month after Cory was born I stayed home. Then I started taking him for walks in a big covered carriage, all bundled up. It wasn't until three months later, however, that I finally saw John. When I went to open the door of our apartment and saw him standing there, my heart just about melted. After he came in, I saw tears in his eyes as he stood there looking down at the crib and his son for the first time. I didn't say a thing, just stood there quietly until he had composed himself. After that, John stayed the night and we had sex all night, but we never talked about any commitment to each other. I was just so glad that he had come to see his son and me. Deep down inside I knew that John still wasn't ready for any kind of commitment to us. When he finally left that next afternoon I felt like I was walking on a cloud, even though I didn't know if or when he would ever come back. Like so many women, I had already learned how to go on with my life.

Pretty soon I was back at work, this time working twice a week in Yorkville as a cleaning lady while Mom baby-sat for me. Although I was still on welfare, it wasn't enough for me to live on. Around six weeks later John showed up again and stayed the night with me, this time having sex for the whole night. I never put any pressure on him, but just enjoyed the few times we had together as much as I could. After that, he didn't come again until Cory was seven months old. When he arrived, I was sitting in the bar two doors down from our apartment having a drink. Mom told him where I was and he came and had a drink with me. That visit he again stayed the night and I took pictures of him with Cory. I was so glad I did, for he never came again. He was getting too attached to his son and that scared him. We do such foolish things in our youth, only understanding them later in life when it is too late. John ran away from the very things he valued the most, because he was afraid of commitment.

My friend Melanie and I decided it would be fun to move to an apartment building on College Street. That way we could live right next door to each other and baby-sit for one another. Her little girl was growing and Melanie needed a bigger place than her bachelor apartment, while I too had been saving money and buying things so I could have a place of my own. Both of us put down payments on apartments, and before I knew it, it was time to move. As Melanie had a free moving truck from welfare, and I didn't have too many belongings, we decided to do everything together. That night, after the truck had picked up all my things, I went down to the new place and there was no Melanie. When I asked the superintendent where she was, he said she told him she had decided to go to New Brunswick instead, and had asked for her deposit back. I couldn't believe it. We had been friends ever since I took her off the street and gave her a free place to stay for months. It just didn't add up. How could she have gone off with all my personal possessions after all we had been through together? When Mom and Bob heard about it, they were disgusted. We called the police to try to track her down, but nothing came of it. I guess they had more important things to do. Then I phoned Melanie's mother in New Brunswick and she told me I wasn't the first person Melanie had done this to. She'd even done it in her own hometown, which was why she couldn't ever go back. Her mother promised to call if she found anything out, but no one ever heard from Melanie again.

In the end, I had to stay with Mom and Bob instead of living on my own. It looked like I would have to start saving all over again. Having known Melanie for almost three years, she sure gave a bad name to the meaning of friend, but I tried not to be bitter about it. Once more, the whole family was suddenly moving, this time to an apartment above a store on the corner of Bloor Street and Magretta. It was a little smaller than our other apartment, with three bedrooms and an entrance off a back parking lot. I worked out a deal with my mother to pay the utilities, while she paid the rent and groceries. Everything suddenly seemed much better at home, with Mom no longer drinking ever since her fall, nor did she ever drink again. If I needed a baby-sitter, she was there, but she let me know that she had raised her kids and had no intention of starting all over again and raising the grandchildren. Instead, we split the cost of a baby-sitter to take care of both Cory and Shane, who was only five years older than Cory.

Despite the improvements at home, I still wanted to live on my own, so I started buying new furniture little by little, putting it on layaway. When each piece was paid for, I would take it home. I was kept busy all the time now, taking care of Cory and Shane. We would go to parks and different attractions, or I would read and play with them. Whenever I bought clothes or toys for Cory, I always bought something for Shane too, never wanting him to feel left out. When I baked, I let them help, remembering all the fun times I had had with Memere doing the same things. Even birthdays were shared because their birthdays were only three days apart. The two of them were growing up like brothers, and I tried to be a good mother and sister to them. I didn't have much to go on except my experiences at Memere and Pepere's, but that must have been the foundation for who I would eventually become, and I tried to put all the things I had learned from them into practice now that I was a mother.

One hot, sunny day I was pushing Cory down Bloor Street in his carriage on my way to my friend Sally's house when something made me look across the street. There stood John leaning against the front door frame of a furniture store. I knew he had recently married, so I just kept walking, but I was aching inside. It hadn't taken John long to get married after we broke up, so he must have thought it was true love. I wasn't surprised when I found out that his wife was Portuguese. That was their usual way, to marry within their own nationality. That was something I couldn't compete with, plus I heard they had no plans for having children in the next several years, preferring to get their careers going first. Although this all looked and sounded good to John, he had no idea how a young girl's mind works. Knowing that I had John's child, his new wife had no intention of waiting to get pregnant. Deceiving him, she was pregnant six months later. So John, who tried running away from me and from the responsibility of having a child, walked right into the same thing again. She was a little smarter than me, though. She managed to get that piece of paper first. What she didn't know was that her deception would be the beginning of the end for them. Two children and ten years later, they would be divorced. Although John loved children, he didn't want his own, not until he was ready to be a dad. All this was still in the future, however, including the personality clash that would finally result in their divorce. All I knew at that moment of seeing him again was that I still felt as in love as I had before, despite everything that had happened to us. As I figured John must be working at that store, I made sure it was closed before walking home that night. After that I always took a different route to Sally's. If John couldn't be part of my life, I didn't want to see him. The hurt was too strong.

Not long after that I met a guy named Gene at one of the Portuguese dances. He was slim, with straight dirty-blond hair and brown eyes. We got along great together and were soon seeing each other on a regular basis, but I could already tell that there was something missing from our relationship, even though I couldn't pinpoint it. One evening, after about a year of dating him, my sister Jody invited me to go with a couple of friends of hers to a gay bar downtown called the Carriage House. All I could think was, why would we want to go there? We weren't gay, but Jody insisted that it was a mixed crowd, so I said okay. When Gene heard about it he bugged me all that week about not going. When I asked him why, he said it was mostly gay and not a place for someone like me. I said I knew, but Jody had said not everyone there is gay and it might be fun. We were only going there once to check it out. Gene was so insistent that I said, "Fine, if you don't want me to go, I won't." Of course, that made me want to go all the more, just to find out why he was so against it.

That night, when we got there, it didn't seem very different from any other bar, except that couples of the same sex were dancing together. The music was great and it was fun, with everyone very friendly. The girls and I were sitting talking when to my horror who should I see in the corner of the dance floor, dancing with a black guy, but Gene. Oh my God, that was why he didn't want me to come here. Grabbing Jody's arm, I said, "Look who's here!" Her mouth almost hit the floor.

"Oh, Gail! Did you know?" she exclaimed.

"Are you crazy? I wouldn't be going out with him if I'd known. He's obviously bisexual." I watched as Gene left the dance floor and started kissing in the corner.

"Wow! Jody," I said," I've seen enough." Just then Gene noticed me and his face went blank. Walking over to our table, he said, "Gail, what are you doing here?"

" I can't believe you have the courage to look me in the face and ask that," I replied. "Go back to your sweetheart. I don't want anything more to do with you. Don't phone me again. It's over—the case is closed." By now, everyone at the table was speechless.

"Do you want to leave?" Jody asked.

"No," I said, "to hell with him. Aren't we here to have a good time?"

Gene drifted away and we all started dancing and having more drinks. That's when I met Vince. He'd been eyeing me all evening and sending drinks to our table. Now he asked me to dance, but first I wanted to know if he was gay or bisexual. No, he told me, a lot of people here were straight. After that we exchanged phone numbers.

The next morning I started to think about the whole bizarre situation. I still couldn't believe it, and just thinking about it made me feel sick. Vince phoned that day and asked if he could take me out. I told him my only available evenings were Fridays and Sundays because of my son Cory. When he asked if he could come over instead, I said no. I didn't want Cory to grow up in an environment of guys coming and going in my life, so I tried to keep my relationships away from home. I already knew that I wanted Cory to have respect for his mother and all women, and felt this was the best way to go about it. Instead, I told Vince I could meet him next week if he liked, so we arranged to get together at the Carriage House again.

Vince was an attractive looking guy, very Italian with a short, small build, dark curly hair, big brown eyes and a chiseled chin. After dating a few times we found we really liked each other's company and became a couple. When that happened I didn't mind him coming to the apartment and being around Cory, because I knew we were serious about each other. Vince liked Cory a lot and had a great time with him, which was important to me. When Cory was two years old and I decided to have him baptized, I even chose Vince to be his godparent along with my sister Jody. Unfortunately, Mom and Bob developed a real dislike of Vince after a conversation they all had together about the building of Toronto into the city it is today. The conversation became pretty heated, with Mom and Bob really offended by Vince's attitude about the important role he felt the Italians had played. He had no idea, but it made him a permanent enemy of theirs, and when Mom became your enemy, you never knew what she might do. The next thing I knew, she wouldn't allow Vince to come over any more, even though by then he had been coming for a year. If he phoned, she would slam the phone down, hanging up on him. She even put a huge padlock on her bedroom door so she could lock the phone in her room when she went out. After a while I figured out how to pick the lock and would go in and get it while she was gone, telling myself that we needed it in the event of a serious emergency with the kids. I would also sneak Vince into my room, but inevitably, all this behaviour started putting a strain on my relationship with both of them.

Finally, the situation came to a head one day when Vince came to pick me up. As he wasn't allowed in our apartment any more, I would wait to hear the doorbell and run downstairs to meet him, but this time he was early and I didn't hear the bell. Peeking out the shuttered window, Mom saw that it was Vince and ran to the bathroom. Filling a bucket full of scalding hot water, she went back to the window and threw it down all over him. Hearing the commotion, I ran downstairs to find Vince standing there in his nice gray suit all drenched with water. I just felt like crying, it was so humiliating. I couldn't imaging being that cruel to someone, no matter how much you disliked them.

Soon after that episode, Mom started acting really peculiar. Bob had gone to PEI to work for a year, so there was no one except me to deal with the situation. Little did I know, but this was the beginning of a gradual deterioration in our relationship until I was finally forced to move out. Mom began stealing groceries, coming home with roasts, steaks, butter, all the most expensive foods. Once she was home, she would take everything out and add up her haul for the day, calculating how much it cost. One time, it totaled one hundred and eighty-five dollars worth of food, and she was so proud you would have thought she had just won the lottery. I couldn't believe she was doing this. There was no real reason for it, other than her distorted sense of control, and it finally caught up with her. The day the police brought her home like a child with her hand caught in the candy jar, I felt a role reversal take place. I was now the mother and she was the child. Unfortunately, she was a child I couldn't control

After this incident, she decided that I should start buying my own food, which I kept separate in a small fridge while Mom put a big chain and padlock on her own refrigerator. Then one day I noticed my food was missing and Shane and Mom were sitting eating it. The next thing she did was nail boards across two feet of my bedroom doorway. When I asked her what in God's creation was wrong with her, she said she didn't want Cory coming out of the bedroom and messing up the rest of the house. The whole thing was crazy, because the only place Cory ever played was on the porch with Shane. He wasn't a child who touched and got into things. There was no reason for her to be worried since I was a cleanliness fanatic and did all the housework. By now, however, I realized that she was just looking for excuses to act crazy towards me. Between the phone, Vince, the fridge, and now Cory being locked in the bedroom, I realized it was time for me to find my own place. I finally found an apartment on Colemine Avenue, just off Dundas Street, part of a house that I shared with a single older man. We had to share the washroom, which wasn't ideal, but the rent was reasonable at one-eighty a month, and I already had all the furniture I needed. Hopefully, I would also now have some peace of mind.

For some time after moving into my own place I was about the happiest I had ever been. Vince was now able to come over whenever he wanted and our relationship was working out just fine, while Cory continued to be an easy child. Although welfare was giving me money, it wasn't enough for us to really live off if I wanted more than a hand-to-mouth existence. Putting Cory into day care, I took a job at Marshall Mattress, starting at $4.75 an hour running a pocket collier. Two other people who started working the same morning as me quit by afternoon, but I was determined to learn how to run that machine. The owner was so happy with me that he arranged to have Cory picked up from day care, the two of us taken home for supper, then brought back so I could work overtime. In the evening, Cory would play right beside me with his toys while I worked, then go to sleep on a mattress when he got tired.

The pay kept getting bigger and bigger all the time, as they gave me a raise every week. Being paid so much gave me a sense of self-worth, and we now had enough money to live off of comfortably. When I started, the pay was less than I had received on welfare, but it was better than staying at home and being trapped in the system. By the time my job ended six months later, I was making double the money I had been paid when I started. Unfortunately, after months of picking up heavy bolts of material, I was finally in so much pain that I went for x-rays and discovered I had broken some ribs. It was a shock going back on welfare while I waited for my workman's compensation claim to be decided on. Once you're used to a little bit of independence and money, I discovered, it's hard to give it up.

After three months of waiting, with still no decision made on my claim, I decided I had to find a job that paid cash so it wouldn't affect my welfare status. Finally, I took one selling flowers from a cart. In the morning I would go to a warehouse where a big truck waited, loaded with flower carts. Climbing inside, all the vendors would be trucked to different locations in the downtown area where we would sell the flowers, keeping ten percent of the proceeds. Depending on where you were located for the day, you might make as much as twenty-five dollars, which wasn't much for standing outside all day in the elements. Most days, however, you made more like five dollars for a day's work. Because I had Cory with me, the owner gave me the better spots, plus I put the price of the flowers up by a dollar a bunch. I would have Cory with me all day, and would let him play outside all bundled up, or inside the doors of whatever building I was working next to. Sometimes people just gave Cory money without even buying any flowers. It was a hard way to earn money, especially in winter when it was a contest to see which was more frozen by the end of the day, the flowers or me.

I hadn't seen my mother for almost a year when I ran head-on into her in Wal-Mart. The minute she saw Cory she started crying. Then she went and bought him a toy airplane. I felt sorry for her, thinking she must be a very sick woman. Perhaps the jump had done more damage than anyone realized. Seeing her suddenly, I realized I had missed her more than I knew. All year I had tried to block my feelings out, including the love I had for my brother Shane. It was hard to be without the people I loved, but I wasn't going to let Mom hurt my own child the way she had hurt us kids. As much as I loved Shane, he would have to take second place over the well-being of my child. He wasn't mine, so I couldn't take him with me. This had been the pattern of my life for so long, with everyone I loved coming and going, that it almost seemed normal. Maybe all this pain and loss were preparing me for what life still had in store in my future. When the real devastating tragedy came, I would be able to handle it.

Bob was back from PEI, so the next night I phoned and asked them to come for dinner. It was so exciting when they came the next evening, with Bob hugging and kissing Cory and me, and everyone loving my place. Bob had no idea about Mom's strange behaviour towards me while he was away, nor did I tell him.

Now that things seemed to be better between us, and I began visiting Mom's apartment again, it didn't take long for me to discover that her latest enterprise was bootlegging. She was making a small fortune, with customers owing her as much as three or four hundred dollars a week. She would sell them liquor on credit, then get paid every Friday, as sure as the sun sets. No one ever tried to cheat her. There was no telling what kind of people they were who paid that kind of money, for to Mom they were just a number on a page in her little black bootlegging book. What kind of work could they be doing to spend that much on alcohol, I wondered, and when were they ever sober enough to work? I even caught Mom watering down the bottles of liquor, so the profit she was making was extraordinary.

As if that wasn't bad enough, having a mother bootlegging, I was in for a shock with Vince as well. I had felt so good about him, finally believing I had found a guy with some kind of values, but the next thing I knew I had contracted a sexually transmitted disease. When I told him, he had the audacity to accuse me of giving it to him. Unless I contracted it from the wind, I said, there was no way on earth I could have given it to him. I had been totally faithful. Now, after two and a half years together, I told him to leave and never come back. It was completely over between us.

That's when my self-esteem hit an all-time low. I felt used and abused and worthless. Wondering what was wrong with me, I felt like first my parents hadn't wanted me, and now even the men in my life treated me like shit. There I was, going through life like I was wading in a pond. When the hell was I going to get wise enough to stand up and realize the pond was only knee-deep? Unfortunately, it wouldn't be any time soon. Instead, I would jump from the pond, bypass the lake and dive into an ocean with waves so big I would lose myself and almost drown. Like so many other women we knew, my sister would do the same.

One nice fall day I walked Cory down to visit Mom's. When I got there, I was shocked to discover Marilyn lying in bed in my old room, with her face all black and blue and a cast on both her hands. Bill had beaten and stabbed her until both her hands were broken. After that, she stayed at Mom's for a while, unable to work or take care of her two children. I knew exactly why she hadn't left sooner, and why she always went back to him in the end. It was fear of the unknown, the same fear that keeps so many women tied to abusive husbands. Although he was a coward, and only as powerful as she let him be, it would be years before she would be brave enough to face the unknown and leave him permanently. Only then would she discover that in the end, it is only you, and you alone, who have the real control over your life.

CHAPTER FIVE

The Face Behind the Number

One day I visited Mom's apartment and discovered the person behind one of the numbers in her little black bootlegging book. He lay there passed out drunk on her couch, with a patch over one eye, his arm in a cast, and snoring like a freight-train. I asked Mom what a drunk was doing there in the middle of the afternoon. Was she having an affair behind Bob's back? "No, Gail," Mom said, "he's one of the numbers in my black book." She went on to tell me that he was a nice man named Fred who'd had a hard life. The woman he lived with had left him one day while he was at work, taking everything with her, including his two kids. He was a tall, big-framed man in his thirties, with salt and pepper hair that was starting to go bald, shifty blue eyes, and a cleft chin. Although she still hadn't made it clear why he was there passed out on her couch, I found out he was out on workman's compensation at the time, having broken his arm.

When Fred woke up, Mom gave him a beer. He seemed a nice enough person, although I could hardly understand a word he said because he talked a mile a minute. Not long after that, another man dropped in, just arriving from work, and Mom gave him a shot of whiskey. He too was a number in her little black book, this time a man with straight black hair and a weather-beaten face. Also named Fred, Mom had given him the nickname of Dunn because he lived on Dunn Avenue. It turned out that Fred and Dunn lived together and were roommates. They were both very comical, buying me drinks and keeping us laughing most of the evening. When it finally got late and I decided to go home, Fred insisted on paying for a cab instead of my taking the bus.

A week later, when I again visited Mom, Fred and Dunn arrived, saying they had come to settle up for the previous week. Fred was very friendly, offering to buy me a drink, which I accepted. Afterwards, I went out with my friend, a Portuguese girl I had met about a year before who I had fun going out with to after-hours clubs and partying. On weekends I was able to go out because Mom and I would split on the baby-sitter fees, having a friend of ours come and spend the night with my little brother Shane and Cory.

The next evening, Vince phoned. He was still trying to apologize, playing games with me emotionally, but I continued to tell him that it was over, that I didn't want to be used. Feeling upset by the whole relationship, I headed over to Mom's and who should be there again but Fred and Dunn, drinking and swapping stories about the east coast with Bob. As Fred and Dunn were both from Prince Edward Island, and Bob was from Nova Scotia, there was no shortage of stories. By now I was starting to understand most of what Fred said, although I still had to ask him to slow down sometimes. Once again, Fred offered to buy me a drink. It seemed strange to be paying for drinks in my own mother's house, but she said there were no exceptions for family or friends when it came to her bootlegging business. A while later Fred asked if he could take the kids and me to a bar and restaurant down the street. I didn't want to because I didn't have much money, but Mom assured me he would pay. I wasn't comfortable with that, but both Mom and Fred insisted, so I finally agreed to go. The truth was, I didn't want to go home and dwell on Vince. I wasn't in love with Vince, I just cared deeply about him and had come to enjoy having him in my life. By now I knew that I would never love anyone as much as I had loved John.

At the restaurant we had drinks, food, and lots of fun laughing together. When Fred went to pay, I discovered he had a charge account there as well. A light bulb should have gone off in my head by that time, for after all, he was the face behind one of the numbers in Mom's black book and by the end of the week, all his money had gone to my mother for alcohol. The truth is, Fred was very smooth and made me feel like I was worth something again. At the time, having first lost John and now Vince, I was feeling pretty worthless, and Fred's obvious interest in me fooled me into thinking he was a better person than he really was.

As Fred continued to show interest in me, I still wasn't sure how I felt about him. He was thirty-five and I was only twenty-one, which meant that we were tampering with the older man / younger woman thing that was taboo in our family ever since Dad ran off with Marie. In my mind, I was better off joining a crazy religious cult than running around with an older man. Fred persisted, however, so I finally agreed to dinner and a movie about a month after meeting him. The second time we went to the movies we stopped at my place afterwards and had sex. I wasn't feeling really good about it, but I knew that it was expected of me if we were to continue seeing each other. Somehow the age thing made it seem dirty to me, like it was a reflection of my Dad's relationship with Marie. I didn't mind Fred as a person, for he seemed really caring in my hour of need, but I didn't like to be seen with him. Whenever we went out, I would walk far behind him like we weren't together. Finally, he put an end to it one day by pulling me closer and holding my hand. I kept looking around and hoping no one I knew would see us. Eventually, however, I got over the age difference issue and we became a couple.

In their usual fashion, Mom and Bob were once again pulling up stakes and moving, this time to a house on Dufferin and Bloor Street with three apartments. Fred and Dunn arranged to share the basement apartment while my mother would have the rest of the house. By now Mom had it really made. Not only could she water down the liquor, she could sell Fred and Dunn a case of beer, then steal the full bottles and replace them with empty ones after the guys had passed out. They were so loaded they never caught on to what she was doing. When I eventually caught Mom in the act, I asked her how she could do such a thing. She might as well just shove her hand into their pockets. I told her they both worked hard for their money and I'd tell on her if I ever saw her doing it again. Mom got mad and told me to mind my own business, but she stopped after that.

When Fred was able to go back to work, he didn't drink as much. He had a good job at the tire factory where he'd been for ten years, so I figured he must not be much of a drunk if he could hold down one job that long. After losing his kids, however, he had gone through a bad time. In the summer of 1980, about eight months after I met Fred, he came back from a two-week vacation to Prince Edward Island and moved out of Mom's place and in with me. All he owned was a garbage bag of clothes and an old radio. Looking back, I wonder why I didn't question or notice things more. Why couldn't I see that something wasn't right when a man with a good paying job doesn't have a thing to his name? I guess I kept on thinking it had something to do with his separation from his wife and kids.

Soon after Fred moved in with me I found a new place. By now the house where I lived was overrun with cockroaches, although it hadn't been like that when I moved in. In August, I found a comfortable two-bedroom basement apartment in a triplex on Harvey Avenue. It was a nice area, with a school right across the street, and at first I thought I was finally going to live a fairly normal life. Unfortunately, I was soon to discover that Fred had a different brand of friends from me, people who drank heavily, gambled, and spent their spare time in strip joints. The honeymoon was over even before it had started. On payday, Fred could never find his way straight home. He would be paid, then spend it all at a strip joint, so half the time he never had money to go to work the next week. That's when I put my foot down, insisting I wanted the money for rent and food, that I wasn't going to pay for a roof over his head. My workman's compensation had run out, I was subsisting on a mothers allowance, and there was no way I was cutting myself off. I told Fred if he didn't pay, he'd have to get out.

After my ultimatum, Fred straightened out a bit, bringing home his pay, and phoning if he was working overtime. Instead of frequenting the strip joints, he would arrive home with a case of beer that he shared with his cronies who began popping in regularly. After a while, the old adage "If you can't beat them, join them" finally worked on me and I started drinking right along with the rest of them. But I always kept on top of things, making sure the place was clean, decent meals were served, the bills paid, and Cory well fed and clothed. Unfortunately, the cycle was continuing, and here I was exposing my son to the very life I had hated as a child, only now I was participating in a different way. Sometimes the drinking would slow down for a while, or Fred would stop all together, working longer hours and bringing home more money. Those were the best times, when it seemed like things could get better and we might be able to live a decent life.

Then Dad came home from Saskatchewan where he had gone to live some years before. After ten years together and three sons, he and Marie had split up, leaving him down and out with no place to stay. As I couldn't see him living out on the street, I let him move in with us. At first it wasn't too bad since Dad wasn't drinking. He would just work, then come home and either watch TV or play cards with Fred. I should have known it wouldn't last. As soon as he started drinking again, all hell broke loose, with him bringing women home who he'd picked up in bars. I never knew who was going to walk in with him. Finally, I had to ask him to leave. "Sorry, Dad," I said, "I'm not going to subject Cory to this kind of garbage." No sooner did Dad leave, than Fred was back on a tear, bringing home people to drink and play cards. After a while I stopped drinking with them and it made me sick to hear how stupid they all sounded and behaved after they got drunk. Not only did I hate the hangovers, but more importantly, I had come to realize that with Cory to take care of, someone needed to stay sober.

About a year after Fred and I started living together, his nephew Dillan and a friend came from PEI and moved in with us. For twenty dollars a week, they started sleeping on the sofa while I was expected to cook and do their laundry for them. Fed up with the situation, I asked for thirty dollars and they said the hell with that and went back to PEI. It was a blessing as I was beginning to feel like a stranger in my own home.

For a while after that we had the place to ourselves until the night we heard knocking on the door. There was my sister Jody, with her face so beaten up that I didn't even recognize her. Once I got her lying on the couch, I wanted to hold her, but didn't dare touch her because she was in such excruciating pain. I asked her, "For God's sake, Jody, what happened to you?" She said Wilfred had beaten her up and thrown her out of the car while it was moving. I felt so sorry for her. It seemed that both my sisters had gotten themselves tangled up with the same kind of abusive men. Despite the terrible injury he had done her, Jody only stayed a few days with me before going back to Wilfred. I tried to make her see that she didn't have to leave, that she had a mind of her own. It must have made an impression on her because, despite having a child with him, she finally walked out on him not too long after this episode.

No sooner had Jody left than the family "halfway house" I was running received its next victim, this time my sister Marilyn with her two kids. I felt like I had a big sign on my head saying, "Come on in, there's room at the inn." After two children and eight years later, Marilyn had finally taken her last pounding from Bill. Although I was really glad she had left him, having her live with me was stressful. We had just painted and wallpapered the apartment and the next thing I knew, her kids were ripping and tearing everything, swearing the whole time, and totally out of control. First Fred moved back to my mother's and then I did too. The whole thing was crazy. Now that I was living at Mom's, I had to take a bus so I could get Cory to school, then I'd stay at my place while Marilyn was at work and her children in day care, then back on the bus to Mom's for the night. In the meantime, Marilyn was obviously finding the whole situation very comfortable, spending her free time going out to bars, bringing guys over to my place afterwards, and not paying a cent towards the rent. Fred paid the rent the first month, but by the time it was due again, I decided something had to be done. Fortifying myself with a couple of drinks, I phoned Marilyn and told her to be out by noon the next day or a moving truck would be coming to get her. Marilyn insisted she couldn't move that soon, but I told her too bad, you'd better get out. She moved the next day to her ex-boyfriend Bill's sister's place, and I vowed never to let things get so out of control ever again. Although Marilyn and I didn't speak for a few years afterwards, I had no choice other than to force her to leave.

The next day it felt so good to be back home again. Fred moved back as well and things returned to normal, or a close to normal as they ever were in my life. At just about this time I met a woman in the next building who would become my best friend. Her name was Jane and she lived with her husband George in a triplex that she owned on the second floor. Jane had blond curly hair and was tall and on the heavy side, while her Greek husband spoke with a foreign accent and was short, very loud and extremely opinionated. Jane warned me about George, saying he had a big mouth, but once you got to know him you discovered his heart was as big as his mouth. Jane had seen me walking with my bundle buggy down the street to get groceries and offered to take me in her station wagon every Saturday morning instead. That was the beginning of our long friendship. On our first shopping trip, we had breakfast at a nice restaurant before getting our groceries. Swapping past histories, I learned that she had married a Jewish man and had a daughter with him, before marrying George. I told her about Cory, that Fred wasn't his father, and about how John was my childhood sweetheart and the love of my life. That's when she told me that everyone on the street thought Fred was my father and my real father was my husband, because Dad looked so much younger than Fred. We had a good laugh over that one. Jane and George were actually Fred's age, but seemed a lot closer to me in age. They both worked in the garment trade, George as a cutter for ladies' fashions and Jane in men's clothing. It was like a match made in heaven.

Jane became both a sister and mother to me, while Fred and George also became best friends, although at first I had my doubts because they were both such hotheads. By now Cory was in school full time, so I decided to go back to work. Someone had reported me and I had lost my mother's allowance. As it happened soon after I made my sister move out, I didn't have much doubt about who could have done such a thing. Fred was supporting me, giving me all his pay and letting me take care of the finances, but I didn't like the hold I felt he had over me. I started selling Avon, Shaklee vitamins, and Tupperware. It didn't make a fortune, but it did give me some mad money. I can remember one time when Fred borrowed Dad's van so we could pick up an unusually large order of mine. Usually I just took the bus. When we reached home again, Fred started unloading the van, cursing like a raving lunatic. Before I knew what had happened, the boxes of Tupperware were flying all over the yard, while Fred raved on about "topper ware" until I was in tears from laughing so hard. He couldn't say the word "Tupperware", and the more I laughed, the angrier he got and the more the boxes flew. It's lucky I wasn't selling fine crystal. That ended my career as a Tupperware lady, and it wasn't long before I gave up on the other two as well. Unfortunately, I was often my own best customer.

Once more out of work, and unwilling to stay home all day, I decided to volunteer at Cory's school. Although Fred wasn't supportive of me going to work, he seemed fine with my volunteering. I realize in retrospect that Fred didn't want me to have any independence from him. By now I had gained about a hundred pounds since meeting him, yet any time I tried to lose weight, he frowned on the idea. It took a long time to figure out how insecure he was, that by me being overweight and unemployed, he didn't have to worry about any other man being interested in me. If I put makeup on and dressed nicely, he would say that I looked like a two-dollar whore. Basically, the only time he ever commented on my appearance was to put me down.

The highlight of my day was when Jane came home from work. Cory and I would go with her when she walked her dog Ralph in the cemetery right behind our apartment building. We'd walk with a glass of wine and chat together as we wandered the meandering roadways. It was so peaceful and beautiful, like an enormous private park just for us. Cory would run and play with the dog while Jane and I laughed together. Jane loved to joke about how she already had a burial plot for herself, bought and paid for beside her grandmother's grave, saying that it was the only real piece of property she had ever owned.

Once again, we seemed to have the welcome sign back out, inviting all the stray relatives to come stay. The first to arrive was Fred's nephew Randy from PEI. Tall and lanky, he liked to drink and play practical jokes. After a few months of having him stay without really working, we gave him the heave-ho, only to have Dad back again. For about six months, things worked out fine, with Dad contributing towards the rent and not drinking. It couldn't last, of course, for Dad could never stay off liquor indefinitely. Coming home one Sunday, he asked to borrow money to go back to the bar. When I said no, he called me a bitch.

"What about the rent money?" he asked.

"No way," I told him. "My rent gets paid no matter what."

Infuriated, he called me a "fucking tramp" then Fred jumped up and hit him. The next thing I knew, they were going at each other, with Dad dancing around on my couch so he could be even with Fred, who was much taller. I finally called the police but Dad left before they got there. The next day when he came home, I had his clothes all packed and told him I'd had enough. No way was I going to get trapped into losing control of my home again.

By now, Marilyn and I were once again talking. It always seemed to be that way in our family. First I would have trouble with one person, then another would become a problem and I'd be back on speaking terms with the first one. I never wanted bad feelings to exist between any of us. It just happened that way. There seemed to be some kind of family curse for as long back as I can remember. Perhaps it is just a stubborn streak, or a defective gene, but no one in my family has ever tried to take control of their emotions. My dad's father and his brothers always lived like this, as has every generation since. Dad and his brother Mikey still do not talk to each other, nor do my two sisters Marilyn and Jody.

One day the phone rang and it was my aunt saying my dad's mother had just died of a massive heart attack. My heart was crushed, for this was my first real close experience with death and I had loved Memere more than almost anyone. She was only sixty-eight and I had just spoken to her a month earlier on her fiftieth wedding anniversary. I even had plans to visit Pepere and her in two weeks. Fred really hurt my feelings by laughing and joking about Memere dying. He could be so cruel and heartless at times. I didn't go to the funeral, preferring to remember her as a person who was always happy, singing opera, cuddling in bed, and telling stories.

The following year, 1984, was to bring about a major change in my life. Cory was nine years old and I found a job at a fish and chips place, although I didn't stay long, quitting after only a month. The tire factory where Fred worked had been bought out and after fourteen years in his job, he was no longer needed. Applying for unemployment while he waited to see if he would be transferred, he insisted on going to PEI for two weeks. When I objected, he put me on a real guilt trip, saying his dad was getting old, and if he died it would be my fault he hadn't seen him. Taking our last money, he went. Soon after he arrived, I phoned and was told that he had gone with his father to see his kids. I didn't give it much thought, as I knew his ex-wife had married again and moved to PEI. What I didn't know was that they had recently separated and she was now living alone with the kids. I found out later that Fred had spent the night there, supposedly sleeping on the couch. At least, that's where he started out, but it wasn't where he stayed.

By the time Fred returned, we were at death's door financially. While waiting for his U.I. money to begin, he got a job cutting down trees which paid cash, something he had done when he first moved to Toronto. It took him three buses to get to work, and it was always late by the time he got home in the evening, but the pay was good. In the meantime, ever since his visit to PEI, he was getting phone calls from the mother of his children. I found this all very strange until my stepfather Bob took me aside and told me Fred was phoning her regularly from a shop down the street and talking to her for a long time. The next time she called I picked up the other line and listened while she begged to come back to Toronto and live with him. When he got off the phone I asked him what the hell was going on between the two of them. We were about to spend the weekend with Jane and

George at their beach cottage, so I gave him an ultimatum. By the end of the weekend, he had to decide whether he was going back to her or not. Otherwise I was going to kick him out. There was no way I wanted to live with someone who was sneaking off down the street to talk to another woman. I'd seen enough of that growing up with my father. At the end of the weekend, Fred said no, he didn't want to live with her. She had put him through enough crap, and he wasn't going back to that. I said then there better be no more phone calls. That night he phoned her and said don't call again.

A month later Fred's youngest daughter Lilly came for a visit. She was a real tomboy who looked just like him, almost like a son. Soon after she arrived, we were on our way to my mother's place in Fred's truck when Lilly asked why Fred hadn't kissed her goodbye the morning after he spent the night at his ex-wife's house. Lilly said she went to say goodbye and he wasn't there.

"Yes, I was," he insisted. "I didn't leave until afternoon. I must have been under the blankets on the couch."

"No, you weren't," she said. "I lifted the blankets and looked."

That's when I put the puzzle together. By now, Fred's face was beet red, and I knew he must have slept with his ex-wife, even though he denied it when I asked him later. After that, we never had sex again. It wasn't much of a loss, as he hadn't been very affectionate, or much of a sexual partner. We were more like roommates than anything else. Maybe that's why I was able to stay with him for so long, despite all the emotional abuse he put me through.

For two weeks Lilly stayed with us while we took Cory and her to all the different tourist attractions. About a month after she went home her mother called, this time to ask if we would take her son from a previous marriage. She was having problems with him and wanted us to take him off her hands. As he wasn't even Fred's son, I couldn't believe the nerve of her. I told her that when my son got older and I couldn't control him, I'd send him to her. That was the last we ever heard from her.

Fred finally found a better job working for the City of Toronto, which he'd worked for years ago. It gave him health benefits and more money, plus he got to work with his brother and friends he'd known all his life. I also got a job, this time working at a hairbrush factory, which was terrible. It was just like a prison. There was absolutely no talking allowed, and you had to put your hand up to go to the washroom. I even hated getting up in the morning, knowing that I had to go there to work. My goal, however, was to gain some financial independence so I could finally leave Fred and escape the continual emotional abuse. Then one day my sister Marilyn called and said there was an opening where she worked downtown at a stock brokers. When I told her I didn't know anything about stocks, she said it didn't make any difference, they trained you on the job. It paid really well, twenty-five dollars an hour, so I applied and got accepted. The offices were in the Sheridan Hotel, right across from City Hall, and I loved everything about the job, with the money rolling in and my self-confidence growing. Plus I was meeting a whole different class of people, ones whose lives were very different from what I had always known. Marilyn was office manager and at lunch hour we would go to the gym together and work out, or swim in the pool. I lost thirty pounds and started to feel good about myself again, dressing nicely the way I always had before meeting Fred. Best of all, my goal of independence seemed more and more within reach.

In June 1985, Fred became a permanent employee of the City of Toronto. We finished signing the papers for all the health benefits, but decided to waive the life insurance. What a mistake that was, for little did we know that our lives were about to change dramatically. On July 4, right after the health benefits went into effect, Fred was on holiday and setting up the barbecue for me. His brother Henry phoned and asked him to come and do a side job for another tree company. Not a big job, just about an hour or so. Fred said he wouldn't be gone long. We could eat when he got back, then take Cory to the CN Tower like we had planned. I asked him not to go, but he insisted, saying he had already said yes to his brother.

After Fred left, I finished setting up the barbecue, then put everything away. It was taking Fred longer than he thought, so I decided to put some mirrored tile I had bought on the bathroom wall. Just as I finished the job, one of the tiles fell and smashed on the floor. Oh God! That wasn't a good sign. By now I was beginning to feel uneasy about Fred. He should have been home long ago, and it was almost too late to go on our outing.

All of a sudden I heard footsteps running down the entry stairs and the door was flung open. It was the owner of the tree company, all in a panic. Hardly stopping to catch his breath, he said that Fred had just fallen off a ladder twenty-five feet above the ground. They'd taken him to Sunnybrook

Hospital, but he couldn't move his neck. Quickly, a friend of mine drove Cory and me to the hospital where we found Fred in emergency. It didn't look like much was wrong with him, other than a cut on his nose where he had hit himself with his pliers. But that was only on the outside. Inside was an entirely different matter. The doctor finally came in and gave us the news. Fred had crushed his T-11 and T-12 vertebrae and was paralyzed from the waist down. He would never walk again. Listening to the news, I felt like a meteor had just crashed to Earth. Fred insisted the doctor didn't know what he was talking about, but I knew he wouldn't say it if he wasn't sure. I was stunned. Fred went on to apologize to Cory for ruining his trip to the CN Tower, but Cory said, "Don't worry, just get better and we'll go another time." In the end, it would be five months before Fred came home.

That was the beginning of a living hell for me. How could I walk out and leave now? I couldn't. All my plans of escaping had come to nothing and I was now locked into a loveless relationship, just as Fred was locked into his impaired body. For the first two weeks, Fred's stepdaughter Jenny came to stay and take care of Cory so I could go to the hospital every day. His oldest daughter Fredia also came from PEI with her six-month-old baby, Fred's first grandchild, and stayed two weeks. She looked exactly like Fred, with dark hair, big blue eyes, freckles, and the same high-speed way of talking. In the meantime, Fred had two steel rods placed in his back so he would be able to sit up instead of being bedridden. That didn't stop him from contemplating suicide, I discovered. The plan was for his alcoholic brother Ryan to bring him a gun. When I found out, I tried to reason with him and help him see the positive side of the situation. I told him that having to do things while he was sitting wasn't all that bad because even healthy people spend most of their day sitting. I said he should count himself lucky when he looked around the hospital and saw how many teenagers, with their whole lives still ahead of them, were now quadriplegics, without even the ability to sit up or move their hands. He was a lot older than most of them and had seen and experienced a hell of a lot more than they ever would. He would still be able to dress and feed himself and do most things they would never be able to do. While they were helpless and would need twenty-four hour care, he would still have his dignity and be able to take care of himself. Plus, we had the added benefit of a big pension because he had been employed by the government. Things could be a whole lot worse, I told him.

The next day when I arrived, I realized there was a difference about him, that Fred had reached a turning point, and all talk of suicide was abandoned. He said he had taken a look around and seen what I meant. After his operation, Fred was transferred to Lyndhurst Hospital, which took me three bus rides and a half-hour walk each way to reach from home. It was located in a lovely part of the city, with enormous rich homes and huge old trees. At night, however, when I finally left the hospital each day, it seemed dark and dreary, with a cold haunting feeling that made me question why people would want to live in such uninviting looking homes. Were they actually any happier than someone in a small, cozy bungalow, and how much of that space did they really need or use? Despite the obvious wealth, I didn't envy them their lives.

During that summer I spent each day with Cory before heading to the hospital, but after school started I could only see him at lunch time and for about a half hour in the afternoon. At first Mom and Bob watched him, until I found out they were actually leaving him home alone while they went visiting, so I made arrangements for an older gentleman to come in each afternoon. Jane also made a point of checking in on things each day. At first Fred's friends and family came to the hospital almost daily, but after a month the novelty wore off and no one came to visit except me. If I had thought I was like a fly caught in a web before, now I felt like I was trapped in quicksand. I was barely twenty-seven years old, had just lost the first job I had ever enjoyed, I hardly ever saw my child, and now I was tied to a man I didn't love, who spent most of his time feeling depressed and sorry for himself. In addition, there was little money coming in, as we were both waiting for our unemployment insurance to begin.

After three months, Fred was able to come home on weekends. His friend Big Jim would pick him up at the hospital on Fridays, bring him home, then take him back on Sunday. He wasn't called Big Jim for nothing, for he stood over six feet tall and weighed about three hundred pounds. Well, I soon realized that Fred might as well have stayed in the hospital on weekends, for all he ever did at home was drink. All his old cronies reappeared, as did the card playing and endless drinking. Now that he was in a wheelchair and had to be catheterized every four hours, once he was drunk and passed out, I had to do it for him. Without knowing it, I had just found a new career, playing nursemaid to a forty-two-year-old man with no pay to show for it. Eventually Fred came home for good, which was nice for him but terrible for me. Now I had to do full-time care for a man who weighed two hundred and twenty pounds. It just about broke my back having to lift him up and down.

The first Sunday morning after Fred came back, George arrived in his burgundy-striped housecoat, which wasn't unusual for him. Dunn and Bob had slept over, and I was busy doing laundry, so before I knew it, I was washing everyone's clothes while they sat around in housecoats drinking beer and playing cards. Suddenly three people walked in, coming straight into the dining room after knocking on the door. They were Jehovah's Witnesses, and the next thing I knew, George started to swear and call them names, then chased them out of the house and down the street in his housecoat. He kept yelling about how they had broken up his first marriage and brainwashed his wife and kids. Later, I thought about how it must have looked, with all these men sitting around on a Sunday morning playing cards and drinking. They probably figured that if there was ever a household that needed help, this was it.

After about a month of staying home with Fred, I decided I needed to get out and work, so I took a job at Cadet Cleaners. When Fred was sober he could cook and look after himself, which meant that my being at work would keep him busy and give him more to do. After a month I was promoted to manager and sent to help reorganize stores that were failing. The job paid for a cab to take me to whatever store needed help, plus I got a raise every month. Once again I felt my self-confidence and self-esteem coming back.

Just before Christmas that year, the family down-and-outs started showing up at my door again. This time it was the last of Fred's sister's sons, Dennis, who arrived all dressed up in his army uniform and saying he was just passing through and wanted to say hi. He said he couldn't stay, but as no one had asked him to, I wasn't disappointed. He said he had just got out of the army and had a job, so I thought great, goodbye and good luck.

The next morning I was starting up the stairs in the inside hallway when something caught my eye. We always kept our garbage bags at the bottom of the stairs and what did I see, but a hand coming straight out from under the pile of green bags. Slowly backing up the stairs, I kept my eyes fixed on that hand, figuring that someone had probably been beaten up and left there. When I got to the top, I started to scream and yell until Fred came rushing in his wheelchair. Then who should appear from behind the garbage, but Dennis. Of course, he had lied about the job. He had no job, or anywhere to go, so before I could stop him, Fred had invited him to stay with us. All I could think was Gail, welcome to your nightmare again.

After about a week, Dennis said he had a car that had broken down and he needed to go pick it up. Of course, it turned out he didn't have a car either, but we would find that out later. In the meantime, it was Christmas Eve and we had been invited next door to Deanna and Al's place where they always hosted a Christmas street party. Our house was spotless, I had all the gifts wrapped and under the tree, and Cory had helped me bake Christmas cookies and string popcorn. It was a tradition I had started when he was small to make Christmas Eve a hustle and bustle so he wouldn't be needling me to let him open any gifts early. Another rule was absolutely no drinking. Christmas was for children and family and I insisted that everyone stay coherent. After my own childhood experiences, I wanted to be sure that this was the one day Cory was guaranteed to have everything happy.

All our preparations were now finished, so we left for the party next door. Everyone had a great time, with people popping in and out all evening, and lots of carol singing, food, joking and carrying on. It was about midnight when a few men finally lifted Fred and his wheelchair down the stairs to our basement apartment. And what to my surprise did I see when we walked in the door, not Santa and his eight tiny reindeer, but five strange people I had never laid eyes on before, sitting in my living room with pizza.

"What are you all doing in my home?" I asked.

One guy was a deaf mute and he started talking with his hands, while Fred got all excited and started using his hands as well. Between the confusion of the one in the wheelchair with a speech impediment, and the deaf mute, I found myself telling the deaf guy to shut up. Finally, a girl spoke up and told us that Dennis had invited them all. As far as they knew, this was Dennis's place, for they had only just met him that evening at a tavern.

"And where the fucking hell," I asked, "is Dennis?" I went into Cory's room and there he was passed out on the bed. That was a serious breach of behaviour in my house. Cory's and my bedrooms were totally off limits. First I told everyone to get out and never darken my door again, then I yanked Dennis right off the bed and threw him out of the room as well.

Unfortunately, he was too intoxicated to throw out on the street, especially on Christmas Eve, but I was tempted to do it anyway.

What a mess I had to clean up that night. Looking in the bar, I discovered there wasn't a drop of liquor left in the house. I had completely filled it in readiness for the holidays, with all sorts of different bottles so I could offer guests a drink when they stopped in to visit. Now I just wanted to sit down and bawl my head off. At least they hadn't walked off with the gifts, although they probably would have if we hadn't come home when we did.

The next morning, Cory woke up and started to open his gifts. His eyes were just beaming, he was so excited, and looking at him, I suddenly realized how much he looked like John. It made me think of how much John was missing out on the joy of experiencing his son, and how different our lives would have been if he were a part of it. I consoled myself with the thought that perhaps John was living a structured normal family life instead of the hell on wheels that I was living. Even after all this time, however, just thinking about him made my heart ache. Cory always knew that Fred wasn't his dad, but I never told him how much I still loved his real father. I only said that we had been childhood sweethearts, that we had been very young and had drifted apart, but that his dad was a very nice person. I wanted Cory to grow up and come to his own decision about how he perceived John.

With all the rattling of paper, Dennis soon woke up. Making a quick phone call, he grabbed his clothes and left. I wasn't interested in where he was going, just so long as he went. He had created his own dilemma and I had no pity for him. After all the gifts were opened, we had breakfast, then got dressed and went to Jane and George's for Christmas dinner. Every other year Christmas dinner had been at my place, with the whole family coming over, but this year I had said no, figuring someone else in the family would offer. Instead, only Jane invited us, which was fine, because as far as I was concerned, she was the best family I could ask for. Her whole family was there and it was a real Christmas experience, filled with love for one another. It made me feel like I was part of a loving family, even if we weren't really related.

That night when we got home, the phone rang and it was Dad. He wanted to know why I had thrown Dennis out on Christmas Day, so I knew where that useless good-for-nothing had gone this time. I told Dad I hadn't thrown him out, that he'd left on his own, then explained what had happened the night before and warned Dad not to take him in.

"Well he's a good worker," Dad said, "so I don't see a problem." Apparently, Dennis had been working for Dad for the past couple of weeks.

"Okay, Dad," I said. "Don't say I didn't warn you. Merry Christmas." I thought Dad was an idiot, especially as he was just getting back on his own feet, not drinking, renting a nice house, and running his own steel erecting company. But he and I were alike that way, suckers for any sad song and backpacker at the door. Dad always seemed to have his share of leeches staying with him, too, now that he had his own place.

Once the holidays were over and I was back at work, Fred quit drinking for a while and was consequently behaving himself. It was one of those grace periods when I could actually entertain the thought that we might live a more normal life for a while. In the middle of January, Jane came over one day and asked if I wanted to go to the Dominican Republic with her sister Diane and her. My first reaction was to say no. Who would take care of Fred and Cory? And where would I get the money at such short notice? George immediately said he'd play nursemaid and mother, while Jane continued to urge me to go, saying I needed the break after all I'd been through in the past six months. She suggested I go ask Gordon for a loan. Gordon was our neighbour two doors down. He was a slim, dark-haired man from Nova Scotia, who was funny as hell, just like a stand-up comedian. He lived with another man, they were roommates, and they were both the greatest friends a person could have. Gordon also owned his own radiator business and was known to always have an abundance of cash on hand, usually stashed in his pocket. He had told us that he had been terribly poor as a child and it made him feel good just knowing he had money on hand and didn't have to worry about it. When I went and asked him for a thousand-dollar loan, he immediately took it right out of his pocket and handed it to me. It wasn't unusual for Gordon to have as much as five thousand on him at one time. I gave him a big hug and a kiss and said thank you. All Gordon would say was you deserve it, kid. Then he told me not to worry about Cory and Fred because he too would keep an eye on things. By the time I got back to Jane with the news, I was bouncing off the ceiling. I had never been anywhere except Canada, and here I was going to the Dominican Republic. Jane, on the other hand, was an experienced traveler and knew the routine, so I had nothing to worry about. That night I went to bed and thought about what fantastic, caring friends I had. Looking back, I realize now that the street we lived on at the time was filled with some of the most incredible people I would ever encounter in my life, people who would do almost anything for you because they cared so much.

When the Sunday of our departure arrived, I hugged and kissed Cory goodbye, telling him I loved him and would he please be good while I was away. On our way to the airport in the limousine, I was exuberant at the thought of an all-inclusive holiday in the middle of winter. Jane took one every year and they always sounded so exciting. Once we were on the plane, I had a few drinks to calm my nerves. Our other traveling companion, Jane's half-sister Diane, was a riot the whole trip. She was very different from Jane, short and tiny and blond, with a rugged complexion. Like me, she had never been on a trip before, and was equally excited. At that point, Jane must have felt like she was traveling with two kids.

Walking off the airplane after we landed, I felt like I'd just arrived in paradise. It was like suddenly being transported into the life of someone rich and famous. We were whisked away to the Jack Tar Village Resort, which had a five-star rating, and no wonder. There were floral paths leading all through the grounds, an abundance of flowers unlike any I had ever seen before, sunny blue skies, mountains in the distance, the ocean, and the warm, seductive tropical air. Our villa had two double beds and a cot, so Diane, as the smallest, was the winner of the cot. Settling in quickly, we went to explore the grounds. Walking around that first day, it felt like we were on another planet. Our first stop was the bar for banana coladas. Then down to the beach for more banana coladas at the beach hut bar. By the time I was stretched out on one of the lounge chairs, I knew this sure beat selling frozen flowers on a street corner. I could hardly believe life could be so different, especially my life. Who would have thought a year ago that I would be lying here in the sun in the Dominican Republic, far from the endless nightmare that constituted my life in Toronto. I was never one to cry over past regrets, always choosing to keep walking, even if I didn't know if the direction was right or wrong. I just kept going. Now, finding myself given the gift of a vacation, I decided not to waste a minute of it. In the end, it might have to last me a lifetime, so let the fun begin.

The next day there were different contests and games taking place, and before I knew what was happening, I heard my name being announced over the loud speakers to report to the pool. Without my knowing, Jane had signed me up for a wet T-shirt contest. I could have killed her. In the end, I won, although I thought the girl I beat looked like a movie star, and as far as I was concerned she was the real winner. I think they let me have the booby prize. Later that day, we decided to rent mopeds and explore some of the island. Up to now, the fastest thing I had ever driven was a bicycle, so I wasn't feeling too confident about this. First Jane got on and gave it a try, ending up in a tumble which I didn't find very reassuring. Then Diane and I tried, and—surprise, surprise—we had no trouble. By then, Jane had managed to smash herself into the curb, so she stayed behind while Diane and I rode off to explore.

The minute we were off the resort compound I knew we had gotten into more than we had bargained for. Trucks and cars whizzed past, with everyone appearing to go at an alarming rate. A moped zoomed by carrying an entire family, including the father, mother, child and a live chicken. Diane and I were laughing so hard we finally had to stop. Somehow we survived the experience, however, finally arriving back at the resort without any major mishap. My guardian angel must have been watching over me, for I never did feel like I was really in control.

That night was the toga contest, with extra sheets left on our beds so we could participate. Everyone at the resort participated in the fun game, so we dressed up in the sheets, with banana leaves around our heads, plus any stray flower we could find. I ended up winning that contest too. Then the next morning I again heard the loud speaker paging me to go to the pool. When I looked quizzically at Jane, she said, "No, it wasn't me." It turned out to be the resort, hoping I would enter the walk-on-water contest, which was going to be written up in a travel magazine. Why not, I thought, and off I went, managing to win yet again. The whole thing seemed just too incredible to be real. It was more like a dream, or something I read about in a magazine, the sort of thing that happens to other people, not me.

The week flew by and suddenly it was our last day. I was overwhelmed when the resort presented me with a T-shirt and a certificate for being the most fun party person, plus a week's free stay. Coming from the life I had been living, the whole thing was almost unbelievable. Jane had told me that once you experience travel first hand, you can get hooked on it like a drug.

I hated to leave paradise, but one thing I knew for sure, I was hooked on travel and already planning our next trip.

Coming home was a real shock. When we arrived there was a blizzard raging and we almost got rerouted to Buffalo, New York. I was so frightened, thinking I might never see Cory again. After circling for an hour, we touched down, still without being able to see anything. About three feet of snow had fallen and it took us four hours to get transportation from the airport into the city. We felt like fools, dressed in our tropical muumuu's, with sandals on. None of us had thought to bring any warm clothes along. By the time I got home, I had to jump straight into my heated waterbed to warm up. Cory and I were so excited to see each other, for we had never been apart for a week in his entire life. He was the one good thing about coming home. Everything else, I knew, would just be the same old grind in this loveless relationship.

A few months passed, and it was the middle of the night in March when I heard pounding on the door. Debating whether to get up and open it, I lay there until the pounding got louder.

"Who's there?" I finally called out.

"It's me, your dad," a voice answered.

Opening the door, I saw six people standing there half frozen, with a TV, VCR, bottles of liquor, and a case of beer. There was a rancid smell of smoke coming off them that made me want to gag.

"Why are you here?" I finally asked as they all came into the house.

"My house just burnt down," Dad replied.

At first, I couldn't believe it. I mean, who bothers to take beer and liquor from a burning house? Just then Fred came rolling in like thunder in his wheelchair, cursing and swearing at all the noise.

"Be quiet," I told him. "My dad's house just burnt down." Taking control of the situation, I told them all to go in the living room and find somewhere to sleep. Then we would talk about it in the morning.

The next day I stayed home from work so I could help decide what was to be done with all these people. There was no way I wanted them camping out here any longer than necessary. Dad told us that someone had dropped a cigarette that went down through the floor grate and ignited a couch in the basement. As they were all probably drunk at the time, I wasn't surprised that no one had noticed until it was too late to do anything.

"I'm sorry for you, Dad," I said, "but you'll have to find somewhere else to stay. I can't keep all of you." I wasn't surprised to see that Dennis was part of the group, still living off my dad. Three of the group immediately found places to stay, but that still left three more: Dad, Dennis and Chantel, my dad's second cousin from New Brunswick. I don't know how she got mixed up with this lot because she was only nineteen. In the end, Chantel went back to New Brunswick, Dad moved in with his ex-mother-in-law Belinda and we were once again stuck with Dennis. This time I laid down firm rules if he expected to stay. No drinking and no company. Dennis must have been feeling desperate as he just went to work and came home, never giving us any trouble.

As always seemed to happen when we opened the door to family, more of them started showing up again. This time it was Fred's sister, and Dennis's mother, who arrived for a visit. One evening I was entertaining all of them, plus Fred's brother and wife, and Jane and George. I had put some finger foods out on the coffee table and everyone was having drinks. Suddenly, for no apparent reason, Dennis picked up the coffee table filled with drinks and food and flung it over on top of Fred, where everything shattered. The men tried to grab Dennis, but he was totally crazed and out of control. They chased him into my bedroom, then back into the living room, with the furniture flying and blood everywhere. When the police arrived, it took six of them to pin him down, cuff his hands, and haul him away. By now my house was a mess, with blood all over my brand-new draperies and carpeting that I had just installed. As Jane helped me clean up, I knew one thing for sure, the Do Drop Inn was officially closed to family. We would never again open our door to a sad song or a backpack.

CHAPTER SIX

Foolish Compassion

It was now the spring of 1986. After work each evening, I would walk over to Jane's so we could watch *The Thorn Birds* together, a TV mini-series being televised four nights in a row. Each evening, George would go over to my place to visit Fred, where they would fight over what to watch. Unable to decide between sports, which was George's choice, and *M*A*S*H*, which Fred liked, they would continually flick the channels between the two. In the meantime, Jane and I were not only enjoying the dramatic story, but also the bottle of Texas Mickey which Jane had received from her stepfather. As he had joined AA and was now a reformed alcoholic, he had given it to her. While we watched the television story unfold, we simultaneously watched the contents of the bottle slowly disappear.

About a week later, after the show was over, George went to look for the bottle, because he had company coming over. Finding it gone, he arrived at our apartment where Jane was visiting and proceeded to rant and rave about her stepfather, who he assumed had taken the bottle back. Jane and I just looked at him, then burst out laughing, it was so funny.

"Gail and I drank it while we were watching *The Thorn Birds*," Jane finally told him.

You should have heard those two men after that, with Fred raving about us like he'd never drunk a day in his life. Then George started stomping his feet like a child having a temper tantrum.

"How can two women drink that much and remember what the hell they saw," he exclaimed. Cursing and swearing, Fred and he finally left.

"I don't know what his fucking problem is," Jane said as she continued to laugh. "He doesn't even drink liquor. Besides, it was given to me, not him, that idiot."

Neither of us ever really took George's anger seriously, because we knew he just liked an excuse for conflict every now and then. Instead, we usually just laughed our heads off. This was an important bond between us, because Fred and George were like two peas in a pod, each one as stubborn and childish as the other. Sharing hotheaded, high-strung men, Jane and I developed a strong camaraderie through our common ability to embrace it all with humour.

During that week between *The Thorn Birds* and the Texas Mickey episode, Jane and I had been checking the newspapers for a seat sale to Prince Edward Island. Fred had been wallowing in self-pity for some time now, saying he wanted to move back to the Island. Jane and I figured that if I took him there for a holiday, it might cure him of his moaning and groaning for a while. Besides, I had never been to PEI and liked the idea of visiting it, having caught the travel bug from my trip to the Dominican. After finally finding a good seat sale, we told Fred and booked the flight. That's when Fred decided to prepare me for the trip by telling me things about his family. His father, sister and her husband were very religious, he informed me, so there was to be no foul language.

Rushing over to Jane's, I said, "You're not going to believe this, but Fred's relatives are a bunch of Bible thumpers." When she started laughing I said, "Don't laugh, Jane, what am I going to do? I don't want to be surrounded for three weeks by a bunch of religious fanatics!" I had nothing against religion, and I believed in God, but I didn't want to be preached to.

Jane said, "Gail, how do you think Fred manages with them when every second word out of his mouth is fucking this and fucking that?"

"I haven't a clue," I said. "All I know is, it looks more like I'm going on a religious retreat than a vacation." By now Jane was really laughing hard, thinking up all sorts of funny things to say.

"Gail," she suggested, "you know it's Easter next week. Why don't we go to church and take a refresher course. Plus, if you have any arthritis, all that getting up and down ought to cure it. Or listen, why don't you say you're into Buddhism. That should take care of things."

Trying not to laugh, I said, "It's not funny. I know what I'll do. If I feel compelled to use some fucking swear words, I'll go outside and howl at the moon." By now, our brilliant idea of giving Fred a taste of PEI to settle him down seemed more like a potential nightmare.

One evening, I decided to have George, Jane, and a nice young man named Lenny over for dinner. Lenny was actually the ex-boyfriend of Jane's daughter, a very funny comic with big brown eyes and a nice smile. As usual, whenever I tried to entertain, things had a way of developing into the downright crazy and comical. I guess the truth was that in my life, you could either laugh your way through things or cry, and I preferred to laugh.

Early in the evening, Fred sent Cory down the street to the store to get him some cigarettes. Back then, there was no law prohibiting young kids from buying them, plus the store was only five minutes away. After half an hour and still no Cory, Fred started to get upset. He had a way of doing this little wheelchair dance, rocking it from side to side, like a child that couldn't get its own way.

Turning to Lenny, he said, "Go get the cigarettes, and if you see Cory, tell him to get the fucking home before I kill him." Next thing we knew, it was an hour later and now Lenny wasn't back either.

Looking at me, Fred cursed and sputtered, "Where the fucking hell did they go? Did the goddamn store move? Gail," he said, "go get me some dirty, filthy, rotten cigarettes right now." By now Fred was all riled up and turning red.

"All right," I said, "I'll go get them, but why don't you quit smoking?"

"Quit smoking," he shouted, "quit smoking! I've lost my hair, I've lost my teeth, I can't fucking walk, and you want me to quit smoking. I might as well slice my fucking throat." After that, I left in a hurry. Anything for a little peace.

Outside, I found Jane sitting on a bench with Lenny, who was back again from the store. She offered me a drink, saying Lenny had brought some homemade wine from his house.

"Lenny, did you see Cory?" I asked.

"Yeah," he said. "He's down at the store talking with his buddies. I told him to get home with the cigarettes," he added. After that, we forgot all about Fred and his cigarettes as we sat enjoying the wine.

About a half an hour later I went waltzing indoors again. And there was Fred, cursing and shouting, "Where are the fucking, mother-jumping cigarettes?" Not thinking much about it, I said that Lenny had told Cory to come on home soon, then I turned and went into the kitchen to check on the food. Well, I must not have been thinking clearly, seeing as how Fred had worked himself into a real passion by now. Blocking the door with his wheelchair, he grabbed a loaf of sliced bread and started slugging me with it. He was sputtering and spitting his words, calling me everything under the sun. The more he hit me, the more the slices of bread went flying all over the place until I was laughing so hard I couldn't control myself. The only pain he was causing me was in my stomach from all the laughter.

Then Jane, George, Cory and Lenny all came in to see what was going on, and Lenny blurted out, "Oh! Some kind of kinky sex." By now there wasn't a slice of bread left and Fred had to retire into the corner puffing like a steam engine. I'll never forget it, for the rest of us just about died laughing. It was like dealing with a giant, oversized toddler that had gotten loose with a loaf of bread. Sometimes I felt like that was my life, dealing with overgrown children who masqueraded as men. The only thing I could do with a life like this was laugh.

Finally it was time to go to Prince Edward Island. Hallelujah, I thought as we flew there in the airplane, let the preaching begin! When we arrived and the plane started circling to land, I looked down and my heart just about stopped. It looked like a Patchwork quilt, with red clay roads, lush green fields, white potato blossoms, and golden yellow hay, all framed by a red shoreline and deep blue water. I had never seen anything so beautiful. Although we hadn't even landed yet, I now knew why Fred liked it so much.

Fred's brother-in-law Patrick picked us up in his blue station wagon and we drove off to Wellington. Patrick was a tall man with red hair, freckles, big teeth and googly eyes with glasses. Fred and he acted like two clowns, joking and carrying on the whole way in the car, while Cory and I just sat drinking in the beauty of the countryside. When we reached the old homestead, I saw it was situated beside a river, with a long tree-lined drive leading up to it. The house was two hundred years old and Fred's family had lived there ever since they emigrated from Ireland. Fred's niece Nora was staying there, Dennis's younger sister. All I could think to myself was, I hope she's not another one who's out of touch with reality, or it will be a long three weeks. She seemed like a nice girl, though, about fifteen and very pretty with dark hair. Apparently, she was living there to help with the cooking and cleaning. Then there was Paps, Fred's dad who was in his seventies and a small man with white hair and a mostly bald head that shook and vibrated uncontrollably. He said, "Good day, glad to see ya', when ya' going back?" I wasn't quite sure how to take that greeting, finally deciding to treat it like, "You're welcome, come on in and stay a while." Next I met Fred's sister Gordy when she came home from working at the fish factory. Her name was really appropriate, for she had a masculine way about her, with straight salt and pepper hair, glasses, shifty eyes, and a crabby look, like someone had stepped on her toe. It also took her a while to unwind, so I began to wonder if we were welcome or not. The only truly welcoming one was Patrick, so at least that was fine.

The next day I tried to be on my best behaviour, feeling out the situation. Paps took off early in the morning, returning in time for lunch. While we were eating, he said "Oh! What a beautiful meeting we had this morning. The nuns were singing just like angels. It was so lovely we're having another one this afternoon." Wow! I thought, they're really religious. By dinnertime that evening, the old man came in singing and smelling like a brewery.

Turning to Fred, I said, "Do the nuns drink?"

Fred started laughing. "What nuns?" he asked. "There aren't any nuns around here."

"I thought your dad was with the nuns all day," I said.

That was too much for Fred. "Don't talk like an idiot. Paps has been at the Legion getting drunk."

That night in the bedroom, Fred had the one small bed, while I had to sleep on the floor. Calling him a liar, I said, "Why did you tell me all that bull about them being holier than thou?" As Fred lay there laughing I added, "I didn't think it was funny. Besides, I wish you had told me that I was welcome to sleep on the floor for three weeks so I could have sent you alone." By this time, I was ready to admit that the Island was a beautiful place, but I wasn't so sure about the people.

As Fred's dad knew how to drive, the next day he took Cory and me to the mall. Every now and then he'd wave, although I didn't have a clue what he was waving at. I didn't see anyone walking down the street. When I asked, he'd say "Oh! That was so-and-so." Cory and I would look at each other in a peculiar way, wondering if he was crazy or what. This whole outing was turning out to be kind of crazy. Paps was so small he had to look through the steering wheel instead of over it, and he shook like a leaf continually. Every time he took his hands off the wheel to wave, I felt sure we were going to end up in the ditch.

Finally arriving at the mall, we did some shopping, then Paps said there was another store we had to visit. By now we had the car filled with groceries and gifts, so I went to lock the door and put up the window.

"What are you doing," Paps exclaimed. "We don't lock anything around here, for God's sake."

Cory and I didn't know what to do as he just walked off towards the mall, leaving the keys in the car and all my bags in the back seat. As we stood there looking at him and back at the car, unsure whether to leave it or not, he started to get impatient.

"Come on, come on," he called, "we don't have all day. I have to get back to the nuns!"

When we got back to the house, someone had rigged a makeshift ramp for Fred's wheelchair. Walking up it, my foot went right through the wood.

Paps turned around and said, "No wonder the cat fucked off."

I couldn't believe it. He was swearing! Plus, I had no idea what he was talking about. What cat? It turned out there was a cat that had been sleeping under the ramp when my foot broke through.

That evening, I went to sit on an old chrome chair and bang, I hit the floor. Paps jumped up and said, "Did you come here to visit or to demolish the place? We just finished the goddamn fucking renovations, but if we'd known you were in the demolition business, we would have waited."

Going into the living room, he came back with a heavy-duty armchair. "Here," he said, "anchor yourself there. If you go through that one, we're shipping you the hell home."

By now I knew one thing for sure, I didn't have to worry about whether I could swear or not. Paps was doing a fine job of it all by himself.

During our visit, Cory and I were at the mercy of Paps as far as travel went. With his drinking problem, he was pretty limited to where he could take us. We went to the beach digging clams and picking quahogs. The ocean was so warm, it was just like a giant bathtub. Mostly, though, we had to spend our time at the homestead. From the little that I could see, however, I knew I truly liked the Island, its tranquillity, the natural surroundings, and the escape from the rat race that typified life in Toronto. Raising a child here, I sensed, would be ideal. Fred, on the other hand, was drunk most of the time and didn't see a thing past the fridge and his next bottle of beer. After all my years with him, I knew better than to expect anything else.

When the three weeks was up we flew home, with Fred sucking back the drinks on the plane at an alarming rate. I asked him to calm down with his drinking. What was he doing, trying to put out a fire? I knew the trouble I would have trying to get him home if he was drunk. Sure enough, he burst his leg bag and the urine went flowing right down the aisle to the back of the plane. By the time we arrived in Toronto he was loaded, reeking of urine and alcohol. Cory and I were so embarrassed. It was a relief to both of us when we finally got home. Jane immediately showed up, saying George and she were lost without us. I assured her it hadn't been the same fun as the trip to the Dominican Republic. The Island was exquisite, I said, but I missed you too.

Not long after our return, Fred started to whine again about moving to PEI. He complained about living in a basement apartment, that if there was a fire, he might not be able to get out.

"I know and understand how you feel," I told him, "but what about me? I have a job here, and friends and family. And what about you, you left PEI when you were fourteen. Things are different when you're on holiday, and always seem better in a place than when you actually live there. What are you going to do that's any different from living here, drink a different brand of beer?"

"No," he said, "I won't drink any more."

"Yeah," I added, "I bet you won't drink any less, either. And where will we get money to buy a house? You need a down payment." That kept him quiet for a while, because he knew we weren't close to having the money for a house.

Fall arrived and the hockey season started up. Cory had begun playing a year ago and loved it immediately. He had never even been on a pair of skates when he started, but by halfway through the season two other teams were fighting for him to play with them. He had won the *Most Improved Player Award*, and had an innate knack for scoring. Big Jim would take him to the rink, or sometimes George, when I was working and couldn't go. Other times Jane and I would go. I couldn't believe how well he played, he was such a natural at it. On one occasion, big Jim, Jane, George, Fred, George's mother, and I all went to the rink to see Cory play. George's mother was in her eighties, a tiny lady always dressed in black ever since her husband died when he was thirty-seven years old. She couldn't speak a word of English, but she loved hockey. On Saturday nights she would sit with her little brown plastic glass of beer and watch it on television. She just loved Gretzky. On the evening that she came to watch the game with us, Cory scored six goals. Afterwards, when his team had won, the old lady hugged and kissed him, calling him Gretzky while we all laughed at her.

That year Cory's team won the tournament and he was named Most Valuable Player. After the game, the coach had champagne in the dressing room for the parents while the kids had pop. After the bottle was opened, champagne was shooting in the air all over us, just like it was the NHL. Cory was in ecstasy from all the excitement, while Jane, George, Big Jim, Fred and I had tears in our eyes. Looking at Cory, I wished that John could have been with me to feel as proud as I did of our child. But I was also thankful to have the best friends anyone could ask for, so they could share his joy with me. A week later there was a big banquet for the team and again we were all there. Cory received two trophies and an embroidered hockey jacket with his name and number on it. It was a moment I will cherish forever.

By March break, 1987, Fred was back on his guilt trip about moving to PEI. His father was dying of cancer, so we decided to go see him while he was still alive. When we arrived, it looked like a winter wonderland, still a patchwork quilt, but a white one. Looking down eagerly from the plane, I could see hints of green in the snowy landscape. Brightly coloured homes dotted the countryside, while glimmers of red clay roads lightly peeked through. The sight of that beautiful landscape was like candy for the eyes and food for the soul; one of those moments that make you stop and thank God for the gift of sight.

When we arrived, we found Paps very frail and unlike his former witty self, with his spark sadly diminished. It was hard to see him like that. After we had been there a few days, a man from the co-op stopped by to talk about the new funeral home being built. Everyone was buying shares in it, so Paps gave the man thirty-five dollars. When the man said how nice it was going to be once it was finally finished next year, I thought to myself, it's a funeral home, not a swanky restaurant. As Paps gave his money, I couldn't help feeling bad for him, figuring he was never going to last until it was built. I'm not sure if Paps was thinking the same thing, but later he mentioned that if someone died before it was built, the share would be passed on to someone else in the family. Paps never talked about how sick he was, or the fact that he was dying.

One day he said, "Gail, if you move here you don't have to worry about driving. I'll take you around."

"That would be nice, Paps, thank you," I replied. "I'll keep that in mind."

Then he proceeded to tell me about how his own dad wouldn't stop driving when he was dying. He told how stubborn his father had been, and how no one could get him to park his vehicle and stop using it. One time, he said, his father had an accident and hit the side of the barn. By the end of the conversation, I realized it was a fucking horse and buggy he was talking about. All that time I had thought it was a car, and wondered why they didn't just take away the keys.

Five days before we were supposed to leave, a blizzard hit, the kind I hadn't seen since I was a child in New Brunswick. Everything came to a complete standstill. Even the plows were taken off the roads and we were storm-stayed. Looking outside, all you could see was a complete whiteout. The feeling of isolation was intense, with the fierce wind battering the house so hard you could feel it move. By the time the plows were back on the road three days later, I had cabin fever and was feeling claustrophobic. Once the road was opened, Fred's brother-in-law Larry came over to take Gordy and me to the grocery store. I didn't care where I was going, all I wanted was out. In some places the snow was up to the phone wires, and we had to walk in drifts six feet high to get out of the driveway. I started to walk on the top of the frozen snow, and the next thing I knew, I was up to my armpits. Unable to lift myself out, I started yelling for help. I could see Fred and Patrick in the window cracking up with laughter, while Gordy and Larry finally realized what had happened and came back to rescue me. Lifting me up, they asked if I wanted to go back, but I said, no way, I have to get out of here. So they literally dragged me through the snow to the car, laughing all the way. Now I knew the true meaning of trapped in PEI.

When it was time for us to leave, everyone was still trying to convince me to move to the Island. They insisted this wasn't a typical winter, that the weather was seldom this fierce. Then we said goodbye and I hugged Paps, knowing he wouldn't be there to chauffeur me around if we moved next summer. On the way to the airport with Larry, we stopped to look at the brand new prefab homes that were being built. They were a nice sixteen feet wide and seventy feet long, with an open concept in their layout that got me thinking twice about living there. And they only cost forty thousand, which wouldn't buy the front door of a house in Toronto. Fred's brother Daniel was willing to give us a half-acre of land to put it on if we wanted. As soon as we were on the plane, Fred started to pester me about moving, trying once again to make me feel guilty about keeping him in a basement apartment. Feeling sorry for him, I finally gave in. "Yes," I said, "we can move to PEI in the summer."

Having made the commitment, I realized one of the hardest things was going to be telling Jane. As soon as we were back home, I took her on a walk and told her. As I had feared, she was very upset.

"Gail," she said, "I'll have no one to go to the grocery store with me, and walk the dog. Who am I going to have for a drinking buddy?"

"Jane," I replied, "Fred's stuck in a basement apartment here, and if we move we can own something. Cory will have the freedom to run on the beaches, fish, and grow up surrounded by nature. That's something he can't do here, and I'll have something to pass on to Cory when I'm dead and gone. I will never be able to buy a home here."

"I know," Jane said. "It's probably better for Fred and Cory. But I'm going to miss you. You're like a sister to me."

"I'm going to miss you too," I told her. "You're like the family I never had. But remember, the Island is only a two-hour flight away. Just think about it. It will only take you two hours on the weekend to get to your cottage!"

The next evening, Jane wanted me to come over to her place to talk. Sitting me down, she said, "I was thinking last night in bed. You're not married to Fred. If something happens to him, you could have a real fight on your hands. With his kids and that family, they will say it's their land

and you will have nothing. They might not treat you like family if you're not married to him."

"I never thought about that," I said. "But I don't want to get married to him."

"You better, to protect yourself and Cory," Jane insisted. "You're not cleaning his piss and shit and living like hell for nothing. He's sixteen years older than you are."

I knew then that Jane was right. I could never even begin to love this man, but marrying might be the only way of protecting my future.

Having made the decision, we fortified ourselves with a few drinks, then went over to my place where George and Fred were drinking and watching TV. Looking at Fred, Jane plunged right in.

"Before you take Gail to PEI, you're going to marry her, or I'm not letting her go."

Fred looked up from the TV. "I'm not marrying that fat bitch," he said.

"Without that fat bitch, as you call her, you would be in a nursing home," Jane continued. "Who the fucking hell do you think cleans and takes care of you when you fall out of your wheelchair, or when you piss and shit yourself. She breaks her back picking you up."

Just then George spoke up. "Fred, I think Jane's right. Without Gail you're screwed, buddy. What the hell," he continued, "you're living with her anyway. You have to give her some security. She's doing this more for you than her. She could have walked out and left when you had that fall. She's a young woman, and you can't give her sex or anything."

Fred must have really listened to them, for the next day he said, "Yeah, I guess we better get married."

"Fred," I said, "what did you have when I met you? Nothing but a green garbage bag and an old radio, and a paycheck that didn't even make it until the next week. Everything we have is because of me. Left to yourself, you would have just pissed everything down the drain."

Jane took control of the plans for the wedding, choosing Friday, June 13 as the only available date. With less than two months before our departure to PEI on August 15, she didn't have much time. Jane was to be the maid of honour and George the best man for the ceremony at city hall, then we would have a reception at their place afterwards with just a few close friends and some family.

In the end, it was a really fun wedding, with about forty people at the reception. Fred parked his wheelchair right beside the bar and didn't move until he was carried to bed, drunk out of his mind. Jane got loaded as well, which left George and me. Our partners always got drunk and passed out, so we were used to it. Afterwards, we sat up all night talking and drinking. George and I always sipped our drinks instead of wolfing them down, which was why we could last much longer than they could. When I finally decided to go to bed, it was eight o'clock in the morning. By then, there were seven people passed out on my waterbed. Normally that wasn't permitted, but I figured it was better than drinking and driving. Plus the marriage was never going to be consummated, so what did it matter. As I didn't feel tired enough to join them, I stayed up and cleaned. By eleven that morning, people started to stop by who hadn't been invited to the wedding, because we considered them serious alcoholics. It made me wonder what I thought the rest of us were. In the end, I didn't sleep until Sunday evening, as I had to keep the place clean and under control during all the partying. Like the others, Fred himself had been up and down like a yo-yo, alternating between drinking and sleeping, and finally I had to ask everyone to leave, telling them the fun was over and it was time for them to go home.

Six weeks before we were to move to the Island, Fred's dad died. We decided not to go to the funeral because it was so close to the time we would be going anyway. Our furniture was sent by transport and then it was the day before our departure. That night we stayed at Jane and George's where they had a big going-away party for us in their back yard. It was a blast, with lots of food and drinks and everyone staying up until daybreak. All the people we had known seemed to be coming out of the woodwork to say goodbye. Finally, in the morning, Jane drove us to the airport. It was so sad to say goodbye to Jane and George, my mother and my sister Marilyn. I was walking away from all the people I loved, and who loved me. And all for someone that didn't love or respect or appreciate me. I was blinded by foolish compassion.

CHAPTER SEVEN

No Looking Back

There is always a price to be paid for a decision made. Fred, Cory and I were starting a whole new life. As I looked out the window of the plane, I wondered if I had made the right decision. Then I looked over at Cory where he was sleeping. At eleven, he was the perfect age, for any older might have been too late to make this move. I still had time to mold him into a country life, before the city swallowed him up. In the meantime, Fred was being his usual crybaby self because it was too early in the morning for a drink. On an airplane, the rules are the same as on the ground; the bar opens at ten o'clock and not a minute earlier. It was a blessing he couldn't drink, for at least I knew he would be manageable when we arrived.

"Fred," I said, "aren't you happy you're getting what you wanted? You're going home, isn't that what you always longed for? Why do you feel the need to drink?"

"Why don't you shut up?" he snapped. "I'm hung over and I need a drink."

"You're not a very thankful person," I replied. "Do you hate yourself, or is it life in general?"

After that, I blocked him out. I was excited at the thought of a home to call my own, and it was all thanks to Lenny who had given us the five thousand dollars we needed for the down payment. He had won ten thou-

113

sand on a scratch ticket and loaned us the money with no strings or interest. Friends like that are priceless. He was even out of work at the moment and could have said no like most people would have. I knew that it would only be a few months before we'd be able to pay him back.

When we finally touched down for the first time knowing it was now our home, I had such confused emotions. In fact, my emotions were as unstable as the plane had felt at times. Trying to feel safe and secure, I also felt like a child learning to walk for the first time. But I knew I would walk, and run if I had to, because this was the choice I had made. Only time would tell whether it had been the right or wrong choice.

Patrick picked us up at the airport and we headed out to Wellington where we would stay with Fred's sister. She was still living in the old homestead, which was left to her when Paps died. I wasn't too pleased about staying there, but our prefab home was being built in New Brunswick and wouldn't be ready for another three weeks. So here I was again, with my bed on the floor, living in a house that wasn't equipped to handle a wheelchair. Also living there were Patrick and Gordy's two boys, Patrick and Malroy, who were five and six years younger than Cory.

One day, about two weeks after we arrived, I found Cory sitting outside on the porch crying. When I went over and put my arm around him and asked what was wrong, he said, "Mom, I don't like living here."

"Why don't you like it, Cory?" I asked.

"I miss my friends and my own room. And it's really boring here."

Then I started to cry too. "Sweetie," I said, "you will have a nice room in just one more week. Soon you'll be going to school and you'll make lots of friends there. Don't cry. I miss everyone, too. We'll go back for lots of visits, and we can always phone."

The next day I took Cory to buy a bicycle at Canadian Tire. He picked out a nice metallic blue one that cost two hundred dollars, but I didn't care. I just wanted him to be happy. He was always so grateful for anything I did for him, kissing and hugging me afterwards. The bicycle gave him something to do, riding it up and down the long driveway, popping wheelies and making himself a ramp.

Fred, on the other hand, was still drinking most of the time, although not so much that he became uncontrollable. The house construction was moving right along, with a well dug, a septic tank put in, and the foundation started. All in all, everything was falling into place nicely. Finally, a tractor-trailer arrived with all our furniture. As our house wasn't finished yet, we had nowhere to put it, so the people who sold us the home put a trailer box in the yard where we could store everything. Cory started feeling better once he saw our things arrive, which made me feel a bit more at ease as well. Then the day arrived when we saw our home coming down the street. We were all so happy and excited. The minute it was set up, Cory went running to see his new bedroom, with me right behind him. After a lifetime living in apartments, having a whole house to ourselves was so exciting. Cory's bedroom was right at the end of the hall, with the dining room next, then a washroom, kitchen, living room, and my bedroom. Not only did I have a house, but also a half-acre of land where I could plant flowers and trees and get lost in nature.

Our new house was right in front of the old homestead. Next door were two boys named Morris and Eric with whom Cory was soon friends. At first, Cory had been a bit reluctant to just go over and meet them on his own, but after their aunt and uncle introduced all the kids to each other, they became fast friends. As the boys had four-wheelers and a small boat for going out on the river, Cory was soon happy again and off doing all the country things I had hoped for.

No sooner were we settled in then who should be at our front door but Randy, Fred's nephew, the one we had already been down the road with. He started hanging around, drinking and sleeping over, which got Fred drinking more as well. I finally told him, "Sorry, Randy, you have a mother and a home and it's not here. You can come and visit, but you can't stay." He left and moved himself next door to Patrick and Gordy's, staying a few weeks until they too sent him packing.

That fall, Cory started school. Unfortunately, the only school in our community was totally French, so Cory wasn't permitted to attend it. At first he was so upset, wanting to be with Morris and all the local kids, but you had to have parents who spoke French at home. Finding him crying in his room one day, my heart ached, but there was nothing I could do about it.

"Mom, I won't know anyone at Miscouche School. All my friends are at Evangeline," he told me.

"I know, Cory, but it will be good for you to go to Miscouche because you will make even more friends. That will give you friends in more than one place."

"I guess you're right, Mom, I never thought of it that way." Happily, another problem was now solved.

At the end of September, we had friends coming from Toronto to visit. Milton had worked with Fred at the tire factory, and he and his wife Carrie were good friends of ours. They both drank heavily, so Fred would be happy having someone to drink with all day. Carrie drank from the time she opened her eyes in the morning until night, but Milton always waited until early evening. The only sightseeing they did the whole visit was at the liquor store. I couldn't believe they drove all that way from Toronto and didn't see a thing. The visit lasted for five days, but that was long enough for me. Having left the city and gotten away from all that drunken commotion, I now found I'd learned to like a quieter pace of life. With Fred now in a wheelchair, I also found that it wasn't easy managing him when he got in a drunken state. We were just settling in, and having guests who brought back all the worst qualities of our life in Toronto no longer seemed fun. It was my first moment of realizing that life on the Island was going to bring about some kind of change in me as a person, that my habits and ambitions and goals would no longer be the same as when I had lived in Toronto.

Our next visitors were George, his friend Joe, and Mutzy, who was Jane's ex-husband. Jane and George were very good friends with Mutzy and his new wife, going on trips together and partying. Jane was one of those people who was a friend for life. Even an ex-husband couldn't shake her great personality. Unfortunately, Jane couldn't come this visit, as she couldn't get the time off from work.

As soon as they arrived and we had all hugged and kissed, Joe asked where the washroom was. We had a little eight-by-twelve shed out in the field which I pointed to and told him was the outhouse.

Looking bewildered, he asked, "What about a shower?"

"Sorry," I replied, "we have to do that in the ocean with a bar of soap."

At that, he turned around and looked at George. "What kind of fucking place did you bring us to, you stupid, little Greek?"

"I didn't know, don't get mad at me," said George.

Then Joe asked, "Is there a hotel we can stay at?"

When he started to walk towards the shed, we all burst out laughing.

Taking pity on him, I called him back and showed him the real washroom. Fortunately he had a good sense of humour, although he said he was just about ready to turn around and leave. We had a great visit with them, taking them out on a lobster boat, going fishing, and doing lots of sightseeing. They loved it. One evening we went to the Legion where they bought rounds for the locals all evening. It started out to be about five people, but by the end there were twenty or more locals gathered there. Joe asked, "Did someone put the word out there were free drinks at the Legion?" No matter how many showed up, however, they kept the free rounds coming. After a few games of snooker and a lot of laughs, we headed for home. George and the guys stayed three days and we had so much fun, I hated to have them leave.

That winter, we had our first Christmas in the country. Throwing out my artificial tree, I decided we would go and get a real one from the woods. Cory and I went to cut one, but the trouble was, we didn't have a clue what kind to get. Choosing one that looked good, we took it home where we discovered it was a different story. Once inside and decorated, all the limbs drooped from the weight of the ornaments. Taking one look at it, Fred said, "That's not the right kind of tree, that's a juniper." At that point, I gave up and went out and bought another artificial one.

On Christmas morning, Cory woke up all excited, but there was an empty feeling as well. There was no family or friends other than Fred's family, who were very different and distant. You never could feel any genuine love coming from them. To me, they seemed to be the type of people who just went through the motions of everyday life, without any real zest or appreciation for it. When Jane phoned from Toronto, her family said it didn't seem like Christmas to them either, without us there. We were all feeling the same loneliness. After that, the phone never stopped ringing all day, with family and friends all saying they missed us. Somehow we finally got through that Christmas and New Year's, but I was glad when it was over.

Then it was January 1988 and the start of a new year. Life settled into a new routine now that we were living on the Island. Fred wasn't home much. He would get up in the morning, go next door to play cards until lunch time, then go back after lunch, come home for supper, and back again until ten or later, staying the whole day with Gordy, Patrick and anyone else who dropped by. I couldn't stand the cards and gossip, which was all it offered in terms of entertainment and excitement. As neither one interested me, I stayed home and cooked, cleaned, crocheted and watched the two chan- nels on TV, passing the time away. Was this what life was supposed to be, I wondered, just getting up every day and passing the time with no real hap- piness? Cory spent most of his time next door with Morris and Eric, which I was glad about, knowing that he was once again happy. But Fred now had me right where he wanted me, isolated and with no friends or family.

One evening there was a storm warning on the radio, telling people to bring in any pets they had from outside. We didn't have any that I knew of. In the meantime, I had just done the grocery shopping and was noticing that the hot dogs, ham and roast beef were disappearing at an alarming rate. I didn't have a clue where the food was going, but figured that Cory was becoming a teenager and was probably eating more. Then the storm hit, and there was this beautiful wolf-like dog lying out on the front deck. It was fairly large, with gray, white and tan colours. As I watched the snow starting to stick and cover it, I remembered the weatherman saying to bring animals inside. Although I was a bit frightened, I finally decided to go out and get the dog, for I couldn't see leaving it out there hungry and cold. Well, it turned out the dog may have been cold, but it definitely wasn't hungry, because Cory confessed that he'd been feeding it for some time. That was where all the meat had been going.

"Cory," I said, "I didn't know what was happening to you. I thought you were eating all that food."

Cory started to laugh. "Mom, are you silly. I could never eat that much."

Then Fred started in. "There's no way you're bringing that fucking mongrel in here, or you're going out with it."

"Fred," I said, "don't you have any respect for life? It will die out there tonight."

"I don't give a fucking shit. You're not taking it in."

"That dog is coming in, and I'm going to get it," I told him. "I won't see it freeze out there. And if you say another word, I'm going to wheel you right out on the deck and push you off. So leave me alone."

After we brought it in, Cory and I cleaned all the snow off the dog and dried it with a towel.

"Isn't she beautiful, Mom?" Cory exclaimed. "Can we keep her? She's been hanging around for a couple of days now."

"If no one claims her," I said. "I don't see why not."

She was trembling all over from the cold, and I had tears in my eyes just looking at her. Fred was mumbling in the background, but I didn't pay any attention to him.

The dog never moved that whole night, while I slept well knowing she was now safe and warm. As no one ever laid claim to her, we kept her and named her Princess. Cory was so happy she was ours. She slept every night at the bottom of his bed. Fred was still complaining about the dog, but it fell on deaf ears.

After a couple of weeks, Princess went missing. Cory and I were devastated, not knowing what had happened to her. Finally, one day when Randy happened to be giving me a ride, I mentioned it to him. Randy turned around with a smug look on his face and said, "The dog? Oh, Patrick and I took it for a swim."

"What the hell are you talking about?" I exclaimed.

"We took it and put a weight around its neck and threw it in Grand River. It's dead."

I couldn't believe what I was hearing. It made me feel like throwing up.

"Why?" I asked. "Are you people crazy? That was Cory's dog."

Randy continued to look smug and unconcerned. "Gordy and Patrick didn't want it in their yard," he remarked, as though that excused everything.

"I don't stop their dog from coming in my yard," I said. "I feed it leftovers when it comes. Who are they to decide if I can have a dog or not?"

I couldn't even think straight at the thought of someone being so hardhearted. When Randy took me home, I cried and cried. That night when Fred came in after his card game, I asked, "What kind of barbaric animals do you have for a family?"

"What are you talking about?" he asked.

"Do you know what they did to Princess?"

"No," he answered, "what did they do to Princess?"

"They took her and drowned her in Grand River."

"Oh! Well, good. We didn't need a fucking old mongrel around here."

"You know what, Fred," I said, "you're the fucking mongrel."

The next day I went to see a neighbour and mentioned what had happened to the dog.

"I think that's the dog Kelly found on her door all wet," she said.

"No, it can't be. It's dead," I exclaimed.

"I'll phone and ask her," she replied.

When she called, the description sounded exactly like Princess. After phoning Fred's sister Millie, we got a ride with her husband Larry to go see the dog. She had been kept in a shed, and the minute she came out and I saw her, I had tears in my eyes.

"Is that it?" Kelly asked.

I could hardly speak, I had such a huge lump in my throat. The dog came running and there I was in snow up to my waist hugging it. Then I picked her up and we brought her home.

In the meantime, Fred knew nothing about me finding the dog. When Patrick wheeled him home and came inside, I was on the floor with Princess petting her. At the sight of us, Patrick's big, googly eyes just about doubled in size, if that was possible. He looked like he had just seen a ghost. Fred and he just looked at each other and never said a word. Then Patrick backed quickly out the door.

Finally, Fred spoke. "Where did you find her?" he said in that phony voice I had come to know so well.

"Like you care," I snapped back. "All that matters is that she's back where she belongs. If something happens to her again, I'll call the Humane Society and report it. So nothing better happen to this dog," I added.

When Cory came in and saw her, Princess went wild licking him. They were so happy together, my boy and his dog. I felt so happy seeing them together, for Cory had a heart that was as big as the outdoors, and now he had a companion to love and care for, filling the void of being an only child.

Sometime after moving to the Island, I realized we had another problem. Fred couldn't drive, and I had never learned, other than riding a moped in the Dominican which didn't really count. With the town forty kilometers away, we were at the mercy of Patrick and Gordy for transportation. When they shopped, we had to shop, with no time for browsing or choosing which stores we wanted to visit. Just run in, get your groceries, and leave. For them, it was a necessity, not a fun family outing.

After six months of this, I finally said, "Fred this can't go on. We need transportation."

"I know," he said, "but how are we going to get a loan to buy a car?"

"Like everyone else, we go apply. What's the worst they can say? No?"

I got right on the phone and started to call dealers, explaining that Fred was in a wheelchair and we had no way to get into town to look at cars. Well, they came right to our door, bringing brand-new cars for us to try out until we finally decided on a 1988 Hyundai Excel. After the loan went through, we now had a car, but no driver. Next, we ordered a hand-controlled device that Fred could use, which allowed him to drive without using his feet. It had a lever beside the steering wheel for controlling the gas and brake.

Despite the purchase of the car, I found I was still at Fred's beck and call. Most of the time he was next-door and not interested in driving anywhere. So I went into plan B. One afternoon when everyone was playing cards at my place and not paying any attention to what I was doing, I took the keys to the car. Figuring out the pedals, I backed out of the driveway and drove to the church and back. My blood was boiling from both the excitement and fear. Then I made the trip two more times, hardly believing I could drive. When I got back the second time, I was beeping the horn continually. Everyone came out side to see what was happening, but I just waved and kept on going. I could see Fred was all worked up, with his hands going one way, and his tongue going the other. When I finally got back, he was furious. So were his sister Millie and Gordy. I just looked at them all and said it was my business what I did. They weren't paying for the car, so they could just keep out of it. I knew that if I didn't teach myself to drive, no one would.

After that, I drove for about five months without a license, just down the country roads and a few times into town. It made me feel like I had escaped from prison. Free at last. The word took on a whole new meaning for me. Now I could go shopping at my own leisure and browse till my feet ached or my purse was empty, whichever came first. While I was out, I would pick up contest forms at the grocery store or the liquor store, wherever I saw them. They were the kind no one pays any attention to, but I figured time was on my side, and it could become a nice hobby if I started to win.

One day, I was about to go to New Brunswick to my grandmother's eightieth birthday party. My one surviving grandmother, she was my mother's mother, the one we did not like to visit. Having grown up and learned more about life, I no longer felt that way about her. Although she could never take the place of Memere, I had learned to love her as well. Now I was looking forward to the party and an opportunity to see many of my relatives again. As it was a five-hour trip, I decided to take the bus instead of driving. I remember it was a Friday morning, and just before I was ready to leave, I went to pick up the mail. At the time, I had decided to take only a hundred dollars with me, because I was between U.I. checks and short on cash. Opening the mail, I read, "Congratulations, you are our third prize winner!" Enclosed was a check for three hundred dollars. It took me a minute to figure out I had won it from a contest sponsored by a rum company. It couldn't have come at a better time. I cashed the check right away and went off to Grandma's birthday.

The relatives came from all over for the event; from Florida, Toronto and everywhere in between. I saw aunts, uncles and cousins I hadn't seen since I was a child. It was fun reminiscing and making a family connection, something I hadn't had since my mother and dad split up. The contest windfall made the trip all the better. After it was over, I realized I had never known my mother's family could be so much fun. Perhaps it was the contrast to living next door to Fred's family that made me finally value my own so much.

By the time I went home at the end of the weekend, I had lost my voice from all the laughing and singing and telling jokes. Fred and Cory came to pick me up at the bus terminal, and I could see Cory from the window as we pulled in. I couldn't wait to hug him. Even two days felt like forever when I was away from Cory.

Then it was spring, and the lobster season was about to begin. It seemed like everyone worked in the fish factory. You worked eight weeks and got laid off so someone else could come and get their eight weeks. Then you collected your U.I. for the rest of the year. That was the system, so you better just go with the flow and not dare question it. I had found all this out firsthand when I went to apply for U.I. after moving from Toronto. When the U.I. officer seated behind the desk saw the amount of insurable weeks I had, he looked at me over his glasses and pounded the desk like I had done something wrong. He informed me I already had too many weeks, and there was a system on the Island that I had better not fuck up. He then proceeded to explain that people here worked eight weeks, then got laid off to make room for the next person. I couldn't believe what I was hearing. In the first place, he was swearing. What kind of people did the government have working for it? By the time I left, I was appalled by what I had heard.

The system here was nothing more than a glorified welfare, a way to keep the people down with no chance of advancement.

Having learned all this already, I knew it was now time to go sign up to work my eight weeks at the fish factory for the season. Little did I know what I was getting into. The regulation attire was rubber boots, a hair net and a white smock. Beginning pay was $5.10 an hour and you worked as many hours as needed, sometimes from eight in the morning until midnight, as long as the lobsters were coming in. When I started, I explained about my situation at home with Fred and said I could only work until five, no later. Of course, everyone at the factory thought I wouldn't last, that I'd quit by the end of that first afternoon. In the end I fooled them by lasting a total of four seasons. My job was putting the little legs of the lobster through a steel ringer to squeeze the meat out, hour after hour, all the time standing on a wet cement floor with no talking allowed. By the end of the day, I felt robotic and in a hypnotized state. During my half hour lunch break, I would drive home like a madwoman to check on Fred. He continually smoked in bed and it worried me. At first, things weren't so bad because Fred would have lunch ready for me. Then he started drinking again and soon had a whole new bunch of cronies to drink with. I would come home and find he had shit himself, or was passed out in bed. Other times he would be waiting for me to come clean him up. There was no excuse for this. The house was wheelchair accessible and he could now shower and clean himself without me. But he would wait, just so he could make me pity him. My whole lunch break would be spent cleaning him up, throwing the laundry in the washer, then driving back. There was no time to eat, so it was a great way to lose weight. This went on for four lobster seasons until I quit. I just couldn't handle coming home to a mess at lunch each day. That was far harder than any work I had to do at the fish factory.

In the summer of 1988, the family and friends came in droves. Now that we lived on the Island, they had discovered a free vacation place to stay, eat, drink and be merry. That summer, I had Big Jim and his cousin, my mother and Bob, my sister Marilyn, her boyfriend, and her three kids. Then Jody came with her husband and two kids. I had a funny feeling that I was going to see more of my family now than when I lived in Toronto. We had now changed from the Do Drop Inn to Vacation Station. All I did that summer was cook, clean and pick up the empties. I was always happy to see my family, but the men all seemed to be heavy drinkers, and not sociable ones at that. My only reward was that Cory was overjoyed at having his cousins visit, spending most of his time swimming at the beach, which was only a five-minute walk away. The kids all played baseball and had a great time.

In the fall, Cory was back into hockey. It was great fun taking him to the games and watching him play. His position was forward and he was getting better and better all the time. The team traveled all over, so it gave the two of us something to focus on while we were seeing the rest of the Island. Sometimes Fred would come with us, but mostly it was just Cory and me.

In February 1988, I had to go to the little country store down the street, about a kilometer away. On the counter I saw a contest from Coca-Cola. "Spring Breakaway in L.A. Win a trip to a beach party with Wayne and Janet Gretzky in Los Angeles." I was so excited, I took eight entries.

Looking confused, the girl behind the cash register said, "Why are you taking so many? No one wins those things."

"I'm going to win," I told her, "and take my son to meet Wayne Gretzky." She started to laugh. "All right," she said. "Good luck."

"You'll be the first to know," I assured her.

When I was walking out the door, I looked back and saw the girl still laughing. She was probably thinking, "That lady is touched in the head."

I went home and filled them out, then sent all eight in and never thought about it again.

Then it was April and I was washing the walls in the living room when the phone rang. It was a call from Toronto, telling me I had just won the Spring Breakaway in L.A. to meet Wayne Gretzky. There were one hundred and four winners from all across Canada. My heart was pounding, but I had two minutes to answer a math question. After I had located pen and paper, the woman on the phone gave me the question and I figured it out. We had won! By now I was walking on thin air, although I could see from the look on Fred's face that he wasn't impressed. He was used to being catered to, and now he was going to have to fend for himself.

After that, I had a hard time finishing up cleaning the walls before to going to pick up Cory from school, instead of waiting for him to come home on the bus. On my way, I stopped off at the store to tell the girl.

"You said you were going to win, but I didn't believe you," she said. "I thought you were a little crazy."

"I kind of figured you did," I replied. "But my gut instinct told me different."

We both laughed as I left the store.

At school, Cory was surprised to see me waiting for him there. "What are you doing here, Mom?"

"What would you say if I told you we were going to meet Wayne Gretzky?" I asked.

"What are you talking about?"

"Cory," I said, "we just won a trip to Los Angeles for two. It's one of those contests I filled out. Remember, I told you I was going to win."

"Are you lying, Mom? I can't believe it!"

"It's true. And we get a brand-new car to drive while we're there, plus five hundred U.S. dollars spending money."

"Oh Mom!" Cory exclaimed. "I can't wait to tell my friends at school. He's the best player there is!"

On May 31, Cory and I flew to Los Angeles. When we arrived, I was surprised that the airport was so empty. It turned out that was because there were eight different terminals. I'd never imagined anything so big. Someone from the Coca-Cola Company was there to meet us and take us into the city on a bus. On the way there the traffic was unreal, much more than we had ever seen on a highway in Toronto. We saw the big Hollywood sign you see in all the movies, so I knew it had to be real. We had arrived.

At the hotel, we checked into our room which had a nice balcony overlooking the pool. Each of us received a kit bag with a shirt, shorts, beach towel and sun visor. After unpacking, we went downstairs for an orientation with the eighty-four Canadians who had won. We were told that we could take possession of our car if we wanted to. By now, I had made friends with a woman named Patty who was here with her daughter Angel. They were from Sault St. Marie, and Angel had filled out the ballot at the local store where they lived. From then on, we were a foursome, which I don't think Cory minded a bit. Angel was beautiful, with dark hair and big blue eyes, while her mother was also very attractive. As it was now time to go sign for the car, I asked Patty if she was taking one, but she said no.

"I can't drive here," she said. "I've driven since I was sixteen, but never in traffic like this."

"Then I'm not taking one either," I told her. "We'll just have to bus it together. I've only had my license for five months and our highway is one lane east and one west, usually with no cars on it."

Then Cory started in. "Mom," he said, "please take it. I know you can drive."

"Cory," I replied, "the highways here are eight lanes. I can't do it! Patty has had her license for years and isn't taking one."

"Oh, Mom, just don't drive on the highway. Try it in the city and if you can't do it, we'll take it back."

"Okay, Cory," I said, "I'll try, but we're taking it back if I get nervous."

"It's a deal, Mom," Cory answered, very pleased with himself.

We were given a Nissan Maxima, which was perfect for the four of us. It was a beauty, all computerized and looking brand-new. When we first got in, I located where everything was, then off we went down the block. Before I knew it, I had made a wrong turn and we were on the L.A. freeway.

"Oh God!" I exclaimed, "we're in trouble now. Where are we going?"

"I have no idea," said Patty.

"How do we get off this roller coaster?"

The traffic was going so fast, I had to just keep driving, with no time to think.

"Let me know when it's safe to switch lanes," I said, keeping my eyes glued to the road ahead.

"Go now!" they all shouted.

Great, we were one lane closer to the exits. Moments later they said to go again. Then wait, then go! In the meantime, they were all laughing their heads off as we inched our way across the lanes.

"I must be nuts listening to you, Cory," I yelled.

"You're doing all right, Mom. Just relax."

"How the hell can I relax? We're on the L.A. freeway, I've had my license for five months and the most I've driven is on the back roads of PEI."

That we finally got off the freeway alive seemed like a miracle. Now the fun was finding our way back to Universal. We must have toured most of the city by the time we got there.

"That's it, Cory," I said. "The car is parked and I'm not driving it. We're taking the bus."

"Ah, Mom, sleep on it," he insisted. "You did great. You'll get used to it."

"Cory, please be quiet. My heart is still thumping!"

I must not have slept on it well, for the next day we were back hitting the road again in the car. We toured all over the place: the Walk of Fame, the Beverly Hills Mall, the Hard Rock Café, where we talked the management into letting Cory and Angel inside. Then the next thing I knew, we were lost in east L.A., where the ghettos and gangs were. While everyone else giggled like fools, I really hit the gas pedal, scared to death by the whole thing.

The next day we took a ferry ride to Catalina Island. Cory and I were seasick the whole way, with our heads down on the table and never moving for three hours. When we got there, however, it was incredible. Best of all was the glass-bottomed-boat we took a trip on. Then it was back again for three more hours of feeling seasick, but it was worth the experience. As sick as I was, I'd do it again.

By now, the four of us were all having the time of our lives, eating, swimming in the pool, and exploring together. The next day we took a bus tour of the movie stars' homes, then ventured out once more with the car to see Rodeo Drive and tour the homes in Beverly Hills, an area we found particularly clean and lovely. Then came another bus tour, this time to Disneyland. It made me so happy to see Cory captivated by the whole experience. And we hadn't even met Wayne Gretzky yet!

Finally the big day came when we were supposed to go to the beach party and meet Wayne and his wife Janet. Early that morning, the CBC radio station on PEI did a live broadcast from L.A., asking me questions about how the trip was going. Then we were all loaded on a bus and taken to a secret location. No one knew where we were going. Everyone was given passes to attend the event, plus passes for two drinks each.

When we finally arrived, it was at a beautiful place near Venice Beach. After about an hour, Wayne Gretzky, his wife Janet, and some of their friends arrived, including the Olympic Champion Bruce Jenner, his wife Lydia Thompson, who was a former girlfriend of Elvis Presley, the actor Matt McCoy, and Wayne's family. Not being a shy person, I went up and asked Janet if we could have a picture taken of the two of us bathing beauties. She laughed and said yes. I was wearing black and white toilet earrings that matched my bathing suit and were creating quite a sensation. Not only did Janet find them amusing, so did the Coca-Cola photographers who kept snapping close-ups. Then Cory asked Wayne and Janet to sign his hockey jacket. Wayne seemed a bit concerned that the signature would never come off, but Cory assured him he wanted it to last forever. Linda Thompson and I chatted for a while, and then she and Matt McCoy also signed Cory's jacket. In the end, we ate and danced until the wee hours of the morning.

After the beach party was over, no one in our group felt like sleeping. Back at the hotel, we Canadians all got together in one of the guest rooms and partied. The hotel management kept chasing us from room to room until it was almost time to get on our plane. No one wanted the party to end, and Cory and I practically missed our flight, along with a few other people. Looking back, I realize that this entire trip was one of the most memorable times Cory and I would ever have together.

On the way home we had a four-hour stay in Toronto, so Jane, my mom, Bob, and Marilyn came to see us at the airport. I was so happy to see Jane because I hadn't seen her since we moved. We laughed and talked all about the trip, and she caught me up on the latest happenings in her life, and how lonely the street now seemed since we had moved away. She told me everyone missed our place and all the great fun we had together. By the time we had to leave, I was agonizing about staying and never going back to the Island again. Everyone was hugging and crying until Cory and I had to tear ourselves away and board the plane. By the time we reached Halifax for an overnight stop, we were both so exhausted we slept from 7:30 that evening until morning, then caught the final plane back to PEI.

The Christmas of 1988, Fred's stepdaughter Genny and her husband came to the Island for a visit. One day they popped into our place with Fred's other daughter, Lilly, and her boyfriend. After about a half hour, Genny said their mother was at the church because they didn't know what to do with her while they were visiting us. They were supposed to pick her up when they left our place, but it was freezing cold in the church and they were a bit concerned. I immediately told them to go get her and bring her to the house because it was far too cold for her to stay there. I wasn't a jealous person, especially as I had never loved Fred and was only married to him on paper, so the prospect of meeting his ex-wife didn't bother me. Plus I was sure she wouldn't still be interested in him now that he was in a wheelchair.

I found Kelly an attractive lady, and pretty soon we were all having a drink and talking together. Everything went smoothly until Fred started flapping his mouth, the way he could, bringing up old wounds about their relationship until I could see that she was getting uneasy. I finally told him to be quiet and leave her alone. By now there was a storm starting outside. There's nothing quite like a winter storm on PEI. Most people just stay right where they are without trying to go anywhere. Lilly and her boyfriend, however, insisted on going, sure that they could make it home. Genny, her husband Tedd, and Kelly were smarter and decided to stay put at our house. I served up a nice dinner of homemade bread and cabbage rolls, as well as some wine, but the glutton in the wheelchair had to have more wine than anyone else. Pretty soon he was back on his sad stories again, putting down Kelly. I finally told him that was enough of his bull, and put him to bed. Afterwards, while Kelly and I sat talking together, I found she was a lot nicer than Fred had given her credit for. Suddenly, there he was again, back up out of bed and shooting his mouth off. I wanted to choke him. This time, after I got him back into bed, I took his wheelchair away so he couldn't get up. But that still didn't stop his mouth. I finally closed the door so we wouldn't hear his endless mumbling. Kelly had a bad heart, having already suffered a heart attack, and I didn't want her hearing him dredge up his worst memories from the past. That was Fred for you, never remembering the good about anything. I suppose after living with him for ten years, Kelly must have already known how repetitious and ignorant he could become when he was drunk.

Ignoring Fred, we continued to sit together talking while the storm built outside. I discovered that her first cousin was married to my mother's sister, which meant that we both had the same cousins. It seemed amazingly coincidental that she was from the Island. Suddenly, Lilly and her boyfriend were back for the night, having found the driving impossible in the snow. So in the end, we had quite a full house.

Six months later, we heard that Kelly had suffered another heart attack, this time a lot more serious than the first. When Lilly phoned with the news, she also told us she was about to have a baby. Could we come visit her mother, she asked. So we drove to Charlottetown, met Kelly at a coffee shop, and followed her to the house. I could immediately see that she was in bad shape. We had a nice visit, though, and just before we left, Kelly gave me a clipping from a plant I happened to like. When we said goodbye, I had a feeling she wasn't going to survive long. Sure enough, a few months later she had a third heart attack. At the same time, Lilly gave birth to a little boy named Eldon, so she and her mom were in the hospital together. Kelly was able to see her new grandson that morning before they transferred her to Halifax, Nova Scotia.

The baby was three days old when I first saw him, and Lilly asked if we could take him for the night. Then a couple of weeks later, she asked if we could take her to Halifax to see her mother. Picking her up in Charlottetown, we caught the ferry at Wood Islands. Halfway to Halifax, Fred's hand controls broke and I had to drive. When we finally arrived, Kelly was in a coma and didn't know anyone. It was so sad. The doctors asked permission to stop the life support system, but Lilly was in denial and wanted to believe that her mother was still going to come home again.

That evening, we left quite late for the return trip. There was a torrential downpour and the road was dark and winding, with only two lanes and the other car lights practically blinding me. I was terrified. Fred kept squawking in the seat beside me about my driving, while Lilly sat in the back rocking her head from side to side. She was making me dizzy with that motion of her head. I could feel it as I drove, and finally asked her to please stop. She would stop for a bit, then start up doing it again until I thought I would go mad. I guess it was something she had done as a child and never really outgrown. When we finally reached home after dropping Lilly off in Charlottetown, I was never so glad to be back and out of that dismal weather.

A few days later, Kelly died at the age of forty-two. At the funeral home, I could see her ex-husband Ely was devastated. Although he had abandoned her about a year ago, he appeared to now be in deep emotional pain. Her kids, however, claimed his mental state had more to do with guilt for having run off than with honest grief. The next thing I knew, Ely had jumped into his car to leave the funeral home, and driven straight into a huge maple tree. Later on that same evening, when we were headed back to the funeral home in Fred's son-in-law's truck, Fred's wheelchair suddenly went flying out the back of the truck onto the street. By that point, Fred and Kelly's kids truly believed their mother was trying to get back at the two of them for the pain they had caused her in her lifetime. To make matters worse, the kids also found out that Ely had gone and bought a burial plot right beside their mother. Two weeks later, we got news that Ely had committed suicide and was buried right beside Kelly.

Over the next few months, I found myself taking care of Lilly's baby far more than she did. Finally, one day when he was seven months old, she phoned and asked if we could come and take him, because she was afraid of what she might do. I told her to hold on right there, we'd be over as soon as possible, and not to do anything stupid. We'll take the baby, I told her. By the time I got there, she was beside herself. At first, I thought she wanted us to take Eldon for a few days, the way we usually did, but I soon discovered she had him all packed up, right down to hospital appointments booked for a year later. Between her mother's death, and being a mother herself at sixteen, the freedom of Lilly's youth had been stolen from her and she just couldn't cope. Caught up in the situation, I knew that there was an innocent baby that needed love and caring for. Whether I liked it or not, I had just become a new mother.

Back home, I borrowed a crib and put it in our bedroom because the house was too small for the baby to have his own room. Fortunately, I was already emotionally attached to Eldon as he had been with us much of the time since he was born. After a month, he started to call me Mom.

Three months later, I learned that Eldon's father wanted him back. His brother and he planned to live together with their kids so they could collect welfare. What a sad reason for wanting a child. Lilly was angry and immediately got a lawyer, but he told us we had no rights unless Lilly was living with the baby. If a mother didn't want a child, the father was entitled to it, no matter how questionable his motives were. At court, the judge said the same thing; that the only way the baby would be permitted to stay with us was if the mother lived with us too. I figured this was just what we needed, perhaps Lilly would bond with the baby and accept her responsibilities as a mother. As much as I loved Baby Eldon, I already had my plate full with Fred.

Unfortunately, Fred and Lilly were like fire and water, fighting constantly. Lilly would lie on the couch, rocking her head back and forth in that way she had, while Fred yelled and cursed. If Baby Eldon messed up all the pots and pans under the kitchen cupboard, Fred would get upset and start cursing at me as well, telling me to clean it up. I asked him what was wrong with Lilly. Couldn't she clean her own child's mess up? I told them both I wasn't there to wait on everyone hand and foot. In the end, my plan backfired, for Lilly wouldn't pick up a thing around the house or watch Baby Eldon. She spent most of her time just there like a bump on a log.

One time, Fred got so mad that he came after me in his wheelchair. I could see he was infuriated. I guess he found it easier to get mad at me than at his own child, even though I was the one doing all the work. When I saw him coming, I ran and jumped in the bathtub where he couldn't get close enough to hit me. If he'd ever gotten his hands on me, I would have been seeing stars, and it wouldn't have been movie stars either. When I finally ventured out, he had stopped his cursing and never even said a word. I had come to the conclusion long ago that Fred had a dual personality, and learning how to deal with it was a balancing act at best.

One day that summer, Jane called. "Hi, Gail, how are you?" I could already tell by her voice that it wasn't good news.

"I'm fine," I said. "How are you?"

"Not good, Gail. I have—" I heard her take a deep breath, then say the most dreaded word in the English language, "Cancer."

"Oh no, Jane, don't tell me that," I exclaimed. "Is it curable?"

"I think so. I have to go for an operation, then I'll know more."

"We'll pray," I assured her, "then you'll be fine."

"Yeah, Gail, I hope so." I could hear the uncertainty in her voice.

"Jane, please," I begged her, "I know it's easy for me to say, but think positive."

We talked for a while longer, then I told I loved her and missed her before we hung up. When I got off the phone I was heartbroken. I tried to think in a positive way, but I knew in my heart that there was still fear and doubt. Fred and Cory were shocked and saddened as well when I told them. All that night I tossed and turned, unable to get my mind off Jane.

Maybe it was hearing about Jane, but all of a sudden I found I had had enough of watching Lilly lie on the couch while I did all the work. It was time for her to get a job, I told her. She soon found one at a restaurant in Summerside, but as she had no means of transportation, I had to drive her to and from work. Most of the time I had Baby Eldon with me as well because Fred was bedridden at the moment. Winter was approaching, and here I was driving Lilly back and forth. She would phone to say when she was finished for the day, but often I would end up waiting as much as an hour in the car with a fussy baby. Unable to stand it any longer, I urged her to get her license, then let her use my car. So even though I no longer had to drive to Summerside twice a day, I had no car. Plus she wasn't making enough money as a waitress to survive on her own. Still, despite everything,

I felt sorry for her. She had lost her mother, and her father didn't have much compassion, or chose not to show it if he did.

Taking control of the situation once more, I steered her into taking a course through Human Resources, which pays you while you learn a vocation. Eventually, she was training at the health center. For two weeks she trained full time, doing heart tracings, eye exams, blood work, and loving the job. So there I was, taking care of her child while she progressed on with her life and I got blamed for all the mess around the house. I was glad, though, that Lilly seemed to be getting her life under some kind of control financially. If she could also get things under control at home as well, and accept some responsibility, my load would be lighter.

One day the phone rang and it was my aunt Lanie. Pepere had just died, she told me. Cory and I had been to see him in the hospital in Moncton two weeks earlier, where he was diagnosed with cancer. Now he had died and I was going to his funeral. I asked Lilly if she would look after her dad and Cory while I was away, but she said no.

"I'm going to the bar with a friend," she informed me. "Eldon is with his dad for the weekend, and I'm not staying here."

"This is a funeral," I told her. "I'm not going to a wedding. I have to go. You can go away next weekend when I'm home." I might as well have saved my breath.

"Sorry, I'm not taking care of him." There was no appealing to her compassion. She had none when it came to her father.

With no real alternative, I asked Fred's sister to check on him while I was gone, as he was still bedridden. Cory was staying as well, but I couldn't rely on him to care for Fred because he had hockey the next morning and also wanted to go to his first dance that evening. Having done what I could, I left for New Brunswick on the bus.

I knew this funeral was going to be painful, for Pepere was one of the people I loved most in the world. When I arrived and looked at him in the casket, I couldn't believe I would never hear the words "Gail of Wind" spoken again. The last link to my fondest memories was now gone. At the funeral, it was very moving when his war buddies sang a song and bid a final farewell salute to him, then draped his coffin with the Canadian flag. Pepere had never mentioned it to us, but his comrades told us of his bravery in helping to save Buckingham Palace during the war. Afterwards, he had been taken all through the Palace and given a special medal of honour.

Pepere would always have a place of honour in my heart, for all the love, guidance and compassion he had given me when I was a child. After the funeral, Lanie, cousin Candy, and I reminisced about our past as children. There were tears and laughter, and suddenly the time had flown by and we had to leave for home. I traveled with Lanie and her husband James as far as Moncton, stopping off at their place for an hour before my bus to the Island. It's a terrible feeling when a funeral is more enjoyable than the reality you have to face when going back home. The only thing that kept me sane was the love I felt for my child. He gave me purpose in life.

Cory was so excited when I got home, wanting to tell me all about his weekend. It turned out he had come home early from the dance because he was worried about Fred being all alone. Lilly hadn't stopped by, or even called, the whole weekend. I was glad to think my child had a conscience and had come home, even if Fred wasn't his father.

Cory's best news was about the hockey tournament. "We won!" he told me excitedly. "We beat the best team, and I scored six goals and one assist. Everyone was cheering and going crazy. I wish you could have been there."

I told him how proud I was, and how much I would have loved to be there too. Then I went in to see how Fred was.

"I'm fine," he told me, "thanks to Cory, and not that fucking tramp."

"Don't say that," I told him. "You never say anything nice to her, so she isn't going to be nice to you either. It doesn't matter if you're her father or not. Sometimes you get what you give, and other times you give but you don't get."

Fred was never one who wanted to listen, though. Instead, he preferred to feel sorry for himself, hoping to arouse pity in other people so he could justify his self-centered behaviour.

About a day later, there was a big headline in the paper on the sports page that read, "Cory Duguay sparks Tyne Valley 7 to 1." Although Cory had been in the paper before, this was the first time there had ever been a big write-up on him.

That Christmas of 1991, Jane wasn't doing well, so I told Fred I wanted to spend it with her. I didn't want my last memory of her to be in a casket. Fred agreed, so without even telling anyone, we drove to Toronto for the holiday, arriving at my mom's at two in the morning. When she opened the door, she was so startled to see us. Bob was overjoyed. After locating some bedclothes and figuring out the sleeping arrangements, everyone went straight to bed.

The next afternoon we headed to Jane's. When we arrived, she had just returned from the hospital. She was so surprised to see us, crying and laughing while we hugged. She had lost weight, and her colour was off, but she was still her straightforward self. Then she lifted her pant leg and showed Fred that she had a leg bag just like him, which made everyone laugh. We were all so happy to see each other. Everyone insisted we stay there over the holidays, but I was afraid it would be too much of a strain for Jane in her condition.

"You're staying here," she insisted. "Then we can walk the dog together, just like old times." It was her mom's dog now, because Ralph had died some time ago.

"We have plenty of space," she continued. "You can take our room downstairs, and I'll sleep upstairs at my mom's. She has two extra bedrooms, so don't worry. I want you here."

"You're staying here, and that's final," Jane's mother added.

While I was there, Jane and I walked the dog and had our drinks together, just like we used to.

"Should you be drinking?" I asked, concerned about her health.

"It's too late. It doesn't matter now," Jane replied. She hadn't come right out and said she wasn't going to make it, but I could read between the lines. It made me have such huge emotional swings inside me. My body felt numb as I heard and felt the pain in her voice, for Jane was everything to me—a mother and sister and a best friend all rolled into one.

It was so nice to be home again where I felt loved and wanted. We went to see Uncle Paul, who was still his same funny self, and Gord, who was delighted to see us. Lenny found out we were at Jane's and came right over to see us too. Then Jane's ex-husband Mutzy, Joe, and all the old gang showed up. No one could get over how much Cory had grown, now that he was sixteen.

One day, while we were in Toronto, Cory turned to me and asked if I knew where his father lived.

"I could find out, if you want me to," I told him. "Do you want to meet him? Have you been thinking about this?"

"Yeah," he answered. "I think I would like to see him if I can."

"If you're sure about that, I'll find him for you," I assured him.

Later that night when we were driving around the city looking at the sights, Cory spoke about it again.

"Mom, I think I've changed my mind. I'll wait until I get older."

"It's up to you," I told him. "Whatever you like."

I wondered if Cory had sensed the hurt in my voice when he'd asked about his father. Perhaps that was why he'd changed his mind, so he wouldn't hurt me. I hoped it wasn't, but knowing him well, I knew Cory would go to any length not to cause me pain. We never talked about it, though, so I guess one way or another, it just wasn't the right time for him to meet his father.

On Christmas Eve, we went to spend the night with my sister Marilyn and her family. What a night it was. Marilyn got drunk. So did her boyfriend Danny and Fred, who both went to bed and passed out. Danny's sister and I were the only ones not drinking. Marilyn's son, Brandon, had a friend over, and the next thing I knew, Marilyn had taken off with this kid who was the same age as her own son. At first we were confused about where she had gone, as we were thinking about Christmas, and wanting to wrap up the gifts for her daughter Cynthia. When Brandon, Cory and I headed out to the car to fetch the packages, there was Marilyn in the hall, kissing the young man. Brandon was so embarrassed and upset, he punched his friend, yelling, "What the fucking hell are you doing with my mother?"

"What are you doing with this kid?" I asked Marilyn. "Come upstairs to bed before Danny finds out." Unfortunately, Danny's sister was with us, so she saw everything. We finally managed to get Marilyn in the elevator, but she was laughing hysterically, which got Brandon so infuriated, he hauled off to hit the elevator and hit Cory instead. Poor Cory was so stunned he almost hit the floor. Brandon felt really bad and kept saying how sorry he was for hitting Cory.

"My mom made me so mad, I wanted to hit the elevator," he explained.

By now I was in tears, holding Cory, and wondering how I could have traveled so far for this garbage. I couldn't believe it was all happening on Christmas Eve. When we finally got Marilyn upstairs and into her bedroom, Danny woke up.

"Why can't you go to bed, Marilyn, when you've had enough, like I do," he asked. And he didn't know the half of it yet.

I had Cory put ice on his eye, which was turning black, got Marilyn to bed, then ended the evening wrapping gifts with Danny's sister. It must have been two in the morning when we were finally done.

The next day, Fred, Cory and I went to Jane's for Christmas dinner. Jane was so upset when she saw Cory's black eye and heard what had happened. "I know she's your sister," she said to me, "but what kind of Christmas is that?" What was so hard for her to understand was the love that still survived in my family, despite the terrible behaviour. I would always forgive Marilyn because I knew she was living in her own hell, always searching for love and never finding it. Like most of my family she would turn to booze to help mask her misery. That was where we all seemed to run for our escape.

In the end, we stayed for three wonderful weeks with Jane and her family. We laughed and reminisced about all the fun we had had together—the Dominican Republic trip, watching *The Thorn Birds*, the Texas Mickey, George and the Jehovah Witnesses, Fred and the loaf of bread, and everything else in between. It also gave us time to get caught up on what each of us had been doing for the last three years.

Finally, our visit was coming to and end and it was time to say goodbye. I hugged and kissed Jane, thanking her for all the hospitality her family had given us, and wished her love and health for the coming year. Our visit had been short and tinged with a cloud of sadness, but some of our greatest laughs and tears were embraced at that moment in time.

On our way home, we stopped off to visit Marie. Despite everything that had happened, she was still the mother of my three half-brothers, and I cared about her. We'd only been there a day when my sister phoned and said I'd better call my mother. Mom said Bob had been hospitalized and might not make it. We decided to immediately return to Toronto, but when we got to the hospital, we saw that Bob's condition wasn't life-threatening. He'd just been drinking too much and not taking care of himself. When he heard why we were back, he was furious at my mother. "I'm not dying," he informed me. "I'm sorry you drove all those hours to get back here."

That's when I put two and two together and realized that even after all these years, my mom was jealous because we were at Marie's place. In the end, we went back for two more days before heading home to the Island. During the drive back, we hit a snowstorm just before Campbellton. Wet snow clung to the headlights, and every now and then I had to get out to wipe them clear so we could see where we were going. It was so dangerous, with only two lanes, hardly any shoulder, and pitch-black everywhere. We were on a winding road along the side of a huge cliff, with a hundred-foot drop on one side down into the freezing water. One wrong move and we would have been history. When I finally saw the Campbellton bridge and the lights of the city, it looked so pretty and welcoming. The lights were reflected in the river, and the homes looked etched into the side of Sugarloaf Mountain. The most nerve-wracking part of the journey was over.

By the time we got back to the Island, it was New Year's Eve. Our furnace had run out of oil and the house was freezing cold. We had been in Toronto for almost a month, since the third of December. It would be a trip to remember, and my last time with Jane.

On January 31, George called up and could hardly speak. "Gail," he sobbed, "she's gone. She just died a few minutes ago."

"Oh God, no."

"She was so glad you came and spent Christmas with her. That was all she talked about."

"That's why I went," I told him. "Because I knew in my heart that it might be her last Christmas and I wanted to remember her smiling. I'm not coming to the funeral, George. I don't want it to be my last memory of her."

George understood how I felt. Much as we loved her, we were glad her suffering was now over.

Jane was such an organized person, she had everything written down, even how long the guests were to stay after her funeral, the food, and the clean-up afterwards. She opened my eyes to a whole new world in the short span of time that our lives crossed paths. I learned that family is not defined by blood alone, but that it's a world of friendship, love and forgiveness that holds the true meaning of family. The day Jane died, I gained of piece of her so she will live on in my heart forever.

CHAPTER EIGHT

Moving Day

In March of 1992, Lilly decided to move out. Her weekend outings had found her a mate, and with the fighting between Fred and her out of control, her boyfriend wanted her to move in with him. She was leaving on bad terms and taking little Eldon with her. It tore me apart to see Eldon leave after having him with us for two years. I was his Nanny, and we would cuddle and watch cartoons together on the couch. Cory and he would play and roughhouse on the floor like the little brother Cory didn't have. We had both become very attached to him.

Lilly moved to Summerside with her boyfriend Sam. He was short with straight dark hair and brown eyes, and he always seemed to be on a bit of a power trip. Perhaps because he was such a slight, small person, he felt he needed to prove himself. At first, everything seemed just hunky-dory. Then one day, about four months after Lilly moved out, I was driving to pick Cory up at school when I happened to go by a daycare. Some children were out walking and I immediately recognized Eldon, who I hadn't seen since Lilly left. Catching sight of me, he started coming towards the car, crying "Nanny, Nanny" over and over again. As I saw the teacher tug him back, it made me feel so sad. I wanted to stop and give him a big hug. I was crying when I drove away, trying to compose myself before picking up Cory.

On the way home, I told Cory what had happened.

"I'm sorry, Mom," Cory said. "I miss him too."

It was only a few days later that I bumped into Lilly.

"Eldon has been asking for you," she told me.

I told her about seeing Eldon at his daycare, and how much Cory and I missed him.

"If you want to come and see him, that's fine with me," she said. "He misses you."

I was glad to hear her say this since she had left on bad terms when she first moved to Summerside, hating both her dad and me—me for trying to motivate her into being a responsible mother, and her father for anything and everything. Visiting Eldon hadn't been an option for me, as Lilly was convinced at the time that Fred and I were the cause of all her problems. Given the healing powers of time and space to breathe, however, she had gained a new and wiser perspective.

After that I began visiting him regularly, going to the dumpy, sparsely furnished apartment on the top floor of a house where Lilly now lived with Sam. Each time I left, Eldon would peer out the window at me until I drove out of sight. As I looked up at him, he seemed so sad, with his big blue eyes, porcelain white skin, and straight blond hair, like a little prince trapped in the top of a tower, with no freedom to run and play outside.

In July, Marilyn, Danny and the kids came to visit, bringing my grandmother with them. Pretty soon the cards and drinks were in full swing, for although my grandmother didn't drink, she loved to play cards. Then my mother and Bob flew in. When they boarded the airplane in Toronto, the stewardess found a pint of whiskey in Bob's pocket and took it away from him. She also took note of his seat number and told him he wouldn't be served anything to drink. He had a window seat, and the man sitting in the aisle asked if Bob would switch seats, because this was his first time flying and he wanted to be able to see out the window. Bob said sure, no trouble, and traded seats. When the stewardess came with the alcohol and asked if anyone wanted drinks, Bob happily ordered a whiskey while the stewardess informed the other man that he was cut off. He looked startled when she wouldn't serve him; he then turned and said to Bob, "I don't know what her problem is."

"Heck, I don't know either," Bob replied.

By the time the plane landed and I met them at the airport, I could see that Bob had had more than his share of whiskey. On top of that, he was in a cast, having broken his ankle by falling over a coffee table just before they left on the trip to the Island. Seeing me, he flung his crutches in the air, hitting someone in the process, then grabbed me and gave me a big hug, calling me his daughter over and over. By now, everyone was looking at him like he was daft, so Mom and I grabbed the crutches and luggage and got out of there at breakneck speed.

Not too long after that, Lilly announced she wanted to move out of Sam's because he was abusing her and Eldon. Marilyn, Danny and I decided to go help her pack up and move back in with us. When we got to the apartment, we found she hardly had anything, just some clothes and a few odds and ends. Sam was there as well, insisting we let him keep things like his underarm deodorant, a toy robot he had found in the garbage and given Eldon, and a big butcher knife. I told him that was fine; Lilly didn't want anything that wasn't hers. I was the last one to leave when we finally headed down the stairs with the last load. Just then Sam jumped out behind me with this huge butcher knife at my back. Danny took one look and said, "Gail, he's behind you with a knife." I was sure at any minute that I'd feel him plunge it straight into my back. Not daring to look around at him, I just walked calmly down the stairs step by step, not saying a word in case I triggered something that might make him snap and use the knife on me. When I hit the last step, I breathed a huge sigh of relief. It was the longest flight of stairs I had ever walked.

Once we were outside, Danny turned to me. "I bet you were pretty scared back there," he said.

"Scared," I replied, "I was terrified! I thought a heart attack was just around the corner. Did you see the size of that knife? It was practically a machete."

"I never saw a knife like that before," Marilyn remarked.

Then Lilly spoke up. "It's a knife for slaughtering animals. He found it in the garbage."

"Why is he always in the garbage?" asked Marilyn.

"He's a garbage man," Lilly replied. "That's his job."

"Oh," Marilyn said, "I thought he just liked to look in the garbage." By now we were all laughing helplessly, mostly from nervous relief.

When we arrived home, we now had two more to add to the crew. I was so glad to have Eldon back again. Right away, I warned Fred not to pick on Lilly. He was her only parent, I told him, so he needed to treat her with respect. In the end, Lilly didn't stay long, preferring to move in with a girlfriend of hers. Fred, I knew, had a hard time showing any kind of affection because he was never shown any love or compassion as a boy. Once he told me a story about how he had worked on a farm, way out in Freetown, when he was ten years old. The farm was about one hundred kilometers away, and he would stay and work on it all week, then come home on the weekends. He'd give his mother ten dollars from his twelve-dollar-a-week pay. One time he was lying on the couch after hitchhiking and walking all the way home, when his mother found him.

"What are you doing lying around here like a big lug," she exclaimed. "You'll never amount to a row of carrots or a hill of beans. Get back to Freetown. You're no good around here." Fred said after that, he didn't come home very often.

I've always believed that if you don't know love, how can you give it. Fred would ask me why I was always kissing and hugging Cory and Eldon. I answered that I wanted them to grow up and be able to show love to whomever they lived with or married, and to the children they might eventually have. If people were not so afraid to show love, I told him, the world might be a better place. Most men, I told him, seem to associate affection with being a sissy, a mindset that serves no purpose other than a destructive one. As I talked, I thought about Memere and Pepere and how they had instilled in me in my earlier years the great gift of love, so that no matter how terrible things got, I could always remember what it was like to really be loved.

After that little speech to Fred, I could see that he was trying to be more affectionate towards Eldon when he came to visit. But Fred always had to have a few drinks in him first.

After two weeks, Marilyn and her family went home, taking a reluctant Grandma with them. "Gail," she said, "I wish I could stay with you. I love this place."

"I wish I had the room for you to stay with me," I told her. When we said our goodbyes, there were tears in my eyes.

One day, while Mom and Bob were still visiting, Bob got drunk and fell over a deck chair, breaking his arm. We had to take him to the hospital three times before they found the break. I was sure they were treating him with a certain amount of disdain because he was an alcoholic. I already knew that alcoholism was a self-inflicted illness, and therefore people thought less of you and often weren't sympathetic. But it never really made sense to me, because cancer from smoking is also self-inflicted, yet people feel such pity and compassion for someone with cancer, doing anything they can to help. I have always felt genuine compassion for a person with an alcohol addiction, for they will live longer with their suffering.

When they finally left for Toronto, Bob cried like a child. He always loved coming to the Island. This would be the last time I would see him because he died two months later. He was visiting a couple he knew at their cottage up north of Toronto when he passed out drunk on the couch and started choking on his phlegm. In her drunkenness, the woman tried to give him mouth-to-mouth, suffocating him. I was deeply upset when I heard he had died. Over the years, Bob had become like a father to us kids, especially as he never had children of his own. He loved Cory and was proud of his achievements in school and sports. When he was sober, he was an intelligent man. I loved and respected him for going through everything he went through with my mother. It was such a waste of a life for him to have drowned in booze.

At first I said I wasn't going to the funeral. I wanted to remember him having fun, and besides, I didn't have the money to go. But my mother's family said Bob would want me there, and all chipped in to buy me a ticket. I really dreaded going; first Jane was gone, and now Bob.

During the summer, Bob had told us that when he died he wanted to be cremated and have his ashes taken to PEI to be scattered off a friend's fishing boat. He also told us that he didn't want any viewing, preferring people to remember him when he was alive. Unfortunately, my youngest sister Jody had other ideas, which she talked our mother into. So his ashes ended up buried in the same cemetery as Jane's. Jody's reasoning was that it gave them a place where they could visit him. Even though I knew this went against Bob's wishes, I didn't feel it was worth arguing over.

At the church, just before the funeral was about to begin, Mom suddenly came hobbling up the aisle, waving a plastic bag and yelling, "Gail! Gail! I got the bank book and his wallet." I was appalled. Everyone was glaring, and rightfully so, it was such a shock to hear what she had just bellowed out in the silent church. And the worst part was that she made it look like I had asked for the bankbook. Bob's family had flown in from Nova Scotia, and were all well-educated with masters degrees and were pillars of their communities. They had never met any of us except Mom. I couldn't imagine what they were thinking. I thought to myself, is that all she's worried about after twenty years together? Bob had just received an inheritance from his mother's estate six months earlier. I guess that was the reason for her concern. She sure wasn't concerned with the time or place. That was one disconcerting thing about Mom. You never knew when, or where, she was going to come out and say something totally inappropriate.

After the funeral I went to see Jane's grave, remembering all the times she had stomped on it, joking that it was the only property she really owned. Neither of us had realized how soon it would be put to use. Then I went to see Jane's mother and daughter. It seemed so silent and cold, with all the laughter and warmth gone. I saw everyone from our old street, then left for home. Marilyn took me to the airport, and like always, I had mixed emotions about leaving. We said our goodbyes, then a few tears later, I was on the plane.

Back on the Island, I was picked up at the airport by Fred and Cory. Once we got home, Fred wanted to get drunk as usual. He had a drinking buddy called Wasted Wally who didn't have a handle like that for nothing. Small and almost bent in half when he stood, he'd had rickets as a child that had left him with a deformed spine. His girlfriend didn't drink, so she and I would watch TV together and chat. Wally's deformity sure didn't stop him from drinking. Fred and he could sit and drink a sixty-ounce bottle of rye in one night. By the end of the evening, Fred would have to be wheeled to bed, half falling out of his wheelchair. I would finally get him in bed, thinking he was asleep, and then I would hear a thump as he fell out of bed onto the floor. He'd start calling for me, and when I went back in, would look up with a pitiful face that he liked to put on. "Can you help me, dear?" he would ask. It was such an obvious act. To make matters worse, by now his leg bag would have busted all over the floor. If Cory was home, he would help me get Fred back in bed. Otherwise, I had to do it alone, cleaning him up and putting him to bed, only to have him fall out again. Sometimes he would do this six or seven times a night just to get my attention. If I tried to ignore him, he would lie there yelling my name constantly until I was practically driven insane. Fred thrived on pity.

Most nights, after Fred was in bed and finally asleep at around eleven o'clock, I would go to my friend Melody's. She was a tall, attractive woman with an outgoing personality. We would sit together crocheting tablecloths and watching the daytime soaps which she taped. I knew that Cory was only five minutes away and going to bed, so it was fun and relaxing going there at the end of the day. She became my Jane on PEI, minus the drinking.

By March of 1993, I had a commercial sign painting business attached to the back part of my house. I had started it about a year ago, and one day I was working with some very strong paint on a bunch of signs. That evening, I suddenly thought I was having a heart attack. Unable to breathe, I jumped out of bed and ran gasping for air to the sink. Cory was watching TV and came running. "Mom! Mom! What's wrong?" he cried. It was a good three minutes before I could speak, as I stood there holding my chest and trying to breathe.

"What's wrong?" Cory asked in alarm.

"I don't know," I said, panting for air. "Maybe the fumes from the paint were too much for me. I'm not sure."

After a bit, I calmed down and started to feel okay, but decided to go see the doctor. I had noticed for the past year that I was having a hard time staying awake in the daytime. After being awake for only an hour or so, I would start to nod off at the most extraordinary moments, like right when I was eating, or while watching TV. Then I would jolt myself awake with the sound of my own snoring. If I didn't wake from the snoring, Fred would yell, "Wake up, you fat bitch!" Even when driving the car, I would have to stop periodically so I could get out and walk around to wake myself up.

After seeing a series of doctors, it turned out I had sleep apnea, a condition where your throat relaxes while sleeping to the point of cutting off your air passages. Either that, or your brain doesn't tell you to breathe. Consequently, you don't get the deep sleep you need called REM. My therapist told me I probably hadn't had deep sleep REM for about six years. I was eventually fitted with CPAP machine, a contraption that fits over your head with a nose mask that maintains a constant of flow of air while you sleep. After three nights of sleeping with the mask on, I woke up and had so much energy to burn, I could hardly believe it. It felt like someone had breathed life into me. Sleeping like this took some getting used to, but it was worth it.

Cory was now getting ready to graduate from grade twelve and the first two years of college, both of which he had completed at the same time. I was so proud of him, knowing what a struggle it had been, with all his friends quitting school at fourteen and fifteen. I could remember the talk we'd had a few years back when he had been so envious of his friends and their jobs at the factory, or on the fishing boats and in potatoes. They all had loans at the Credit Union, cosigned by their parents, and were buying old trucks and cars. I'd explained to Cory that his friends had jobs that only lasted for eight or ten weeks, then it was the unemployment line until the next season. I'd told him how the loans for the cars and trucks would still need to be paid off, and the only way they could do it was by living at home with their parents. With a loan like that, they would never be able to move out on their own and afford the rent, money for food and clothes and gas, plus the repairs on old vehicles. They would have to deal with all that responsibility without any steady employment. Their whole lives would be like that, with no opportunity to get any further in life. In the end, Cory had listened to what I had to say.

It was now three years since we'd had that conversation, and his friends were all being caught for impaired driving, losing their licenses, smashing their vehicles, and struggling with paying off their loans. Often they were paying off loans for something they no longer even had.

One day, Cory and I got talking about what had happened in the last three years to ninety percent of his friends.

"Mom," he said, "I'm so glad you talked me out of quitting school back then, when I see what's happened to most of them. My future is still ahead of me, but theirs is what it is, and it's only going to get worse for them. Thank you so much, Mom. I love you."

"Cory," I answered, "I want to thank you for being a good son and paying attention to the advice I gave you. Soon I'll stand proud and watch you graduate, something no one in our family has ever done."

Cory now had a night job working at the factory. Before he started work, I told him that if I saw him spending money on crazy things, I would charge him rent. I wanted him to put fifty dollars a week in the bank, so he could learn how to manage his money. That way, when he moved out some-day, he would know how to keep enough money to pay his rent and bills.

Now that he was working, Cory would go to school for half the day, then catch the school bus to the French school where I would meet him and drive him to the fish factory. He worked alone in the old part of the factory, cleaning and spraying the place down with highly toxic chemicals. We had no idea how toxic they were, as he wasn't told to wear a mask or anything.

Sometime after Cory started working at the fish factory, Fred began picking on him to mow the lawn. All we had was a push mower for a half-acre of land, and Fred insisted on it being mowed every three days. That had been okay when Cory didn't have to work and go to school each day, but now it was impossible.

"You're nothing but a lazy bum," Fred would say to Cory, just like his mother used to say to him. "You're never going to amount to anything." I finally went maniacal. It takes a lot to get me angry, but I couldn't believe what was coming from his mouth.

"Fred," I said, "I've heard enough! That poor kid is going to school, working most nights until three in the morning, and all you can say is that he's a bum. You must be wild in the head." By now, I was really warming to the topic, ready to vent all my pent-up frustration with Fred's negative behaviour. "I'll do the fucking lawn," I continued, "when it's windy and there are no mosquitoes outside. And if you can't wait, then I'll hitch your fucking wheelchair up to the lawn mower, and I'll turn it on and watch you go to it. You can try to degrade me and tear away at my spirit, but I won't let you do it to him too. Don't make me choose between you and Cory, because you will be out the door. He's my child and I have to protect him and guide him. I put him on this earth and he's my flesh and blood; just remember that, Fred. I won't let you treat Cory the way your mom treated you." After that, Fred shut his mouth and never spoke to Cory that way again. For once in his life, he must have been listening.

On the day of Cory's graduation, we came home in the afternoon after his rehearsal to find Fred shivering and shaking in bed. Although I could tell he hadn't been drinking, he wasn't making any sense at all. Running to the phone to call an ambulance, the first thing that came to my mind was that he was dying. On top of everything else, he had completely lost control of his bowels and was in a terrible state. When the ambulance drivers arrived,

I apologized for the mess, as he was too delirious for me to clean things up. I told Cory to stay and get ready for his graduation, as I'd be back to pick him up as soon as Fred was in the hospital.

As I followed the ambulance, I thought about how many times in my life I'd done this before; with my mother, when Cory was small, with Fred. Maybe I was meant to be some kind of caregiver in a hospital, as I always seemed to be surrounded by some sort of medical condition or illness. Perhaps "The Gail of Wind" wasn't the right pet name for me. It should have been "Florence Nightingale".

At the hospital, the doctor confirmed that Fred was in septic shock, and in another half hour he would have been dead. Once he was in intensive care, I left to pick up Cory, knowing that Fred was now in good hands and there wasn't anything more I needed to do. Back home, I threw all the bedclothes in the garbage, washed and disinfected everything, took a shower and left.

On the way to the school I looked over and realized that Cory was crying.

"What's wrong?" I asked.

"Mom, I'm graduating and Fred, or my real dad, isn't going to be here, only you and me. All the other kids have grandparents and family." I told Cory I understood how he felt, but I reminded him that Fred's daughters were going to be there to see him graduate.

"Besides," I pointed out, "you received a telegram today from my Aunt Yvette, and one from my mom, so we're really not alone. There are people thinking about you that are proud and happy for you even though they can't be here."

Later, as I watched Cory standing to receive his diploma, I wished John could have been there for him. Those were the times I felt guilty for denying him a father, but that was adult hindsight, now that I was no longer young and hurt. Not for one moment did I think I shouldn't have given Cory life. I just wish I'd thought more about the kind of life I had created for him.

CHAPTER NINE

A Thousand Tears

School was over and Cory was still working at the fish factory. He had applied at other places for welding jobs, the skill he had learned in college and was anxious to put into practice. In between driving Cory to work and visiting the hospital daily, my plate was full, plus Fred always insisted on me bringing home cooked food for him and the other men in the ward. I don't know who Fred thought I was—Martha Stewart? I still had my sign painting business to tend to as well, with a continual stream of vehicles parked in the driveway, waiting for me to do the lettering on them. Cory had a talent for art and would help me, which gave us some quality time together. I loved it when we worked together as a team.

Just about the time Fred came home from the hospital, Cory started to cough a lot and complain about night sweats. I thought it was because he had quit smoking, which he knew I really disliked. I would try to scare him by saying he'd get cancer if he kept smoking, telling him he was probably more susceptible than most because of his allergies and asthma. He would quit for a while, then start up again.

After a while, when Cory's coughing started to get really bad, we decided to go see the doctor. All the doctor did was give Cory some medication, telling him it was just a bad cold. Another few weeks went by with still no change. In fact, Cory seemed to be getting worse, sweating so much at night that he had to change the sheets. Back we went to the doctor again who decided it must be pneumonia and gave Cory a different medicine, but nothing seemed to make any difference. The cough just kept on getting worse until it was so constant it was unbearable for everyone. Then one afternoon, I heard Cory yelling for me.

"What's wrong?" I asked, coming into his bedroom.

"Look at my chest," he said. "It has a lump on it." I felt his chest area, looking for a small lump, but couldn't find anything. Then he stood sideways in the mirror and showed me. Oh my God, the whole right side of his chest was deformed by a lump the size of a fist. Trying not to look alarmed, I said, "We'd better go and see the doctor again." I'd noticed his chest the other night when he was lying on the couch, but had thought it was just the way he was lying down.

At the doctor's office, Cory showed him the lump while I waited outside.

"Are you sure you weren't born like this?" he asked. Cory assured him he wasn't. If he had been, we would have noticed long before this. On our way to have an x-ray done, my mind was racing, wondering what was wrong with Cory. I kept thinking it was pneumonia.

A few days later the doctor called and asked Cory to come in right away. Standing in his room we both started to hug and cry, knowing deep down in our hearts that it wasn't good news.

"I'm coming with you," I told him. "Did he ask you to bring anyone?"

"No," Cory answered, "he didn't."

"Well then, don't worry," I said. "If it was bad he would have said bring someone."

"Yeah, that's what I was thinking. If it was bad, he wouldn't want me to go in alone, would he?"

Trying to reassure each other, we drove to the doctor's with Lilly, who had been visiting at the time of the call. At first, the doctor just looked at Cory's hands without saying anything, and then pressed on his stomach. Going back into his office from the examining room, he immediately hit us with the nightmare.

"Cory," he said, "you have Non-Hodgkin's Lymphoma." Well, that still didn't tell me anything, because I didn't know what it meant. When I asked him, he said it was what NHL player Mario Lemieux had. At first I thought it must be a hockey disease that only hockey players got. It wasn't until the doctor added that Cory would have to have a biopsy that my brain registered he was talking about cancer. For a moment, my stomach felt like it had just been turned inside out. I was holding Cory, and Cory was holding me until I wasn't sure who was holding who up. Then the doctor told us to make an appointment with the secretary, and walked out without another word.

Back in the waiting room, Lilly took one look at us and helped us into a private room.

"What is it?" she asked. "What does Cory have?"

"Cancer," I told her, hardly believing I was saying the words. I could see the blood draining from her face, she was so white. Finally, we pulled ourselves together enough to leave, with Cory and me still holding each other for dear life. I just kept thinking, please someone tell me I'm dreaming. I knew I had to give Cory some comfort and hope, but I didn't know how I was going to convince him when I couldn't convince myself.

Back at home, we told Fred and listened as he tried to tell us it must be a mistake. Here was Cory, just seventeen years old, diagnosed with cancer. I had always thought of cancer as something which older people got, not teenagers. Pulling myself together, I told Cory we would take this day by day and deal with each issue as it came. Then I went out and got some movies to watch to take our minds off things. While Fred got drunk as usual and went to bed, Cory and I huddled on the couch and watched *Weekend at Bernie's*, alternating between laughing and crying. The laughter was from the movies and the tears from the fear of the unknown.

When we finally went to bed, I found I couldn't sleep. I kept thinking about the doctor and how he'd asked a seventeen-year-old to come to his office to hear something like that, without telling him to bring someone with him. I just couldn't believe it. Thinking about everything, I kept tossing and turning until Fred started flying out of the waterbed and landing on the floor. At first I thought he was doing it on purpose until I realized it was my restlessness that was causing the waterbed to move. The next thing I knew, Fred was awake and yelling for me to get him beer, then his leg bag burst and I had to clean everything up. By now I didn't have to worry about how I was going to get to sleep, because the night was just about over.

I started thinking about family and friends and the phone calls I needed to make, plus it was five days before Cory's eighteenth birthday and I'd planned a huge party for him. My first thought was that I'd have to cancel it. Getting out of bed, I found Fred seated at the table, already pretty loaded and talking a lot of stupid nonsense. Not in any mood to listen, I wheeled him back to bed, and then started making phone calls before Cory woke up. I called my sister Marilyn first, then Jody. The first thing she said was, "Gail, I think John should know about Cory having cancer. He's his real father, so he has a right to know." I told her I didn't know a thing about John now, only that he'd gotten married two years after Cory was born and had another child. John hadn't seen Cory since he was seven months old and I didn't want to interfere with his life. I didn't even know where he lived now.

"I can find out for you," she said. "I know where his mother and father live, so I can start there." Somehow, I didn't feel ready for this. I had loved John with all my heart, but the only way I could keep from being hurt was to put him out of my mind as much as possible. It was bad enough when Cory looked at me certain ways and I saw the strong resemblance to John.

"I think I should discuss this with Cory first," I insisted. "Let's just leave things alone for now until we find out more. I have enough to deal with already."

After I hung up, I thought to myself that John's family had probably moved by now and she wouldn't be able to find them anyway. Besides, Jody had finally agreed to wait until Cory and I had talked.

Once the phone calls were over and I had time to think straight, I wondered how I was going to manage with an alcoholic in a wheelchair, a child with cancer, no family nearby, and only one friend. My one close friend on the Island was Melody. As soon as she came over, I told her about Cory's illness. After assuring me that she would be there to help as much as I needed, she suddenly asked about Cory's surprise birthday party.

"Isn't it this Saturday?" she asked.

"Yeah, but I guess I'm going to cancel it."

"Why don't you have it anyway," Melody suggested. "It might help take his mind off things, and yours too." I wasn't so sure, but after thinking about it for a while, I could see that she was right. We couldn't just stop living, I thought. That would be the worst thing we could do.

On Saturday, Fred's sisters came over and helped clean up my sign painting shop so the party could be held in my studio at the back of the house.

While Cory was in the shower, thinking he was going out for the evening with his friend Drake, all his friends came in through the back door. Then Drake arrived and asked Cory if they could go out back for a moment and lift something for me before they left. The minute Cory walked through the door and turned the light on, everyone yelled, "Surprise!" The look on his face was amazing.

All evening I could see from the living room window what a great time they were having. If laughter was the best medicine, I thought, Cory was getting a good dose of it. A couple of times I went in to take a few pictures, and could have cried later when I discovered none of them had turned out. What if this was his last birthday, and I didn't have any pictures to remember him by? Later the next morning, Cory told me it was the best time he'd had with his friends in years, just like the old days when they were younger and they all hung out together.

That Sunday, I had to take Cory to the hospital for his biopsy, followed by surgery on Monday afternoon. Who would have ever conceived that, on his eighteenth birthday, something like this could be happening? After checking him in, something I was certainly experienced at by this time, I would have stayed the night if I hadn't had Fred to worry about, especially the fact that he insisted on smoking in bed. Sometimes it seemed worse than having a two-year-old in the house.

The next morning, after a sleepless night, I went straight back to the hospital where I discovered Cory had already been operated on. Although I didn't say anything, I was really upset because I'd been told the operation was scheduled for the afternoon, and had wanted to be there so he wouldn't feel so alone. Cory finally awoke around six in the evening. On the way to the hospital, I'd stopped at the post office to pick up a gift for Cory's birthday from my sister Jody. Once Cory was awake enough to sit up, I gave it to him. She'd sent a gold chain with "Number 1 Nephew" on it, which Cory loved. Unfortunately, he couldn't come home that night like he was supposed to, because the doctor said he was still too sedated, so I left at around eleven that night. As I was leaving, Cory told me to please drive carefully. He'd never said that before to me, I realized, as I kissed and hugged him goodbye.

Once outside, I noticed how lit up the sky was, with stars everywhere. The night was freezing cold. Driving home, all I could think about was

Cory. Then suddenly, just as I was passing the school near our home, I hit a patch of black ice and started to spin out of control. Panicking, I tried to hit the brake, stepped on the gas pedal by mistake, and sent the car heading straight for a light pole. I was screaming as the car hit the ditch two feet from the pole, spun around fast, and bounced back out into the road again. The speedometer, I noticed, was at one hundred and five kilometers when I just missed the pole. I was screaming to God to please, please do not take me now. Cory needed me.

When the car finally came to a stop, I was in the middle of the road, facing the right way to drive home, and without a scratch or dent. If someone had driven by they would have thought I had just stalled there in the middle of the road. It didn't look like a thing had happened except for the skid marks. For a few minutes I sat there, unable to believe what had just happened. I'd never known what black ice meant. Now I knew.

Back home, I found Fred still up, and actually sober. Taking one look at my pale face, he asked what was wrong with me, so I told him what had happened. I shouldn't have bothered, because all he did was give me shit for stamping on the gas instead of the brake. I might have known he would say something stupid. I told him that wasn't exactly what I needed to hear right after almost getting myself killed.

The next day I went to pick up Cory. The doctor said it would be a few days before we knew the results of the biopsy, but in the meantime we needed to go and get familiar with the oncology department, and with the doctor who would be doing the treatment there. On the way home, I told Cory about my experience with the black ice.

"You know what, Mom?" Cory said, "I don't know why, but last night I was worried about you driving home." After a minute, he went on. "Mom, you know how when you found out you had sleep apnea; you said that if you didn't have your health, then you didn't have anything? You said look at Fred, how even though he's getting a big pension, he'd rather have the use of his legs and be able to work for his money, and that money and possessions don't mean a thing if you're not healthy. I didn't really understand what you meant until now."

"I'm sorry you had to find out the hard way," I told him. It was a tragic way for such a young person to have learned one of life's biggest lessons.

A week later, Melody came with us to the hospital. Sharon, the main oncology nurse, was a tall, thin, very attractive lady with a feel for her job. The other nurse was Melissa. She had dark hair, was thin and also attractive. Both nurses were very compassionate in how they handled their patients, making you feel that there was hope, and keeping your spirits lifted. I knew it was their job, but I thought they took it one step further so you didn't feel like just another patient with a medical card. It was all I could do to hold back the tears when Sharon explained the procedure. At one point I even left the room so Cory wouldn't see me so torn apart. It was an information overload, and I found it hard to digest. By the time we left, however, they had made me feel some comfort by believing that there was hope. Melody helped us to try and understand things a little clearer as well. By the time I went to bed that night, loaded down with information from all the different pamphlets, I knew I was getting some on-the-job training in understanding the medical treatment for cancer. It wasn't anything I'd ever wanted first-hand knowledge of, but if there was ever a reason to learn, this was it. I had to educate myself so I would have the courage and strength to pass on to Cory, to give him the hope, love and the will to carry on. Sometimes the choices in life are made by us, but other times the choices are made for us, whether we want them or not. This was one of those times.

CHAPTER TEN

The Kindness of Strangers

It was getting close to Christmas time, and my sister Jody, her husband Gary, their two girls Sasha and Lorraine, and their dog were all coming to spend the holiday with us. I was pleased because having them there would make it more bearable for Cory and me, instead of being alone with Fred. When they arrived, everyone was in high spirits. I couldn't get over the change in the girls since I'd last seen them five years ago. Sasha was now twelve years old, a tall, blond-haired, brown-eyed beauty, while Lorraine was ten, cute and looked a lot like her handsome dad. Fred was thrilled to have Gary there, for they had worked together in Toronto, cutting down trees for the city. That's how Jody and Gary had first met, and they were still crazy about each other. I was happy for Jody because he was a good man. He drank, but he never got out of control. Jody, who was tiny and weighed about ninety-five pounds, would run around cleaning like mad. During their visit, it always seemed as though we were laughing and having a great time, just what we needed to get through Christmas.

Shortly before Cory's first chemotherapy session, on December 24, we got a call from my mother. She was visiting our grandmother in New Brunswick and the family had decided that Mom was a burden and would be better off staying with us. They wanted to get rid of her and I was the next best thing, I guess. Under the circumstances, I couldn't believe that they would even consider sending her to me, but before I knew it, the ticket was bought and she was on her way. If I thought Fred was a two-year-old at times, Mom wasn't any better. It wasn't that I didn't love her; it's just that right now wasn't the time for her company. In a way, I pitied Mom because her family never wanted her around, she was such an embarrassment to them.

Now I had serious visitation overload, especially after I discovered that Mom and Jody weren't on speaking terms, and whatever Jody did, her kids followed. Suddenly, we had a house full of people who were mad at each other. Even the dogs were fighting over the food and territory. Princess was a typical big country dog and very territorial, while Jody's was a little citified lap dog, right down to its red boots, gem-encrusted collar, and variety of sweaters. One time, Jody decided the dog needed to go out for a walk. It was storming outside, and she had the dog all dressed up. If I had not known any better, I would have thought she was about to enter it in a dog show. Between the dog and Jody's weight combined, a hundred pounds would have been stretching it. When she got to the end of the ramp outside, a gust of wind and drifting snow picked her and the dog up and spun them around, just like Dorothy and Toto in the *Wizard of Oz*. The next thing we knew, we couldn't see her any longer. Gary had to go outside and find her and the dog before they got totally lost in the storm. By the time Jody got inside again, she was as mad at the weather outside as she was at Mom, and when Jody gets mad, she stomps her feet while she walks until that ninety-five-pound frame turns into a three-hundred-and-ninety-five-pound elephant. The whole house shook.

Meanwhile, as Fred only ever managed to like my mother for the first hour of her visits, there was soon nothing but name-calling and arguing between them. On top of that, because Mom liked to chew ice cubes, she had brought an ice cube crusher with her, and the racket was soon driving us all nuts. After a few days of this, Fred said he would see what was wrong with it, why it made so much noise. Unfortunately, Fred was no more mechanically inclined than a ballerina. Having taken it apart, he threw it in a bag and headed for the front door. When Mom saw that, she jumped up off the couch, yelling and screaming, "Where the hell are you going?" Fred just sat there laughing like a fool, while I was ready to kill them both. As no one knew how to put it back together, Mom now started going outside to get her ice. Leaving the door wide open in the middle of winter, she would bend over with no coat on, half in and half out the door, and hammer at the big bags of ice she started buying, trying to break off cubes in minus thirty-five degree temperatures. She also took to drinking all Cory's ginger ale, and the more I bought, the more she drank. By now, what with all the ginger ale and beer I was having to buy, we were wearing a path from our house to the store.

If that wasn't enough, Mom started going into Cory's room to make phone calls. Calling all her friends and family long distance, she would tell people down to the last detail what he was going through, making up what she didn't actually know. Poor Cory would be right beside her in his bed trying to sleep. Jody was mad because Mom liked to stay up most of the night chewing ice and driving them all crazy, while they were trying to sleep in the living room. After keeping everyone awake at night, she would then sleep all day. Mind you, she had a way of sleeping during the day with one eye open so she didn't miss a thing.

One time, Mom got in a real huff and took off to my studio, wrapping herself in blankets like an Indian. It was so cold in there you could see your breath. After a while, I went in to see what she was up to and found her huddled on a bed, still wolfing down ice and wondering why she was so cold. When I asked her what was wrong, she said everyone was mad at her and Fred broke her ice machine. Assuring her I'd give her the money to buy a new one when she went home, I sent her off to my bed with Fred so everyone could finally get some sleep. Fred was so drunk he didn't even notice. Not until the next morning, that is. Then he was raging mad, yelling and swearing that the fucking chipmunk wasn't going to sleep with him again. That did it; I sat everyone down and asked why they'd come if all they were going to do was drive me crazy.

"You better start talking," I told them, "because I've had just about enough. You can all never speak to each other again when you go back to Toronto, but right now, please stop it. Cory is sick and I don't need all this stomping around and mad faces. It's Christmas time, so grow up and get along and get your emotions under control."

I guess my little outburst was worth it, because after that they seemed to see what distress they were all causing and made an effort to get along together as much as possible. Nothing could ever truly be normal when my family got together, but things were a lot better than before.

On December 24, Jody and I drove Cory to Charlottetown for his first chemotherapy. Poor Cory vomited all the way there, and was totally drained when we finally arrived after the hour and a half drive. It broke my heart to watch as the different foreign substances entered his body through the needles in his arm, while I wondered if it would all be for nothing. He was sick the whole way home as well. Princess could sense Cory's pain, staying beside him every move he made, and waiting outside the bathroom door for him.

On Christmas Day, Jody and I cooked a big dinner. Mom never helped, preferring to lie around and expect service with a smile. At the dinner table she suddenly decided to say something while we were giving thanks.

"Here's to lots of health and happiness," she said. "I hope Cory doesn't die and is with us next year." I can't say it was exactly what I wanted to hear, and I saw Cory's face drop, along with everyone else's. After dinner, I spoke to him.

"Don't mind your grandmother," I told him. "She means well, she just comes across wrong sometimes."

"I know," Cory said. "We were all probably thinking the same thing anyway." Cory knew she was a sick woman, and he felt sorry for her. She was the only grandmother he knew, so he had no other to compare her to.

The next week Cory had another appointment. When they x-rayed his chest first before the chemo, the x-rays came back with no sign of cancer. The lump was gone. The doctor was so astonished, he called down to the lab to make sure there was no mistake, but they were Cory's x-rays. I cried when I heard the news. It didn't mean we were out of the woods, far from it, but it gave us a glimmer of hope and something to smile about.

By the New Year, Jody and her family were leaving for home. I was sorry things had been so chaotic, because it was nice of them to have come. Mom was also ready to leave, and although I hated to feel this way, I was relieved she was going. After everyone had left, I went to bed that night and couldn't believe all the commotion that had taken place. As much as I loved my family, seeing them one on one was always best and created the least amount of emotional upheaval.

By now, Cory had been so continually sick from the chemo that he was down to skin and bones. On the next visit to the doctor, somehow the conversation came around to medical coverage. When the doctor found out we had insurance, he told us about a drug to help control the nausea. He said he hadn't told us about it before because the pills cost twenty-five dollars apiece, and Cory would need four a day. I got him on them right away and it was like a miracle. The vomiting stopped and Cory began to gain back all his weight until he looked healthy and happy. That poor child, to think that a doctor would take it upon himself to withhold medication because of the money involved. He also told us about a needle Cory could take to bring up his white blood cell count so his chemo could be on time and not delayed. He'd also be less susceptible to infection. Again, he hadn't told us about the needles because of the high cost. I'd like to know who makes them judge and jury when it comes to finances, or the treatment of people. It made me wonder how people on welfare get treated. Do they even have a fighting chance? How does a doctor know who can and can't afford medication? I realize that it can be hard to find the money but when it comes to a life, there are always things like family, friends, a bank loan, or a second mortgage on a house. Here on the Island, people always put on a benefit dance and auction for times of hardship like this. I have always believed that where there's a will, there's a way. Here I was with an eighteen-year-old, my one and only child, with his whole life ahead of him, and nothing was going to stop me from trying to keep him alive.

At the end of January, we were told that Cory would need radiation on his head, so for three weeks we would have to find a place to stay in Charlottetown. The drive would be impossible, because we had to be there at eight in the morning for his treatments. As the cheapest hotel I could find was forty dollars a day, I didn't know what to do or which way to turn. Finally, I found out about the hospital lodge which was only twenty-five dollars a night and had cooking facilities. We could manage that, but only barely, mainly by putting some bills on hold. Cory and I would be in Charlottetown for three weeks and only able to go home on weekends. I wasn't sure how Fred was going to manage, but there was no alternative. He would have to look after himself. I just hoped he wouldn't drink and burn the house down smoking in bed.

When Cory and I arrived at the hospital lodge, we found it was very nice, with a bedroom, a downstairs living room, kitchen, laundry facilities, and a house-mother who was a sweetheart. The next morning, Cory was scheduled for his first radiation treatment. Having no idea what to expect, I was told to wait in the hall where I could watch on a TV monitor. It looked like he was just lying down in a big round tube. What alarmed me wasn't so much what I could see, but what I couldn't see. With no one allowed in the room, and the radiologist completely covered, I wondered how strong the radiation was that was penetrating Cory's body. Standing there watching, the tears started pouring down my face. No matter how much I tried to hold back, sometimes it just consumed me and I lost control. Just then, a pretty, dark-haired lady came by and noticed me crying. Stopping to talk, she asked what was wrong, so between sobs, I explained the situation with Cory. When she asked where we were staying, I told her at the lodge.

The next day there was a knock at the door of the lodge and there was the same lady asking to see me. Handing me an envelope, she said she hoped it would help. Then before I could say anything, she disappeared again. Inside the envelope was a card from the Ladies' Auxiliary, wishing us all the best, plus a hundred-dollar bill. I was totally overcome at the kindness of these ladies I had never even met. I hadn't mentioned a word about the hard time we were having financially, as it's not something I would ever discuss with a total stranger, yet they had wisely known how difficult things must be for us. Now, every time I see the Ladies' Auxiliary raising money, I gladly donate to their cause, always remembering the help this one woman gave me that cold, lonely morning in the hospital corridor.

Finally the treatments were over and it was time to go home. The day we left, a storm started about halfway home and soon we were driving in a complete whiteout. I was frightened to death driving in such terrible weather, with Cory sick beside me. There were times when I was just guessing if I was still on the road or not, using the telephone poles as guides when I could glimpse them through the blowing snow and drifts. Slowly we inched our way home, while the winds howled, tossing our little car around in the blinding snow. There was no point in stopping, as I couldn't see a house in sight and had no idea where anything was. I never said anything to Cory, but I really thought this was how we were going to die, on that dark and stormy night together.

After what seemed like hours and hours, we finally made it home. Fred had taken good care of himself and greeted us in a genuinely caring way.

But I might have known he couldn't keep up the civilized charade for long, and a few hours later he was back to his miserable self.

Plans were soon underway by the community for a benefit drive to help Cory. People were unbelievably generous. A dance was planned, with an auction, food sale, raffle tickets, and donations from local businesses. When the night of the dance arrived, Cory wasn't old enough to get into the Legion where it was being held, so I asked the manager if an exception could be made. All of Cory's friends were going to be there, plus most of the community. He said it was fine, as long as Cory didn't have any alcohol in front of him at the table.

When we arrived at the table where Cory's friends were, they all stood up and everyone had a ribbon tied to the loop of their jeans. It was ribbon from Cory's birthday party that they had all kept as a souvenir. Neither Cory nor I had any idea they'd done that until we saw them wearing it at the dance. It was a very moving gesture from such a young group of people.

That night the community raised forty-five hundred dollars. I was amazed at the time, effort, and tenderness shown by the people of the community. I couldn't speak, as I was so astounded by it all. So Cory did the honours and thanked everyone. That night, as I lay in bed, I thought about how the rest of Canada refers to the east coast as the "have not" provinces. What they lack in material wealth, I now knew, they more than make up for in generosity and kindness and, to me, that is a far more valuable asset.

Someone had mentioned to me that Cory might be able to get a wish granted from the Children's Wish Fund, so I decided to phone and find out what the requirements were. I didn't tell Cory about it in case he was too old, or didn't meet all the requirements, but I was told the child had to be between the ages of three and eighteen, with a life-threatening illness and a doctor's evaluation. After I got the ball rolling, I asked Cory what he wanted for a wish. At first, he couldn't make up his mind, one minute thinking he'd like to see the mountains, then wanting a trip to Jamaica. We only had until his nineteenth birthday on December 6, so there wasn't much time, as the trip would have to be completed by then. Cory finally decided on a one-week trip to Jamaica, beginning November 1, 1994. As there was a stop in Toronto, we could make the whole trip longer; spending one week in Toronto, a week in Jamaica, and a final week back in Toronto again, visiting family. Since Cory had no brother or sister to take, and Fred wasn't coming to Jamaica, Cory asked if his cousin Brandon could come, and I asked my sister Marilyn to come with me. Normally, only people living in the same household can go, but our circumstances were unusual, so they bent the rules a bit.

A week or so after the benefit dance; CBC TV came and did an interview with us about the benefit, the Wish Fund, and the story of Cory's battle with cancer. I was very impressed with the interview when I saw it on TV, the only exception being Fred's little debut which was rather embarrassing. Cory had handled himself really well in front of the camera, and I hadn't found myself nearly as nervous as I thought I would be.

The whole benefit couldn't have come at a better time, for I was now able to pay our taxes and settle all the bills. Although we had medical coverage, it didn't cover everything. Fred had two thousand dollars worth of medical needs a month, and Cory's medications were four hundred a day. By Easter time, despite the medical coverage and benefit money, we were once more falling behind on the bills and I was at my wit's end wondering what to do. That's when I decided to start bootlegging, as I really had no other choice. It went against everything I believed in, but getting a regular job was out of the question. I simply couldn't work and still manage Cory and Fred. First I fixed up the back studio with a fridge, bar counter, chairs, couch, and a table. We already had a separate washroom, so after adding some music, I was open for business. Fortunately I had an idea what it was I was getting myself into, having been surrounded by alcoholics all my life. The word wasn't out one night before I had them pounding down the door first thing the next morning. I figured, what the hell—Fred always had people over to drink anyway. Now at least I would get well paid for it. I couldn't believe the people who came, even the other local bootleggers who would close shop on Saturday night to come and pay to drink at my place. It was a happening spot. With its own separate entrance out back, it didn't disturb a thing in the front of our house. If anyone got too drunk, I drove them home, or they passed out. When I wasn't there, Fred took charge, drinking with his buddies, but always keeping himself in control. He loved being the bartender, and always waited until I got home before getting drunk. I told myself that it wasn't much different than opening a bar, except it wasn't licensed, and it stayed open all night. At least I made sure no one left drinking and driving, which is more than a licensed bar does. They don't care how you get home as long as they have your money. There were never any fights at my place either, just a friendly atmosphere where the local guys and gals could come. Eventually, it did get nerve-wracking, but at least the bills were finally getting paid.

By now, Cory was really starting to feel and look good. My mom decided to give him some of the inheritance from Bob's mother's estate so he could buy a car. He already had his eye on a 1974 Dodge Duster in car show condition, and Cory couldn't believe it when she gave him the money. After he bought it, he loved that car so much that when he went to clean it he'd take his shoes off. I would laugh at him, saying I wished he'd clean his room like that. With the car, he now had the freedom to come and go as he pleased. I was so happy for him, for he seemed so healthy and happy again.

One day that spring, Jody phoned and asked if she could contact John. I told her I didn't see the point, as Cory was now feeling good. Well, she went ahead and did it anyway, finding John's brother Charlie and his wife. She learned that John was now divorced and living at home with his parents in the same house they had always lived in. He had two children from his marriage, a daughter and a son, who lived with their mother. Charlie was really upset when he heard the news about Cory, because when Cory was small, Charlie had come over weekly, spending time visiting and forming a real bond with Cory. That had all happened back before Fred came into the picture and I moved away. Having found out that John worked as a bartender at his brother's bar on Dundas Street, Jody and my brother Shane decided to go find him there. The minute he saw them, he knew them right away. When they talked about Cory, John said he was saddened by the news, but didn't know what he could or should do after all these years. I was completely unaware of all this until Jody called to tell me what she'd done. Of course, she had to tell me what he looked like now, insisting he hadn't changed except for a small bald spot. There was no point in getting mad at her, as she had done it now, and there was no way to change it.

Now she had me thinking about John. Going into my room, I took out the few pictures I had of him. Without really looking at them, I still had a clear memory in my mind and heart of what he looked like. Reminiscing about our past, I wished things could have been different for the three of us.

When Cory came home that night after Fred went to bed, I told him about Jody and Shane going to see his father. The look on his face when

I told him was sad, and then he started to ask questions. He told me he'd been thinking about his dad for a while now, and wishing he could meet him, but he hadn't said anything because we lived so far away.

"Mom," he said suddenly, "do you think that as part of my wish, I could meet my father?"

"I don't see why not," I said. "We're going to be in Toronto anyway."

It was now Father's Day coming up and Cory wanted to phone John, so I gave him the number and told him to go ahead if he wanted to. Using the phone in my bedroom, he dialed the number and a woman answered. It was John's mother. The minute she heard it was Cory, she began screaming over the phone in her heavy Portuguese accent.

"You my grandson!" she exclaimed excitedly. "Me love you! I tell John, he comes home from work. Thank you, my grandson. Me love you too much. I pray for you." She went on and on, with Cory beaming with happiness.

"Wow, Mom," he said as he hung up, "she said she loves me."

"She's your grandmother," I said. "She knows you're her blood, and it obviously means a lot to her. If she said she loves you, I'm sure she means it."

I could see that Cory now wanted to make a connection with his father. He sent a letter, telling him about our visit to Toronto in November, and including some pictures and a newspaper article about our trip to L.A. to meet the Gretzkys. Little did I know at the time what a turning point this would prove to be in my life.

A few months passed, and John still hadn't made any contact with Cory. The summer had rolled by, with Cory now finished with his chemotherapy. A bunch of his friends came over one evening and started joking and carrying on. Some of the guys had blond curly hair, and some long straight hair. There was even one with a big round face, freckles, and red hair. Going into the back room later to check on them, I discovered a scene that looked right out of *Star Wars*. There wasn't a head with hair on it anywhere. All seven of them had shaved their heads bald. As I looked around the room for a familiar face, I had a hard time recognizing who was who. What happened here, I asked. The reply was that his friends didn't want Cory to feel bad about losing his hair again, so they had all shaved their heads too. You guys are the best, I told them. One of a kind.

Cory was still on medication, but he was now in remission. The last day of his chemotherapy, he bought some fireworks and let them off in downtown Summerside, jumping up and down and yelling out, "Chemo is over! Chemo is over!" All his friends were there celebrating with him. By the time the police arrived to find out who was setting off fireworks, they had run inside the arcade where they hung around and said they didn't know a thing about it. Even the owner denied seeing anything. I never saw a kid so happy. It had been a long year of both elevated and dejected emotions, but somehow we had pulled through day by day.

Now it was time to get ready for our trip. We were still surviving on the bootlegging business, which had become a real burden, because Fred was drunk morning, noon and night. I guess he would have been drunk anyway, but it just seemed to be getting worse. Then he fell out of his wheelchair and broke his leg. I couldn't believe it after all the times he'd fallen, or thrown himself out of his wheelchair or bed. Just as we were getting ready to leave on our trip, he broke his leg and had to wear a cast that went clear up to the groin area. Leaving him alone for three weeks was out of the question. As his family wouldn't help care for him, he would have to come to Toronto with us and stay with Jane's husband George. That way, I would only be away from him for one week, as we would be staying with George during our two weeks in Toronto.

One evening, two weeks before the trip, a carload of Cory's friends showed up, saying they had brought him something they thought he'd need on the trip. It was a brand new camcorder, which they'd chipped in and bought together. Handing it to him, they said they didn't want us to ever forget our trip. I had tears in my eyes thinking what a great bunch of friends Cory had.

Sitting down with Cory one day, I talked to him about meeting his father for the first time. We still hadn't heard from John, perhaps because he didn't know what to say, or was just waiting to meet face to face. Talking to Cory now, I wanted to prepare him for what a difficult thing this could be for everyone.

"Cory," I said, "I want you to know that sometimes when a parent and child meet for the first time, it doesn't always work out. I haven't seen your father since we were kids, so I don't know what he's like. I do remember how kind he was to Shane whenever he came over, but I don't want you to get your hopes up in case it doesn't work out."

"All right, Mom," Cory said. "I'm glad you told me. I understand."

I couldn't believe that John was going to meet his son again after all these years. I couldn't hope for a father and son relationship, that was too late, but I hoped they would become friends. It was too bad that it had taken a tragic illness to bring them together. If things did work out, how much time would they have to spend together, I wondered. Although Cory was in remission, that didn't guarantee he was cured. Only time would tell.

The night before we were going to leave, Fred went on one of his self-pitying trips, saying he didn't want to come with us. I told him he was coming with us because there was no one to take care of him at home, and he wasn't responsible enough to stay alone. He'd probably burn the place down. Then I told him the Children's Wish Foundation had already paid for the fare, the money had all been raised from donations, and it had taken a lot of time and effort. So if he thought he was going to waste a ticket, or ruin Cory's wish, I had news for him. That was the last I heard out of him.

Trying to sleep that night, I found myself worrying about everything. Had I forgotten anything? Would John be welcoming to Cory? Would he make him feel loved? I knew that Cory would be loving towards John, because he was a loving soul, but maybe John would hate and resent me after all these years. I couldn't blame him if he did, for I took something from him that he didn't want to give. On the other hand, he knew how much I had wanted his child, and hadn't protected himself from that happening. I guess he was young and his hormones were what ruled him, not his head. With me, it had been my heart that ruled me. What was I going to say to him? Would I get weak in the knees? After all, I knew that I was still deeply in love with him. As I lay in bed, my mind ran a marathon over a hundred different scenarios. Some consisted of great endings, and some were sad and heartbreaking. Finally I thought, why am I doing this to myself? Whatever happens happens, and this is for Cory, not me. As much as I loved John, I would have to keep my emotions in check and under control. All the time, however, I was thinking, "Will I be able to do this?" Finally, I decided the answer was *yes*. After the past year of such emotional upheaval, this should be a walk in the park, or perhaps a walk in the dark. Whatever happened, I believed one thing for sure, that in any grave adversity, the magnanimity in humankind always prevails in the end.

CHAPTER ELEVEN
A Wish To Remember

At last it was morning, and we were on our way to the airport. As usual, Fred was in a pissed-off mood, trying to ruin Cory's and my fun, but I wouldn't let it happen. This could be Cory's last wish, and I wanted to make sure it was a memorable one for him. At the airport, we were met by the head of the PEI Children's Wish Foundation, a nice man named Lee who gave us all the necessary documentation for our trip, plus six hundred dollars extra spending money. As we stood talking together, I realized I could never have imagined what an impact the Foundation would have on our lives.

Suddenly it was time to board, and what a job it was getting Fred on the plane with a cast on and grumpy as hell. In the meantime, Cory was all excited and I was nervous at the thought of meeting John. Jody had visited John's mother and father and discovered that he and his brother Luke were going to be at the airport to meet us.

When we arrived at Toronto, there was Marilyn, but I didn't see any sign of John. All I could think was that this was downfall number three. First had been the Father's Day phone call, which John hadn't returned, then the letter Cory sent that never received a reply, and now no John at the airport.

"Where's my dad?" Cory asked.

"I don't know," I said. "Maybe he's working or something and couldn't make it."

We hopped into Marilyn's car and drove to George's place, where he now lived with Jane's daughter. We were all so glad to see each other — George, Jane's mom, and the daughter, Jenny. Everyone was happy to have some life in the house once again. Finally, after about an hour, I said we'd better get ready and go see Cory's dad. Having left the phone number at home, I decided we might as well just take a cab to the house and arrive unannounced. I couldn't imagine how he was feeling, maybe fear or maybe anger at the thought of meeting us after all these years. It felt like a lifetime ago since we had been teenagers together. Does time heal all wounds, or create new ones, I wondered.

Driving there in the cab, I could feel my stomach tying itself into knots. What kind of a welcome were we going to get? Were all the failed attempts to contact John his way of telling us something, that he wanted nothing to do with us and our problems? Suddenly we were there, on the street where John lived. As we made our way down the road, getting closer and closer to his house, I felt my heart in my throat.

"How do you feel right now?" I asked, turning to Cory.

"A little nervous," he admitted.

Then we were there, and I was paying the driver and feeling suddenly numb. Looking up at the house, I saw someone peering out the window from upstairs.

"You get out first," I told Cory.

"No, Mom, you know him."

"But Cory, he's your father." By now, the cab driver was looking at us like we were mad.

"Are you getting out here, or what?" he asked.

Recognizing Cory's desperate appeal, I finally got out and went up to the front door, followed by Cory. Taking a deep breath, I rang the doorbell. And then there was John and his mom, and I was looking into his eyes and feeling all the love I had ever felt for him come surging back like a tidal wave. John put his arms around me and said, "Hi, Gail," and gave me a kiss on the cheek. The energy from his body made me tremble as I drank in the fragrance of him.

"Come in, come in," his mom was saying.

"Hi, John," I said. "This is Cory." But his mother already had Cory in her arms, hugging and kissing him. And then John was hugging him too and we were following them down to the basement apartment where we met John's dad. I could see that John got his looks from a combination of both his parents. Sitting down at the table, we waited while his mother put food out—Portuguese soup and wine and bread. As we sat and ate, they made us feel welcome, and I could see how well Cory fit in, like he'd always been there. It was where he belonged, not living the hell-on-wheels life we led with Fred. He seemed so happy and comfortable.

Every now and then, John would glance over at me. Our eyes would lock and my heart would liquefy. I could already feel that John and I were lost in each other souls, as if not another person was in the room. I felt so drawn to him, it was almost an hypnotic state. Finally, I felt the others' eyes on us and snapped out of it. We spoke about Cory's cancer and our trip, then John filled us in on his life, working for his brother Luke and managing the bar.

"Gail," John said, "do you mind if I take Cory shopping tomorrow?" I told him that would be fine once we'd rented a car. John's mother was so excited, she just kept touching Cory and looking at him. Our visit lasted about four hours, then we were all kissing and hugging goodbye. Each time John put his arms around me, I got weak just from the touch of him. Watching him hug our son gave me so much satisfaction. All those years I'd always thought of Cory as just part of me and my family, but suddenly I realized he was part of John's family as well.

Once we were in the cab, I asked Cory how he felt about them.

"I really liked them, Mom," he told me. "They made me feel part of them. And you know what?" he added, "For some strange reason, my grandmother's face looks familiar. I mean, I feel like I've seen her before."

"I got that same impression too," I said. "Like I have met her some-where already."

"She's a really nice lady."

"What do you think of your dad?" I asked.

"I like him. He's a really decent guy. I'm glad we met at his house for the first time, instead of the airport. Like my dad said, the airport would have been too impersonal, so it's great he waited for us to show up at his house. I hadn't thought of it that way, but it made sense."

We smiled together, sharing our euphoria that it had all gone so well.

That night, we sat up for hours talking with George and Jane's mom. George told me he had met another woman, and then showed me a picture of her. I couldn't believe my eyes, for she looked just like Jane's twin. I felt it was best not to mention it to him, however, because I didn't want him to think I was comparing the two women to each other. He told me he wasn't staying at his house very much anymore, preferring to live with his new woman at her place.

"There's no way I can move my girlfriend in here," he said. "It wouldn't be right." I knew what he meant. This would always be Jane's home, even though she was no longer with us. And besides, she had left it to her daughter Jenny when she died, with the understanding that George could always live there if he wanted.

When we finally went to bed, Fred started in with his little innuendos and snide remarks. It hadn't taken me long to discover that he was feeling jealous, knowing I had been with John.

"Fred," I said, "Cory met his father for the first time, and his grandparents. Can't you show some excitement for him? Why do you turn everything around into pity for yourself? Just go to sleep!"

As I lay there trying to sleep, my heart broke knowing that Jane was buried just outside in the cemetery, the place where we had walked and talked for so many hours. Now here I was sleeping in her bed because Cory had cancer and his wish was to be here and meet his father. I knew she would be glad that we were here, but not under these circumstances. Then my thoughts shifted to John, and the evening we had just spent together. It had all gone so well, and despite Fred's inevitable bad behaviour, I was having a hard time coming down from all the excitement.

The next day I rented car. Not wanting to spend a lot of money, I got a Rent-A-Wreck, and what a wreck it was. But as long as it got us around from A to Z, I didn't really care what it looked like. Arriving at John's, we were met by him at the door, dressed in nice jeans, a black T-shirt, and jean jacket. He looked so appealing; I could hardly take my eyes off him. His mom and dad were both home, so I sat and talked with them while John finished getting ready, then left with Cory to go shopping. Although John would take Cory home later, I decided to stay and talk with his mother a while longer. She spoke broken English with a heavy Portuguese accent, but

I did my best to try and understand her. That's when she told me she had seen Cory as a small boy.

"When did you see him?" I asked her, startled.

"At Dufferin Mall," she replied.

"How did you know who I was?"

"Luke tell me that's John's boy," she answered. "I tell Luke, I go talk to girl. Luke say no, you no talk to the girl. Leave girl alone. You sitting at table eating, and me sit down beside you. I say you have nice-a boy. I touch Cory's hair, same like John's. Cory jumping up and down, you say eat Cory. When I touch Cory again, you look at me and take Cory in you arms. I no say I John's mother. You think maybe this crazy lady, why she toucha my boy. Then I say bye, you have nice-a boy, thank you and leave. Me like to tell you I John's mother, but Luke say no, Mom, you say nothing. But Luke, I say, this my grandson. He look like John. After I go home, I cry. I love John's boy."

Her broken English must have been contagious, because by now I was speaking to her the same way.

"You know what?" I told her, "yesterday when Cory and me leave, Cory say to me, Mom, I see my grandmother's face before. I say to Cory, me too. This lady's face I see before."

"Ah, Gail, this long time ago. Maybe Cory have only three years old."

"I know," I continued. "Maybe that's why Cory remember you face, and me too. I wish you tell me you like to see Cory. I think you don't know John have Cory."

"Ah, yes," she said. "John no tell, but Charlie tell me. He say, Mom, you know John have one baby boy? Baby one year old. What's the matter, I say to Charlie. Why you no tell me before? Mom, he say, John no like me tell you. Ah! I kill John. Why he no marry this girl? Charlie say, John no want baby right away. Too bad for John, I think, why he no think before. Gail, you nice-a girl. I like John marry you. Lotsa years now, but I see you love John."

I just looked at her and smiled, wondering, was I that transparent, or was it just a woman's intuition.

When it was finally time for me to go, she invited us back to eat at their house the next day, then she hugged and kissed me as I left. Driving back to George's, I thought what a nice lady she was. I'd have given anything to have a mother like that. I wondered if John knew how fortunate he was. Then my mind went back to John and Cory, father and son going out together. I couldn't have asked for a better wish for him. I thought of how great John still looked after seventeen years. It made me realize how I had let myself go, and gained all that weight. But I was still going to Weight Watchers, and was down seventy-five pounds, so I had something to be proud of. I had also started going to the gym and feeling good about myself, even though Fred was calling me a slut, and every other name imaginable. When I would go to the gym, he'd ask if I was going for an orgy. He was so insecure even before his fall, it made him a very angry person, and it consumed most of his energy being like that. I felt sorry for him because he was imprisoned by his own self. He couldn't step away from himself and appreciate what I was trying to do. I was only thirty-six years old, but I felt like ninety with all that extra weight.

Later that evening, John, Cory and John's brother Luke arrived. Coming inside, they met Fred and stayed for a drink. Suddenly, John turned to Fred.

"Thank you for taking care of my son all those years," he said. "You did a good job. He's a great kid."

"He's not your son," Fred retorted. "He's mine."

John looked at him. "Yeah, I guess you're right. You raised him, but he's my blood."

I felt like strangling Fred. Cory and I were so embarrassed.

As soon as Luke left, John took Cory off to meet his other brother Norman. Fred started right in on me.

"You didn't' fucking tell me he looked like that!" he exclaimed.

"Looked like what, Fred?"

"A fucking movie star," he yelled.

"Well, was I supposed to tell you what he looked like? I didn't know he looked like a movie star. He looked like John to me, and I can't help the way he looks."

"I thought he was a fucking old man," Fred continued.

"Why would you think that? John and I are the same age. Besides, you've seen the pictures I have of him with Cory."

"A picture is different than the real person," Fred insisted, like this was somehow my fault for misleading him.

"Stop being so stupid and childish," I said, wheeling him into the bedroom. Getting him into bed was always my way of finally shutting him up so I could have some peace and quiet.

Later that evening, Marilyn showed up for a visit. We talked about the trip, and she said her son Brandon was really excited about going to Jamaica, and so was she. By the time she left, it was about one in the morning and John and Cory still weren't back. Then all of a sudden I heard the most hideous noise coming down the street. It was John and Cory returning with the Rent-A-Wreck car. Parking it in the school yard just across the street, they came in laughing like two fools. They said the motor had stuck in first gear all the way home and was smoking and making enough noise to wake the dead. Apparently, they'd turned the music on full blast just to drown out the noise.

"You sounded like the Beverly Hillbillies coming down the road," I informed them as we all laughed hysterically. Then they filled me in on their day. Every now and then as we talked, John would look into my eyes and I'd feel myself melting like ice cubes in the middle of the desert.

"Gail," John said suddenly, "we made a nice-looking kid. Would you like to try for another one?" Cory started to laugh, and I was floored by what John had said, even though I knew he was just joking. I don't think John knew how much I still loved him. Then he was gone, with promises to see us tomorrow.

The next day we scrapped the wreck, which had blown its engine, and rented a van instead for the rest of the week. Cory and I drove to John's where plans were made to meet friends at the local bar down the street. John's mom served a nice meal of fish and potatoes that was delicious. Again, while we ate, John kept gazing at me across the table.

"I don't remember you having such beautiful green eyes," he suddenly remarked.

"Well, it was a long time ago," I replied. I didn't mention that I'd never forgotten his gorgeous brown eyes, or anything else about his looks. I could see that John's parents and Cory were hanging on every word we said to each other.

After we finished eating, I dropped John and Cory off at the bar and went to Marilyn's house for a while. Later, when I finally returned to George's, Fred had company over and was drunk, so we put him to bed. It wasn't too soon, either, for he started right in calling me a tramp and every dirty word he could think of. A short time later, John and Cory showed up and we sat talking about his life and his kids. After a bit, John wanted a cigarette, so he asked me to go outside with him while he smoked. Outside, the sky was black, with stars twinkling and a full moon. I was standing against the building, with John standing over me, when suddenly he had his arms around me and was trying to kiss me.

"What are you doing?" I exclaimed. "I'm a married woman."

"A married woman to that guy," he said. "What the hell are you doing with him, anyway? I can see you don't love him. You're just his nurse."

"I know," I admitted, "but I'm still married."

"Come on, Babe," John said, "you want to kiss me as much as I want to kiss you." As he pressed his body against mine, I couldn't resist his kiss, as our mouths met for the first time after all these years. I felt alive again, and whole. I'd forgotten what it felt like to be held by someone you passionately love. Then out of nowhere, a cloud came over us and warm mist started to fall ever so gently. I wouldn't have cared if it was a torrential downpour. Nothing was going to pry me from his embrace. Finally coming back to reality, John looked at me seriously.

"Gail, even after all this time you still love me, don't you?" When I didn't say anything, he continued. "I never stopped thinking of you either. I thought of you and Cory often."

"John," I said, "I think we'd better go back in with Cory. He's sitting there all by himself."

Pulling me into his arms one more time, he kissed me, then winked. Looking up in the sky, we saw there wasn't a cloud in sight. It had disappeared as if it had never been. But the cloud had been real, and so was the kiss. I felt like I was on top of the world. No one and nothing was going to change it, not Fred, or any guilt. Guilt was the last emotion I should be feeling after all the terrible things Fred had said to me over the years.

Back inside, John admitted he had seen Cory and me one time years ago. We were walking down Bloor Street, he said, and he was driving in the car with his wife, her aunt, and his daughter when they stopped at a light. He said his heart was in his feet when he saw how Cory looked just like him at that age. But he couldn't do anything because his wife was so jealous. On more than one occasion she had accused him of visiting Cory, and giving us money.

After John went home, I found Fred still awake and smoking in bed. Then the foul mouth started up again, calling me a whore and making all sorts of wild accusations. In the end, I took some blankets and slept on the floor. Lying there, I replayed that kiss and his words over and over in my mind. I was so happy; it was like I was fifteen again.

The next day we were going to visit Charlie's house and have dinner. I couldn't wait for the time to go by. When we arrived at John's house to pick him up, he was standing on the front verandah waiting for us, dressed in a nice black suit.

At Charlie's, we met his wife and kids for the first time. As we sat eating, Charlie kept looking at John and me, shaking his head in disbelief.

"I can't believe you're sitting here with John and Cory in my home," he remarked. "This is great. I love it. It should have happened a long time ago."

Charlie wasn't the only who couldn't believe it. I was in total rapture. We had a wonderful evening, eating a delicious meal and getting to know Charlie's Italian wife and three kids. In the end, we stayed quite late, and then finally headed back to George's where we found him still drinking with Fred. John came in for a while, waiting while I put Fred to bed. Then it was time for me to drive John home alone, as both George and Cory had gone to bed.

On the way back, John asked me to stop in the school yard by his house so we could sit and talk. We talked, listened to soft music, and then made love to each other. Married or not, I couldn't resist him. I had never dreamed I would ever lay eyes on John again, let alone make love to him. I hadn't had sex in ten years, but with John it wasn't just sex, it was love. A fierce and passionate love. We talked a while more, and then I finally drove back to George's alone. Thank God the streets were empty at three in the morning, because I was in no state to drive. I was so high, not from booze or any kind of drugs, but from the euphoria of love. No man had ever made me feel like John did.

The week was now almost over, with only one more night before we were off to Jamaica. It had all gone by too fast for Cory and me. On our last evening we went to John's brother Joe's house. Cory still couldn't get over how many cousins he had, all around his age. Joe had a son, two daughters, and his wife Fredericka, who spoke mostly Portuguese. John told us they had been childhood sweethearts since they were fourteen back in Portugal, and were still very much in love with each other. I could sense the love in that home as soon as I walked inside. After visiting for a while, the night was still young, so we went to Marilyn's apartment where we found her and Brandon all packed and ready for the trip. Finally leaving at around five in the morning, Cory drove the car back to John's house while John and I kissed all the way there. Then, with promises to call from Jamaica, we left.

It was quite a rush from there to the airport, as our plane was due to leave at eight in the morning. While Fred cursed and swore a blue streak, we grabbed our suitcases from George's, drove over to pick up Marilyn and Brandon, and rushed to the airport. Neither Marilyn nor Brandon had ever been anywhere except PEI, so the whole trip was incredibly exciting for them. Brandon was a nice companion for Cory, two years older, and tall, thin, blond and nice looking. By the time we got on the plane, we were all relieved and ready for some sleep.

After a four-hour flight, we arrived in Jamaica. As we were walking to the shuttle to board for the resort, people kept stopping us and asking if we wanted ganja. Well, I didn't have a clue what they were talking about until Marilyn filled me in that it was grass. "No thanks," I said, "I don't want that stuff." That was the last thing I needed. I had tried it before when I was a young teenager, but like smoking cigarettes, it wasn't for me. I just didn't like smoking anything. By now, I was realizing that it was different here in Jamaica. Everywhere I looked there seemed to be people drinking on the street, even on the bus. It was kind of crazy. All I could think was, where in the hell have we come to? It was nice and hot, but the bus was very stuffy and bouncy, and Cory got sick from all the motion. After that, everyone looked at us like we had just murdered someone. I wasn't overly impressed with the drive to the resort. It was bumpy, and the scenery wasn't breathtaking like other places I'd been. It was actually very poor, and quite depressing to see people living like that.

Getting to the resort was a relief, and seemed like a world apart from the rest of Jamaica. It was a five-star hotel, very beautiful, with nice rooms, and a view from the balcony that was like paradise. Changing quickly, we went down into the resort grounds. There were exotic birds, palm trees lining the walkways, waterfalls, pools, and flowers everywhere. It was the nicest resort I had been to so far. Later that evening we went to the resort disco, where it didn't take Cory and Brandon long to meet some pretty girls and have a great time dancing. Marilyn and I danced as well and had lots fun too. After that, each day we went on a tour, while every night we went to the disco and danced. One time we went to Dunn's River Falls, where a guide took us climbing up the rocks to the top while we all held hands. Cory, always the daredevil, was willing to try everything, starting with jet skis. Although he had never been on one before, you would never have known it, he looked so professional. The next day he tried parasailing while I taped it with my video camera. As I stood taping, I couldn't help the tears trickling down my cheeks, seeing how happy he was experiencing all these new adventures. How happy we all were, yet I had to ask myself why we had to go through such pain and sorrow to be able to be so happy. It didn't seem fair, but I had learned a long time ago that life isn't always fair, and you have to make of it what you can. I thought about how Cory had at least gone into remission, or we wouldn't have been there in the first place, so there was plenty to be happy about.

After the parasailing, we decided to go on a tour to the mountains, for that had been part of Cory's wish, to see the mountains. We ended up in a magnificent rain forest where we saw the most amazing tree that was four hundred years old. Cory and Brandon swung from it like Tarzan, hooting and hollering. Then we went into a waterfall where we were surrounded by the most unbelievable flowers of all shades and sizes and shapes. What a day we had, finishing off at a little restaurant at the top of the mountain that served jerk chicken, a local specialty that we had never eaten before, very hot and spicy.

That evening as Marilyn and I walked along the beach, we watched the sun setting in a glorious blaze of colour. As the sun sat cradled on the waves, slowly fading out of sight, the sound of Caribbean music softly echoed in the background. That's when thoughts of John came rushing back, as I found myself wishing he was here walking beside me. Thinking of the love he had showed Cory, I knew I was happy for the first time in years.

Our time was running out and the trip was quickly coming to an end. We swam, danced, talked, laughed, ate amazing food, experienced a different culture and lifestyle, and knew we would return home wiser from our adventure. Our last night, desperately wanting to hear John's voice, I phoned him to tell what time we would be arriving in Toronto. He told me to phone as soon as we arrived at George's so he could come over. Afterwards, I couldn't sleep from all the joy and bliss of having talked to him.

The trip home was long and tiring, with numerous delays as we waited for overdue flights and endured three hours of waiting in Toronto while the authorities searched everyone's baggage for drugs. Finally arriving at George's, we discovered Fred in his usual foul mood, half tanked and in company with his stepdaughter and her husband. I had always liked Fred's stepdaughter and her husband, but by the time John arrived and everyone had visited for a while, I was ready to put Fred to bed and no longer have to listen to him. As I wheeled him into the bedroom, he started up like an announcer at a racetrack. "How many black guys did you sleep with while you were in Jamaica, you and your tramp sister?"

"Sorry, Fred," I replied. "If I'd known you were interested, I would have kept count."

With that, I bundled him into bed and hurried back into the living room where I found Cory and John laughing over some of our Jamaican stories. After a while, Cory went to bed and John and I were right back where we'd left off that night in the van. It was six in the morning before he took a cab home and I fell asleep on the couch.

At around nine o'clock, I went in to see if Fred was awake and ready to get up.

"Where were you last night?" he exclaimed. "You didn't come to bed."

"I slept on the couch," I told him truthfully.

As I put him in the wheelchair, he grabbed me by the hair and hit me in the side of the head, yelling abuse the whole time. Pushing him out of the room, I slammed the door shut, jumped into bed and went back to sleep for a few hours.

Later that night, Fred and George wanted to drive to George's favourite hangout, the Spadina Hotel. As John was visiting at the time, George asked us to join them for a drink, but I told them we had to go pick Cory up and go out. Only part of that was true since Cory was planning to spend the evening at my sister's visiting with Brandon. It seemed almost too good to be true, as that left John and me free to do whatever we wanted. Driving to the Drake Hotel on Queen Street, we sat drinking together, reminiscing about our youth and feeling a bit strange once more being together in the same bar we had gone to when we were young and in love.

Later, when we picked Cory up, John asked if he'd like to spend Christmas with him, but Cory said he'd rather be home, especially as it was already the third week in November and he didn't want to leave home that soon again.

"Why don't you come to PEI for Christmas," I suggested as I drove John home after dropping Cory off at George's. "We won't tell Cory and surprise him."

"What about Fred?" John asked.

"What about him," I said. "It's my house too."

"I wouldn't feel comfortable," he admitted. "I mean, I don't think he likes me very much."

"You know what, John? Fred doesn't even like himself. And if it was up to him, Cory would never have gone on this trip." After all I'd gone through, I really didn't feel like I owed Fred anything.

"Did he get like this after his accident?" John asked.

"No," I said, "he was always like this."

"So why did you marry him?"

"Out of pity, I guess."

John sat for a minute without saying anything. "I'll think about it," he finally decided, "but you'd better ask Fred first."

"Okay," I agreed. "I'll ask him and we'll talk tomorrow."

The next morning, I ran the prospect past Fred of John coming to PEI for a visit.

"What's wrong?" were the first words out of his mouth. "Two weeks wasn't enough time for the two of you bastards? Now he needs more?"

"It's for Cory," I said, "not me. Why would he be interested in me, the way I look all overweight like I am." I must have convinced him with that, feeling the way he did about me and always carrying on about my weight.

"Do what the hell you want," he finally said. "I know you will anyway, you bitch."

I didn't care what he called me any more. It was wasted effort on his part, now that I had John back in my life making me feel like a desirable, worthwhile person again.

Later that evening, I told John that Fred had agreed to the visit, although I admitted he hadn't been overly joyous at the prospect.

"I really want to spend time with Cory, meet his friends and see his surroundings," John said. "It would be nice, but I still don't know about Fred."

I assured him that it was what Cory and I wanted, and that was more important than Fred's feelings about it. After all, it wasn't as though we had ever been in love, and he'd been verbally abusing me for years.

The next day, John bought a ticket to PEI for December 26. The plan was for him to come for two weeks as a surprise for Cory. At the time, he had no idea how drastically his life was about to change by coming back into our lives, and neither did I.

That same evening my sister Jody and her family came for a visit at George's. I had no idea what Fred had told her husband Gary, but I immediately sensed a strain in the atmosphere. Fred and Gary had always been good friends, and no one could spin a yarn to suit his own good better than Fred, always making everyone else look bad so they would have pity on him. Not only did everyone fall into his trap and believe them, but Fred even believed his own lies once he had told them enough. I could see something was bugging Jody, and knew that if there were sides to be taken, she was going to take Fred's side, even if she was my sister. Like many people, she liked Fred, never realizing that his funny, charming side was phony, because she didn't have to live with him and see the real man that lay behind it. She never witnessed the emotional abuse I suffered daily with him. I knew, though, that whatever happened, it was because she had found John and brought him back into our lives again. When she did that, she never thought about what would be the consequences of her action.

Suddenly our last week was up and it was time for us to go back to the Island. Dropping off the rental van and taking a cab for the last time to John's, I felt my heart aching because I didn't want to leave. Every time I went to Toronto I didn't want to leave, but this time it was especially hard. I'd had a taste of what life could have been with John, Cory and me living together, and I didn't want it to end. At John's house, we said our goodbyes with tears, hugs and kisses. As we drove away, I felt a real sense of family love and belonging for both Cory and me, something I had never known or felt in my life. It was wonderful to experience, and the perfect finish to our trip.

As we sat together on the plane, talking about our trip and meeting John after all these years, Cory turned to me.

"Mom, I always felt like something was missing inside of me. I didn't

feel complete and now I do. It's like I've found the other half of who I am."
Then Cory smiled at me. "I'm so happy to see that you and my dad really
cared for each other, and I wasn't just conceived without love."

"I'm glad that everything worked out for you," I told him. "As the lamb
comes back to the fold, in life it's never too late, and we're never too old."

CHAPTER TWELVE
The Welcome Home

Arriving in Charlottetown just after midnight, we hired a cab to take us the hour and a half drive home. It was about 2:00 A.M. when we finally arrived, unloaded the taxi, and carried our bags into the house. Immediately, I noticed that something didn't seem right. To begin with, where was the guy who was supposed to be staying at our place? There was no sign of him. Then I walked into Cory's room and found potatoes all over the floor, his dresser drawers open, his stereo in our laundry hamper in the middle of the room, and bottles of liquor piled underneath. It didn't take a detective to see that something had spooked whoever had done this, causing them to leave in a hurry before they could take the stereo and liquor.

"I think we've been broken into," I exclaimed, heading for my bedroom. Here, too, I discovered the dresser drawers open and clothes thrown all over the floor. Looking around, I felt as if I had been raped. All our personal possessions had been rummaged through and touched by someone's dirty hands and mind. Our private space had been opened and exposed to someone we didn't know. It made me sick to think of people rifling through my clothing and personal papers. Calling the police, I reported what had happened and was told someone would be out in the morning. As the cab driver was still there, he assured us that he would be a witness if we needed one.

The next morning, I looked out the window and suddenly saw what had happened to our three cars. All of them had their windshields smashed. Rushing outside to take a closer look, I discovered that Cory's was the most damaged, with the back window broken as well, the tires slashed, and the car all gouged along the sides. I couldn't imagine who could hate us so much that they broke into our house and damaged every car we owned, especially Cory's car that he took such good care of.

Just then Reggie, the nice man who was supposed to house-sit for us, showed up. Quickly explaining the situation, he said he hadn't been able to stay at our house, because in all the excitement of the trip, I'd forgotten to leave the back door unlocked, and he couldn't get in. According to Reggie, the story going around was that Fred's oldest nephew had done the damage. I had a hard time making sense of all this, because I'd paid him to look after Princess our dog and couldn't imagine why he would be so angry with us.

As Cory wasn't awake yet, I dreaded telling him about his car. It was hard to believe that this had happened after such a wonderful vacation. It made me feel sick to my stomach. He came over to visit every day without fail, probably because Fred would pay attention to him. He liked to talk a lot, and Fred always seemed willing to listen.

Fred's sister showed up shortly after Reggie left and admitted that her son had done the damage, but we were to blame. In no uncertain terms, she announced that it was because her son didn't like us bootlegging. That was Fred's sister for you.

Well, I thought after she left, that certainly didn't make sense. If he was so upset with the bootlegging, then why was he here every day after school to visit? I always kept the bootlegging completely separate from our home.

As soon as Cory woke up, I sat him down and broke the news as gently as I could. It didn't make it any better, however. He went wild, running outside to look at the cars, then crying and screaming. I had never seen Cory show such anger.

"Why would he do this, Mom," he cried. "I've never done a thing to that kid but say hi and bye."

"I really can't answer that," I told him. "Don't worry," I added, "we'll get everything fixed and straightened out. I'm going to call our insurance and see what can be done."

A police officer finally showed up that afternoon. Walking inside the house, he just looked around, checked the ashtrays, and remarked that I had a nice set-up. I mentioned to him about the cars, but he insisted it was two different episodes, and wasn't done by the same kid. That's the way things are in rural communities. Everyone always seems to know who's done something, even if they're not saying. Anyway, I could see the police officer was far more interested in my bootlegging set-up than anything else. That was a fine how-do-you-do, I thought as he left. As far as I could see, he hadn't accomplished a thing, other than informing me that the police would have to press charges. I started cleaning everything up and trying to assess what our losses were.

A few days later I phoned the insurance company and told them what the damage had come to. Their first reaction was that I'd arranged to have myself robbed. That did it. I wasn't going to stand for this kind of thing. I already had enough to deal with in my life—a husband in a wheelchair, a child with cancer, and a trip that was my child's last dying wish. Where would I have had the time to even imagine such a ridiculous scenario? The authorities might have thought I was a criminal for bootlegging, and in all respects I was, but that was done strictly out of desperation, not greed. Getting a lawyer, I eventually won the case so the insurance was settled. After months of scrutinizing every inch of our lives, however, the insurance company canceled both our car and house insurance, making me feel more a criminal than an innocent victim. It was only a claim for three thousand dollars, and I should have said, "Forget it," but by now it had more to do with my dignity and the principle of it all. Even though I won my case, I felt totally violated by the insurance company.

The case with the vandalism was another matter, and had to be settled in court. When the judge asked why the boy would damage other people's property, the defending lawyer said it had to do with the bootlegging. That really got the judge angry. He asked what kind of excuse was that. Who was he to take the law into his own hands? He added that it was none of anyone's business what their neighbours might or might not be doing on their own property, and that there were laws to take care of such matters. People couldn't go around trying to be vigilantes.

The boy was charged and told to pay damages, plus he couldn't come on our property without written permission from us. I didn't really want him charged, but it was beyond my control. After that, Fred's family, who had never had much to do with us, now severed all ties. Although I was willing to put the whole thing behind us and forget about it that was kind of hard when they lived close by.

Fortunately I had happier things to dwell on, now that Christmas was close at hand and John was coming to visit. He phoned every night, wanting to know how Cory was doing and telling us he missed us. Feeling like a schoolgirl in love, I would talk with him for hours on the phone late at night when the rates were cheaper and Fred was asleep. A few times, Fred was awake when John phoned and the war was on. I'd say John had called to talk with Cory, not me, and turn a deaf ear to Fred's tirade.

When December 26 finally arrived, I was just beside myself trying not to tell Cory that John was on his way to the Island. While Cory was out with his friends that evening, I drove to the airport to pick John up. I was so excited to see him again. Arriving back home after the long drive, we came in the back door where Fred was drinking with a few customers. I'd warned John about the bootlegging business so he wouldn't be shocked, explaining why I'd had to do it to pay Cory's medical bills. Going into the front part of our house, we sat talking until Cory showed up with a few friends. The look on his face when he glanced through the front door window and saw his dad said it all. Rushing inside, he grabbed John and hugged him so hard I thought he wasn't going to let go. He was so happy he was speechless.

"Merry Christmas, Cory," John finally managed to say.

"How long are you here for?" Cory exclaimed.

"Two weeks."

After all the introductions were made, Cory and his friends went into his bedroom to watch TV. Fred came wheeling in to go to bed, but John and I stayed up most of the night talking and making love. Later, when I finally crawled into bed, Fred spoke out of the darkness.

"Are you happy now you got what you wanted, tramp?"

He spoke to deaf ears. I was far too happy to care what he said from now on. For the very first time in years, I felt safe with John around. I felt like everything was going to be all right.

Most of the time during John's visit he went out with Cory to meet his friends. Some nights I went along too, but mostly I wanted John and Cory to spend time together, as that was the important part of his visit — for them to get to know each other. Plus it kept Fred and his emotions a little more under control.

On New Year's Eve I decided I was going to go out celebrating with my son and his father, no matter what Fred thought. We asked him to come, but he refused, saying he didn't like New Year's Eve. I already knew this was going to be the most fulfilling night of my life with the two people I loved the most. Cory was also to have the best night of his life, for he met a girl that night and they fell totally in love with each other. We had wine and champagne and danced and kissed. After the bar closed, John and I went home and finished celebrating alone together, staying up until eight in the morning.

The following evening, Cory brought his new girl over for dinner. Her name was Brenda, and she was so pretty, with long black hair and big blue eyes. It turned out she was niece of the Deputy Chief of Police in Summerside. That was a match to take note of, the bootlegger's son and the Deputy Chief's niece. She was to be one of the best things to happen in Cory's life, and I was so happy for him. He had always had my love, but now he had the love of his father and a wonderful girlfriend. Brenda had come to the Island for a vacation to see her grandmother, but when she met Cory, she didn't want to go back to Vancouver where she lived. She knew he had cancer, but it didn't make any difference to her. When she phoned her mother to tell her about meeting Cory, her mother warned her not to get serious in case something happened to Cory. Brenda told her mother she was going to be with him no matter what the outcome, or for how long. She was in love, and at twenty-two years old, she knew what she felt. I could understand all this, because this was how I had always felt about John, but like her mother, I was a bit worried. Right now Cory wasn't receiving chemotherapy and was fine, but Brenda didn't know what the demands of cancer were all about. I only hoped if the cancer came back, she wouldn't bolt out the door and hurt both herself and Cory.

One day, close to the end of John's two weeks, Cory told me he wanted me to ask John to stay another week.

"Why do you want him to stay?" I asked him.

"Since he's been here, I feel real safe for some reason," he replied. "I don't really know why."

"I feel the same way," I told him. "But I think you better ask him. It might have more meaning coming from you."

That afternoon Cory asked John to stay and he said, "I guess I could change my ticket for another week." None of us wanted the visit to ever end, except Fred, of course. He blamed the whole thing on me, insisting that John's staying was all my doing.

A few nights later, Fred was in bed and John and I were in the back room together. Despite a storm raging outside, it was nice and cozy, with a wood fire going in the stove. The snow was drifting up and you could hear the wind howling. John held me in his arms and I felt swept away by the sounds of the fire and the wind. I was lost in the moment and time, with a love I thought would never be mine.

Looking outside, John said he had never seen anything like it. It looked like a winter desert drifting across the open landscape. He was captivated by the Island's winter blanket, saying it looked like something from a storybook. He was right, and I felt like the princess who had finally found her prince. Eventually, I knew, the fairy-tale would come to an end and John would have to go home, but for now I was happy and so was Cory. We both had love in our lives from this man. Cory had already asked John to come back for the summer, and John had said, "Sure, I'd love to spend the summer with you both." It was all so overwhelming, I felt guilty for feeling so happy. Why should I have felt that way? Why did I always feel I wasn't deserving of love and happiness in my life? The question should have been, why was I denying myself happiness? It all came back to the past and my feelings of abandonment and rejection and betrayal by everyone I had loved—my father, my mother and all my boyfriends. It was a long trail, but somewhere it had to stop. I had to take control of my life and feel good about myself. It didn't mean I had to stop caring for other people, it just meant I had to include myself in the final happiness, not just everyone around me. A person, I finally realized, should never feel guilty for being happy.

CHAPTER THIRTEEN

Back with a Vengeance

John had gone, and the house was now quiet except for Fred's ramblings and carrying on. It was January 1995, and Cory was starting to think maybe we should give up the bootlegging business and go into a legitimate line of work, opening a little country store. There hadn't been one for five years in this area. I thought it was a good idea as we were getting fed up with all the drinking and late nights. The money was good, but the medical expenses were getting more manageable, so there was no real reason to continue with the bootlegging. To finance it, Cory said he would put his car up for a line of credit, while Brenda said she would help on her days off from work. Soon we had the ball rolling, finding wholesale companies and renovating the bootlegging shop. We were set to open the 15th of February, and as usual, Fred wasn't happy. If I'd listened to Fred, I'd never have done anything in my life.

On Valentine's Day, John sent me a card. What a sweetheart he was, so loving and different from most of the men I had known in my life. That same day, Fred got a friend of ours to take him out. I had no idea where or why he was going, but a few hours later he was back with a huge bouquet of flowers, a bottle of wine, and the biggest card they could possibly make. I guess with John coming back into the picture, Fred was feeling threatened, and maybe even a little guilty for the hateful way he'd treated me over the years. When he gave me the presents, I wanted to laugh, but I couldn't also help feeling sorry for him. Why couldn't he have done this before? Why did it take the threat of another man to make him act decently to me? Not wanting to hurt his feelings, I said thank you, but that night, after he'd had a few drinks, the real Fred reappeared as I knew it would, and the words weren't the ones he'd written on the card.

Our store opened right on schedule and the customers immediately started to come. By the month's end, things were looking very good, making me feel like we had made the right decision. Both Cory and I now had a job we liked, and even Fred reluctantly learned how to run the cash, finding he liked it once we'd forced him to learn. The store was good for him, for it kept him busy and sober for the first month after we opened. That was better than nothing.

By April, Cory wasn't feeling well and had a lump on his neck. Once again I took him to our family doctor who insisted he didn't know what it was. He liked to call Cory his Mystery Man. I couldn't believe it. What is the mystery, I thought. Cory had cancer, so the chances were that this was related. Ignoring the doctor, I took Cory back to the oncologist who sent us to Charlottetown for an x-ray. I was upstairs in the gift shop when Cory came up with a look on his face that wasn't good.

"Mom," he said, "the cancer is back."

I just grabbed him and we both started to cry.

This time the cancer was back with vengeance. The doctor told us they would have to get the cancer under control so Cory could have a bone marrow done. So now we knew it was back to treatments again and all the torture that came with it.

The first thing I did was call Fred to tell him, but he was so drunk, all he asked was who I was having sex with. I just hung up. On our way home, we picked Brenda up from work. She was devastated when Cory told her. Last of all, I called John.

"I'll come back if you want me to," he said right away.

"I think you should," I answered. "Cory is scared, and so am I."

So on the 15th of April, 1995, John's and our lives were changed forever when he arrived back on PEI.

Once again our lives revolved around going to the hospital for chemotherapy, but this time Cory and I had the love and support of two other people, John and Brenda, and somehow it made all the difference in the world. The fear was more bearable this time because we could share it with them.

In May, on Mother's Day, Cory bought me some gifts, and then John and he took me out to dinner. Fred stayed home, drunk as usual, and Brenda had to work. It was the first Mother's Day I had ever spent with John and Cory, and it meant the world to me. After dinner, while Cory went to get Brenda, John and I went to the beach and made love under the stars. After all the love-making, we talked until the sun came up. John told me how he never forgot the last night we had together.

"No woman has ever made me feel the way you did," he said. "For some reason, there is chemistry between us, Gail, that I can't explain, and it's still here after all these years."

"If I mean so much to you, why didn't you ever come back?" I asked.

"I was afraid. I think if you hadn't gotten pregnant, I would have stayed around longer. But then, I turned right around not long after us and got married. Go figure," he added.

"I'm glad to know that I meant something to you besides just sex," I added.

John looked at me. "I just wish it didn't have to take such a tragedy for us to find each other again. Gail, I ran the first time, but I won't run now. I'll be here for as long as you want or need me. I want Cory to know I love and care about you and him."

I knew that John was speaking from the bottom of his heart. There would be no turning back now. We were finally bonded as a family.

This time around, Cory's cancer was fighting mad and wasn't going anywhere. On the days when Cory's white blood cells were low and he had to be hospitalized, Brenda would stay right there with him, never leaving his side. She'd order the TV, phone for a cot to sleep on and take out food. She was such an angel, booking time off from work so she could be with him. God works in mysterious ways, and it seemed as though John and Brenda were in our lives for a reason.

In between the chemotherapy treatments, John, Cory, Brenda and I would go dine out, or go dancing in the evening and have fun. One night, on John's birthday, he and I went to a quaint little restaurant in Charlottetown. It was an old Victorian home redone as a restaurant, but it had kept the same ambiance as the bygone era. We were given a table in a nice private corner with a window that overlooked other old Victorian homes on the street. As we ate, the rain gently fell, tapping on the window like it was Morse code, giving us a message that John wasn't ready to receive. The message was coming in loud and clear, and I was hearing it. I had heard and felt it long ago. Now I was preparing myself for the tragedy that was going to unfold, but how can one really prepare for the most devastating pain a mother can have? John and I had talked about the possibility of Cory dying, but I could see he was still in denial. Not wanting to ruin his birthday, I tried to think positively without leading him on. In the end, we had a lovely time together, dancing together after dinner, and then going to the beach for an intimate night under the stars.

In the end, the evening was as perfect as it could possibly be until I went home and Fred was on the warpath. I can't say I blamed him. When I look back at that time now, I wonder if I was in my right mind. I think it must have been a diversion reality, and probably what kept me sane through the whole ordeal.

By now, Cory was up and down with his chemotherapy, having his good days and his bad. In one of his up times we all decided to take a trip over Canada Day weekend and see the Cabot Trail in Cape Breton, stopping off in Halifax first. After we arrived, we walked along the waterfront, popping into some of quaint pubs along the way. The next day we went shopping, with John and Cory going off to men's stores together, and Brenda and I to the ladies' shops. When we met up with them later, Cory was all excited about a nice sweater he had bought for the fall. As soon as I saw it I thought he probably wouldn't ever get to wear it. It made me feel so sad inside.

That night Cory started to cry, telling John he was afraid to die, and how much he loved having his father coming into his life. It was so emotional to see the two of them that Brenda and I started to cry as well. We were all trying to be so strong for each other; it was good to finally be able to cry together. It was really what we needed, to just let some of the pain out. After that, it seemed as though we all felt much better and were ready to have fun on the rest of the trip.

The next morning we drove to Cape Breton and found a place to stay in Baddeck. While Cory and Brenda went for a swim in the pool, John and I went down to the beach. There was a bonfire going, with people sitting around it listening to a girl from the resort tell stories about the town's history. It was a fun evening, sitting around the fire with everyone cuddling up to someone special in their lives, all of them from different parts of the world. Looking back, I realized that the whole weekend, I felt like I was on another planet. Cory and Brenda were happy, and so were John and I. Later that evening, John and I had a candlelit bubble bath with wine and soft music. It was such an emotional balancing act between the pain of losing Cory and the ecstasy of gaining John. And then there was always the thought of Fred hovering in the background waiting to bring me back to a harsh reality.

When morning came, we started our scenic drive on the Cabot Trail, and what a scenic drive it was. I had never seen such beauty, like Mother Nature at her very best. We kept stopping for pictures and videotaping. Then the funniest thing happened. Cory was driving and John was beside him in the front, with Brenda right behind Cory next to me in the back seat. Brenda's nickname for Cory was puppet, and just then she said, "Puppet, I miss you." We all turned and looked at her like she had lost her mind.

"Brenda, I'm right here," said Cory. "How can you be missing me?"

Then we all started to laugh. Just then, the song "I'm Your Puppet" came on the radio and that really set us all off. We were all laughing and singing as we traveled up and around the winding Cabot Trail, with its lush green mountains, the blue sea, and the whitecaps out on the water. We were all having the time of our lives and I didn't want it to ever end.

"I have an idea," Cory suddenly said. "I can see Mom is really happy, so let's stay another night. I'll phone Fred and tell him."

We were all so excited. When we got to the hotel there weren't any rooms available so we had to take housekeeping units. Brenda took one look at the place and went crazy; she was so excited over the Jacuzzi and the kitchen. She kept running back and forth telling us what the room had in it.

"Why are you so excited over the kitchen?" Cory laughed. "It's not like you're going to cook in it. We're only here one night."

"And Brenda," I said, "our room is just like yours, so you can stop running back and forth because you're getting me dizzy." By now we were all laughing at her, it was so funny.

The next day, on the way home, Cory played the gambling machines on the ferry and won three hundred dollars. Somehow it just seemed to cap off the whole trip perfectly, like nothing could ever go wrong as long as we were all together and having fun.

Arriving home, it was back to reality, with Fred doing his usual abusive tirade at night, and Cory beginning another round of chemotherapy. By now he was starting to swell from the steroids and his looks were changing. The doctor hadn't confirmed that he was going to die, but as a mother, I knew in my heart that it was coming.

In August, there was a family reunion over in New Brunswick, so we decided to go for the weekend. John had never seen where I was born, and neither had Brenda. On the way, we stopped in Moncton as it was getting close to my birthday and it turned out Cory wanted to buy me something. At the time, I had no idea why we were shopping; just thinking they all wanted to see the bigger shops than the ones on the Island. Even when we went to a jewelry store, I didn't realize Cory had bought me anything.

When we arrived at my Uncle Tommy's camp, just over the border into Quebec, Mom's whole family was there, including my Mom who had come on the train from Toronto. Everyone was drinking and playing guitars and having a great time around a bonfire. Then the next day, we went to see my dad's brother Zeb and Aunt Jan. They lived in a small, dilapidated trailer with cats and dogs running wild around the place, and to top it off, dozens of pigeons on the roof. It always seemed strange to me that Zeb and Jan lived that way because her first husband had died and left her money and his pensions. When we arrived we could hear Jan yelling, "You black bastard!" As we couldn't see who or what she was yelling at, John and Cory thought it was the dogs, but I knew differently. I had heard those words often enough as a child when my mom said it to Dad and the uncles. Then suddenly there was Zeb coming out from behind the woodpile. He was laughing his head off, and still as dark as could be, with green eyes and straight black hair. You could clearly see the Indian in him. He told us he always went up behind the woodpile to hide when Jan was drunk and on the rampage.

As we sat outside at the picnic table, Jan appeared with some fresh-picked hazelnuts, and suddenly the floodgates of my childhood memory opened wide. It's strange how food can do that to you. Jan, we discovered, was still one heck of a character, about eighty pounds, with bleached blond hair and the inevitable cigarette dangling from her lip. Half drunk, she was soon telling us about Zeb's hut up the mountain behind their trailer where she claimed he slept with whores. Zeb insisted it wasn't true, that he had the shack up there to hide from her. By now Cory and John were crying with laughter at the two of them. Jan was really nice, insisting on feeding us before we left. She felt such pity for Cory, having lost a daughter to cancer years back.

Then next day Cory wasn't feeling well, so we called the hospital in Charlottetown where they told us his white blood cells were very low. We had to cut the trip short, but I had videotaped most of it and was really glad I had, for it would be the last time I saw Jan before she died a year later.

On our drive home we laughed all the way, reminiscing about the visit. John couldn't believe where he had just been. "Nice roots you have, Babe," he remarked.

"I know. I'm glad we moved to Toronto when I was a child, or I'd still be there in hillbilly heaven. I still loved them," I added, "although in a different way. The alcohol and lack of education have made them what they are."

"I have to say, it's one hell of a scenic place," John said.

"I know. That's why I love it."

"Hey, Mom," Cory remarked, "How does that cigarette stay glued to Jan's lip?"

"I don't know," I confessed. "It's been that way since I can remember."

We didn't know it at the time, but this would be the last of our great laughs together. After this, it was to be all downhill for Cory, as little by little he slipped away from us.

One morning, not long after we got back, Cory woke up and couldn't see from his left eye. The cancer was moving quickly now. John, Brenda, Cory and I all went to the hospital to see what was wrong with his sight. After some tests were done, the doctor hit us with the news. She said she was sorry, but they'd hit a brick wall. Cory wasn't going to make it. The tears started to run down our faces and I could feel myself beginning to shake inside as I stood and watched my child cry from the reality of it. Brenda left the room to go out for air, and when she didn't come back, Cory asked John to go look for her. When he found her she was outside, having a panic attack. He finally calmed her down while I tried to find the right words to say. How was I going to calm anyone down when I was in a state of panic myself? I had known it was coming, but until you actually hear something like this, you try to suppress it as much as possible. I was his mother, and no matter how much I loved or felt for him, it wasn't going to save him. I felt like I was tied to a chair, and all I could do was watch while my only child's life was slowly tortured to death before my eyes. All the praying, love or money wasn't going to change it.

We finally all got under control and headed for home. On the way, a song came on the radio with the lines, "I've got my poor old gray-haired daddy driving my limousine." Cory, who always had a great sense of humour, looked over at John and started laughing, After that, it helped change the mood.

From that time on, Fred wasn't sober for even one day. It got so bad he wasn't even getting out of bed. Thank god the health nurses were coming in daily to take care of him, although I still had to put up with his drunken state. His friends would come visit and bring him moonshine until I finally put a stop to it.

On my birthday, Cory was so excited to give me my gift. It made my heart melt when I saw it. It was a heart-shaped locket with diamonds all over it. I had tears in my eyes as I looked at it. Why was God taking such a wonderful and loving soul away? It didn't seem right.

Leaving Cory and Brenda at home, John and I drove to Charlottetown where he had booked a private dining room at the Delta Prince Edward Hotel. It was so beautiful, with candlelight and soft music playing. The chef even came and prepared some of the food right in front of us. When John told me how beautiful I looked, and gazed into my eyes, he made me feel beautiful inside as well.

Stopping at a pay phone afterwards to phone home, we overheard a gentleman from England talking about working on something called the Human Genome Project that researches the human gene pool and what genes do in the body. When John told him about Cory, the man said they were halfway through with their research. He explained some of their findings concerning the causes of cancer, and the big one was runoff from the chemicals sprayed on the land and into the waterways. It was poisoning our fish, among other things.

After phoning home and hearing that Cory was fine, we went for a nightcap at a bar in Summerside, then to the beach to watch the stars. As we looked out onto the water, the waves lapping the shore made their own special music.

"Its funny how life changes," John suddenly said. "I would never have imagined I would be with you after all this time."

"I know it's strange," I replied. "I wish it had been under happier circumstances."

"Babe, it feels so unreal at times, and so unfair."

"John," I told him, "I believe there is a reason for all things in life. It may seem unfair at times, but it takes a while before the puzzle is solved. That's when we stand back and take that final look, and it's only then that it all becomes so clear, we wonder why we never saw it in the first place." Telling him this seemed to help, just as it helped me to believe it.

Three days later Cory was in the hospital, and as usual, Brenda stayed with him. By now, Fred had been sober for a while, because no one was bringing him any booze. Suddenly, he decided he was going out, and off he went in the car, not even bothering to take his wheelchair. That evening John and I were just sitting down to eat when Fred's sister from next-door came in the store door and said Fred was in the driveway on the ground. Then she closed the door and walked away. I was so shocked that she would just walk away and leave him there on the ground, her own brother. When John and I went out to pick him up, he was completely drunk. I got him some food and he went to bed in a tirade of cursing and swearing at me. It was quite an education for John to see what my life had been like tied to Fred.

It was now September and Brenda's birthday, so Cory asked me to go get her a nice gold bangle as a present from him. She was so happy with her gift, not knowing that I had picked it out. It wouldn't have mattered to her, but this way she could think that Cory had chosen it specially. Fortunately, he was out of the hospital in time to take her out somewhere nice for a birthday dinner.

While Cory was home this time we had a talk about his will. The courage and strength he had was incredible. I couldn't imagine what he must be feeling at nineteen years old making out a will and deciding what he wanted done with his body. Then came the time for me to go and prearrange his funeral. I didn't want to wait until he died, for it would be that much harder for me to do. One afternoon, when I felt like I was strong enough, I went to the funeral home alone without telling anyone. As I walked in, I stopped and took a deep breath, not knowing if I could really do this. I picked out an urn with a picture of mountains on it, for Cory had always loved the mountains. When I left, I couldn't believe I had just bought the container that would hold my child's remains forever. This was one of the final steps to accepting the inevitable. Getting into the car, I cried, then pulled myself together and went home. When I told John later what I had done, he just held me without saying anything. John knew there were no words that could make this any easier to endure.

At the end of September, Fred was drunk for an entire week. As he refused to get out of bed, the bedroom was filthy, with an unbelievable smell of urine, smoke and vomit. The smell had gotten so bad; it was starting to smell in the kitchen as well. Every time I went in to try and clean up, he would throw bottles of liquor at me and call me names. Finally Cory said he couldn't stand it any longer and told me to call an ambulance to get him out of there. We'd already had him taken to detox a month earlier, but he wouldn't stay. By the time the ambulance arrived, Fred was in septic shock once again, and had to be put in intensive care. At least I could now throw everything in the bedroom out and disinfect the place.

A few days later, Cory ended up in the hospital as well, right in the same room until I arranged to have Fred transferred to Charlottetown. Phoning his daughters, I asked if they could take him, as I didn't want to leave Cory's side, but both of them said they were too busy. Even knowing about my situation with Cory, they didn't want to do anything to help their father. So in the end I had to take him myself.

By now Cory needed a wheelchair, as he could no longer walk. The top half of his body was getting so swollen, he was almost unrecognizable. Despite the fact that Fred was alone in the hospital with no visitors, I told him my priorities were with Cory. I felt sorry for Fred because not one member of his family ever went to see him, not even his kids.

Cory's friends were coming to the house to see him daily. One girl asked, "Can't they do anything more for you?"

"No," Cory said. "I guess it's time for me to check out." Everyone was silent. The amount of friends he had was incredible.

When Cory was in the hospital a month prior, he had met a woman who also had cancer and was dying. She had given him *Embraced by the Light* by Betty Edie, a book passed on by other cancer patients who had died. Each one had signed their name after reading it. Brenda and Cory were reading it together, but I had noticed that the bookmark hadn't moved for a while. One day I asked him about it.

"Why aren't you reading the book anymore?"

"Because I'm afraid when I finish it, I'll die," he said. "I feel like I'm postponing my death somehow."

I had a numbing sensation in my stomach and a lump in my throat. "If that's how you feel, honey, then don't read it," I finally managed to say.

The next day I discovered he was reading it again. By now he was really in pain and the morphine was stronger. He wanted to have a shower, so Brenda took him in and showered him. On his way out he lifted himself up from the wheelchair and looked in the mirror. He hadn't seen what he looked like for a week. When he saw himself, he started to cry like a baby.

"Mom, I look like a monster," he sobbed. I didn't know what to say, so I just held him in my arms and cried with him.

I finally knew it was time to call the priest and give Cory his last rites. When the priest came, I told him Cory no longer looked the same, and not to be shocked. As we all gathered around Cory's bed, the priest spoke to him about his cancer and Cory told him he had accepted his fate and was ready to die. Then the priest gave him the last sacrament and we left the room. As I walked out, I could feel someone holding my shoulder from behind and sobbing uncontrollably. Thinking it was John; I turned around and saw it was the priest. He thanked me for letting him know of Cory's appearance beforehand.

"Of all the people I've given the last sacraments to," he said, "all of them were old, never young like this, and no one ever acknowledged that they were dying, or ready to go. He's a brave young man."

Later that evening, Cory came and sat on the couch and I told him how much I loved him and was glad to be his mom. I told him I couldn't have asked for a better son.

"As much as I love you," I said, "it's selfish for me to want you to stay and suffer just because I don't want to let you go. We'll be together again someday."

"Mom, you're the best mother I could have asked for. You gave me love and a good life. All I want is for you to go on with your life and live it as long and happy as you can. Don't sit and grieve for me. Maybe I have to die for you and my father to be together."

"Cory," I said, "as much as I love your father, I would rather not have seen him again if it means losing you."

"I'm worried about what's going to happen to you and Brenda." he told me.

"We'll be fine, Cory. Don't worry about us."

"What if Fred dies? You'll be alone. And I worry about Brenda going back to Vancouver. Her dad might try to sexually abuse her again."

"Brenda is older now," I assured him. "She'll be all right. He won't harm her."

Then he spoke to John, telling him to take care of me, and saying how sorry he was for not having been with him as a child. Finally he turned to Brenda, asking her not to go back to her dad, and telling her he loved her. Those were the last words we would ever hear from him.

The next morning the health nurse came and said he should go to the hospital. Now that the morphine was stronger, he slept most of the time. His friends kept coming to visit, but Cory was heavily sedated. The doctor said his heart was strong and he could linger for weeks like this.

"No," I told him. "Don't do it like this. I want you to give him more morphine and let him go faster. You wouldn't let a dog suffer like that, and you're not going to do it to my son. Let him go." By now we had been in the hospital with Cory for three days and I needed a shower and clean clothes, as well as my breathing machine. When John and I went home for a quick chance, we found Princess grieving and howling. As soon as I saw her I turned to John.

"Cory is going to die tonight."

"How do you know that?" he asked.

"Look at the dog," I replied. "She knows."

Showering quickly, we left in a hurry. I was so scared I wouldn't make it back in time, and didn't want him to die without me.

That night Cory's friends all came until the room was full. At four thirty in the morning, just after his friends left, Cory died with his dad, Brenda and me in the room—the three people who loved him the most. As Cory gasped for his last breath, he sat straight up in bed. His eyes were wide open and he looked toward the corner ceiling as if he saw something spectacular. We all kissed and hugged him and said goodbye. Then he was gone.

Now that Cory's suffering was over, mine was about to begin, a very different kind from what I had been going through for the last two years. My sister Jody and her two daughters flew in for the funeral, as well as my Aunt Lanie, her husband and his mother. Fred's friend Big Jim drove all the way from Toronto. Then the day before the funeral, Fred's sister called and asked if the family could come. I couldn't imagine the nerve. They never so much as paid a visit to Cory in the hospital, or at home, so why would they want to come to the funeral? They obviously didn't want to look bad in front of the neighbours.

The day of the funeral there was standing room only at the funeral home. So many people came they had to open the adjoining rooms. Although it wasn't finished yet, there was a painting which represented a collage of Cory's life. Cory had seen it while he was in the hospital and asked if his dog and car could be added. Right in front were his ashes in the urn I had picked out, with the picture of the mountains on it. Sasha, my niece, read poems written by Brenda and me, followed by the song "Seasons In The Sun" by Terry Jacks. The priest read a sermon, and then the service was over. It was amazing to see how many young people had come, all friends of Cory during his short lifetime.

That evening, Cory's friends came over to watch videos of our trip to Jamaica. As we all laughed together, I knew this was how Cory would have wanted it. Then I took all his friends into Cory's room and showed them his collection of baseball caps. All his life he had worn caps until he had thirty-six all together, including the ones he'd worn after he'd started to lose his hair. They were now spread out all over his bed and I asked each of them to take one in remembrance of him. They all seemed to have different reasons for taking a particular one. Each of them would reflect back to a different time or place that they had been with Cory, a time that stood out in their minds and they remembered which ball cap he had been wearing. It was touching to see how each ball cap had a special meaning to his friends. In the end, after everyone left, I thought about my son. I knew I would always miss him dearly, for I had given him the gift of life, if only for a short while. But he had given me the most precious gift of all, the gift of love.

THE TIME HAS COME

The time has come to let you go
God loaned you to me
For a short time you know
But don't be sad just be glad
For the special times we had
I know it's hard to say goodbye
Without a tear in your eye
You're going where the sun shines bright
And the moon and stars dance all night
So sleep, my child, the loan is now due
And that means God is calling you.

CHAPTER FOURTEEN
Deception 101

The day after the funeral, I decided to sort through and give away Cory's clothes. Coming across his red sweater that I'd given him at Christmas, I picked it up and got chills down my spine, for it still had the scent of his cologne. It took all I had to hold back the tears. Then I thought maybe I should have waited and done this later. Was I rushing myself, I wondered. How much time was supposed to lapse before you did something like this? Is there a right or a wrong time? Who could you ask, I thought. Or is there a book for this? If there is, I didn't know about it. Finally I realized that what was right for one person wasn't necessarily right for another, so what good was a book anyway? Sooner or later I would have to do it, so there didn't seem much point in postponing it.

Fred's daughter Lilly showed up to help, and my sister Jody stayed after the funeral as well. I decided to keep all his trophies, plus his awards from school posted all over his walls. Moving out his bunk bed, I turned the room into a den, with a couch and entertainment center. After fixing it up, I was always drawn to that room; watching TV, listening to music and reading in there. Even the plants seemed to flourish. Not only did I feel more comfortable in the den, but so did our guests. Reluctantly, they would agree to spend the night in there, then say it was the most peaceful sleep they'd ever had, so I knew the feelings I felt in that room weren't just in my mind.

The next day, after Jody and her daughters left, Fred's friend Big Jim asked John behind my back what the hell he thought he was up to. "Why are you staying here?" he insisted.

"I came here for my son," John replied. "He wanted me here. Fred was no help to Gail, and you weren't here, so you have no idea what she has gone through with Fred and Cory. When I see Gail is all right and Fred is back home, I'll leave. I can't just walk out on her. She has no one here, and she's just been through hell and back."

John then came and told me what Jim had said.

"Don't worry about him," I told John. "He's drunk, and it's none of his business."

Jim left the next day without my ever mentioning the conversation to him. I didn't want any bad feelings between us, because it was nice that he had driven all that way for Cory's funeral.

That night I had a dream about Cory. He was standing in a open doorway, wearing his red sweater, with his arms stretched out wide. Behind him a blinding yellow light radiated out from the doorway. There were no words, just his presence. I had an overwhelming feeling that he was asking me to join him. When I awoke I noticed that my breathing machine had come off of my head, and my heart was racing a mile a minute. The dream felt so real, I wondered if it was a dream at all, or had I stopped breathing for a moment and had a vision of the afterlife? Whatever it was, it gave me a feeling of calm inside of my soul.

With Fred still in the hospital, I now found myself going back and forth to visit while John stayed and watched the store for me. The doctor told me it was touch and go whether Fred would pull through this time, as there wasn't much they could do for him. He kept being shifted back and forth between Charlottetown and Summerside, and every time I had to visit him in the Summerside Hospital I had to walk right by the room where Cory had died. I tried to put it out of my mind, but it was always there in my heart.

Two months later Fred was once more back in Charlottetown. December 6 came, and all I could think about was how this would have been Cory's twentieth birthday. Lilly and I went to visit Fred, and there he was in one of the rooms Cory had spent a lot of time in. I felt like I had just lost my breath when we walked in. Fred immediately started to moan and groan about how he was getting shipped to a hospital in Halifax that afternoon.

"Stop complaining," I told him. "At least you're still alive. Consider yourself lucky. You still have hope that you'll get better."

"When is that fucking jerk going home?" Fred shot back at me.

"John's waiting for you to come home so he can leave. He's not a jerk. He's watching the store so I can come and visit you. Would you like me to be there alone, suffering in grief? Then again," I added, "who has time to grieve when I have to run back and forth daily to bring you and the other men in here food and cigarettes and everything else!"

After Lilly and I left, I cried most of the way home. Everything was finally catching up with me, all the running back and forth for someone who didn't care about me, while the one person who really did care was gone. It seemed so unjust for it to be that way. John didn't want to go home, but he knew I wasn't going to leave Fred. I wanted to be with John, but I felt compelled to take care of Fred, whether I loved him or not.

Once home, I went to pick up the mail and, as usual, a bunch of junk flyers came with it. Combing through them, John suddenly looked up at me.

"Look Gail, here is a ballot to win a diamond ring. Why don't you fill it out, you're so lucky at those things."

The ad said the ring was valued at eight hundred dollars, but didn't describe what it actually looked like. Although at the moment I didn't want to do it, I did it to please John. Nothing like that seemed to have much meaning at this particular moment in my life. Here I was, dealing with the loss of Cory, and Fred in the hospital expecting me to cook for everyone, and having to walk past the room where Cory died, and John leaving me soon so there would be no one left but Fred. Even Brenda was leaving for Vancouver to go back and live with her mom. Thinking about winning something material like a diamond ring just didn't fit in.

A week later John and I decided to do some Christmas shopping in Charlottetown. Before we left, John made sure I filled out the ballot for the ring. At the mall we split up to buy each other gifts, then finished up our shopping together. As we were leaving, John asked if I'd dropped off the ballot. Discovering that I'd once again forgotten, he went back to put it in himself. All I could think was good, now he'll stop mentioning the draw to me, and how lucky I am.

On Christmas Eve, it was about three o'clock in the afternoon. John was asleep on the sofa, and I was wrapping presents. The tears started to flow as I remembered how happy Christmas once was for me, and how it would never be the same again. No more Christmas music playing, no stringing popcorn for the tree, no smell of cinnamon rolls in the air. Princess loved it when I baked cinnamon rolls. She would sit by the oven, waiting for her share. And no smiles on Christmas morning from my child's face, the face I had grown to love and adore. Just then, the phone rang. It was the jewelry store in Charlottetown telling me that I'd won the eight hundred dollar diamond ring. I was in shock, having forgotten all about entering the draw. I asked the woman when I could pick up the ring and she said the store was open until five o'clock. By now I was jumping all over the place, I was so excited. Running out to the car, I drove straight to the store. When I told the clerk who I was, she said she was glad it was me who'd won, because she could see that I appreciated jewelry. When she took the ring out of the box and showed it to me, my heart just stopped. I couldn't believe my eyes. The ring was called "The Stairway to Heaven", and I felt sure it was a gift from Cory. He was trying to tell me, "Mom, I'm in Heaven, so please don't worry about me." I showed the clerk the diamond heart locket Cory had bought me for my birthday, and the diamond watch he had given me just before he died. Now he had completed the set.

Leaving the store on a cloud, I went to the mall and ran smack into Brenda. When I showed her the ring, she said, "Gail, it's from Cory. He sent it to you, I just know it."

"That's the first thing that came to my mind as well," I told her.

In the end, I must have shown it to everyone I knew in the mall, telling them that Cory had sent it to me. It made me realize that Cory was now in good hands, the hands of God.

That evening, Brenda came over and the three of us had a toast to Cory as we sat and had a reflective evening, remembering all the fun times we'd had together over the past year. I mentioned that I wasn't a great believer in the afterlife, but winning that ring had just opened my heart and eyes to it all. There seemed to be no other explanation for it. If it had been any other ring, I wouldn't have thought anything of it, but the name said it all. "The Stairway to Heaven." Later in the evening, John went into the store and played the gambling machines, something he never normally does, and won three hundred dollars. Brenda had also won some money at the bar the night before, as had Cory's best friend, so we figured Cory was sending us all a little something that Christmas to let us know he was with us.

Christmas morning, John and I went to open our presents to each other. Opening his first, John laughed, "Are you sure these are men's gloves?"

"Yes," I said, "I bought them in a men's store. Don't you like them? They're real nice leather, and they'll match your coat."

"Open your gift now," John said. Taking one look at it, I began to laugh as well.

"Are you sure these are ladies' gloves?" I asked.

We'd bought each other the exact same pair of gloves, even though neither of us had mentioned what it was we wanted. It made me realize again how close we were, and how much we thought alike and understood each other. It was a bond, I realized, that nothing in life would ever break.

After opening our presents, John and I went to Lilly's for Christmas dinner. It was a fun dinner with her husband and kids, but I couldn't help thinking about Cory, and Fred alone in the hospital in Halifax, too far away for anyone to visit. I should have saved my compassion when it came to Fred. Two days later I was shopping in the mall when I ran into two of my neighbours who specialized in being the community gossips. They asked how Fred was doing, so I told them he was in Halifax and holding his own. Looking at me strangely, they told me he had been in Summerside for days. Denying it, I found out later that they were right. It turned out that Fred's family had weaseled their way back into Fred's life and were busy stirring up as much trouble as possible. They weren't doing it out of genuine love, just to stir up trouble, and they succeeded in poisoning his mind against me. I may not have been an angel, but I was willing to give up any chance of happiness with John, just to honour my commitment of marriage to Fred. I didn't have the heart to leave him in his hour of need.

Going to the hospital to visit and give him his gifts, I noticed that Fred never explained why he had kept it a secret that he was in Summerside. Instead, we talked about an invitation I had from my cousin in Florida to come visit any time I wanted. I'd already talked to my family doctor who said there was nothing I could do for Fred. They didn't think he was going to make it out of the hospital, so I might as well go to Florida.

"Go on the trip for your own sanity," he told me. "You can't keep coming to the hospital and walking by the room where Cory died, day after day. Fred shouldn't expect that of you."

When I spoke to Fred about it, he said I should go for a while.

"It'll be good for you, dear," he said, putting on that fake voice of his. "Pick up something for my grandchildren from Disneyland."

Having found a friend to watch the store, John and I went to the hospital to say goodbye to Fred.

"Thanks for everything," John said. "I'm leaving and won't be coming back. I hope you get better soon so Gail won't be alone when she gets home from Florida."

Then I gave Fred some money and we left.

When John and I got to Toronto, we stayed at his place for two days. It was so nice seeing his mom and dad again, plus it just felt great being away from home after everything I'd gone through. I hadn't realized how much I'd needed it. Then it was time to go to Florida and everything seemed so exciting. Neither John nor I had been there before, so it was all new to us.

To begin with, there was a two-hour delay while the officials tried to track down the source of a foul odor on the plane. It turned out to be some homemade wine, smelling more like vinegar that one of the passengers had in her luggage. When it was discovered, another passenger asked why she hadn't said something sooner, why hold us up for two hours? Looking at the rest of us, she laughed and said she didn't mind, it was just a little delay. John turned to me. "Maybe she might not mind just a little slap in the face," he hissed. I started to giggle. I'd never heard John talk like that before.

The rest of the flight was great. I couldn't believe that John and I were actually going together to Florida. It felt like I was on my honeymoon. At least it did until we landed and no one was allowed to get off the plane. We were detained for over an hour and a half, though God alone knows why, because the rest of us sure didn't.

My cousin Macy met us and whisked us off to her place in West Palm Beach. Macy was very attractive, with blond hair, blue eyes and a nice smile. I hadn't seen her in years, and although our mothers were sisters, believe me, that's where the similarities ended. Unlike my own mother, my Aunt Rosette was educated and sophisticated, as well as financially well off. She'd kept herself in shape, and at sixty, she looked like a forty-year-old.

My grandmother always said she didn't know where Rosette came from. Even as a little girl she'd always seemed so different from the rest. Rosette was quite prim and proper, while my mom would swear like a sailor, and never knew how to behave. I guess Rosette got it all, while Mom got short-changed in the class department. But she was still my mom, and no matter what, I loved her, class or no class.

Macy's home, where we were going to stay, was lovely. When we arrived, my Aunt Rosette was there, baby-sitting for Macy's little three-year-old daughter Molly. With her blond hair and blue eyes, she looked just like her dad, Barry.

The first couple of days John and I went shopping and sightseeing. Then my mom's sister Yvette showed up for two weeks, along with my two cousins Maureen and Darlene from New Brunswick. They were all serious party animals, so the party was on. Each day we would go to a five-star hotel and lie on the beach, getting served nice tropical drinks from the hotel. For lunch we'd go dine at the best places we could find where I enjoyed people-watching. At one restaurant, I saw five ladies seated together who all looked exactly the same, like quintuplets. They all had the same bleached blond hair, done in some kind of bouffant, and faces that were so pulled from plastic surgery, if they got pulled one more time their eyes would be in the back of their heads. I figured they must all have the same plastic surgeon, and he was laughing all the way to the bank. Maybe it was a new look called "The Clones Are Coming". We all got a great chuckle out of it later. By now, home was but a distant memory. Thank God for all the fun I was having, because it was about to come to an abrupt halt, and a new nightmare would take place.

That evening, John and I walked down to a lake in front of Macy's home. The night air was calm and the waters still as we sat on a small boat dock with our glasses of wine. Cuddling in his arms, I felt safe and loved as we reminisced for hours, talking about our past and what we had just been through for the last year together. It felt like we were on our honeymoon, although no vows had ever been spoken. Happy to have found each other again, we were still both devastated by the grief we had suffered, and the loss we had endured. It seemed ironic that it was Cory's birth that had separated us, and his death that had reunited us.

After talking for a while, we decided that John was going to stay in

Toronto, while I went home after our trip. I didn't feel it would be right to just walk out on Fred in his condition. The best we could do at the moment was planning to talk on the phone and stay in touch. John's life and work had been put on hold long enough. He couldn't stay stuck in limbo any longer. He had definitely done his share in being part of our lives when the road got rocky, and that was more than I had ever expected. As much as I loved and wanted to be with him for the rest of my life, however, for now it wasn't going to be so.

Two days before we were scheduled to leave, we decided to go out for a night on the town. Stopping at a bank machine so I could get some cash, I went through the usual ritual, but to my surprise, my joint account had the large amount of zero in it. I was flabbergasted. Trying again, I got the same result—no money. Fred was still in the hospital and didn't even know our account number, so why would he need money, or even be able to access it? There was no point in phoning home, for the girl staying in my house and working the store wouldn't know a thing about my bank account.

Although we went out that evening, I couldn't get my mind off what had happened. Here I was in a foreign country without a cent to my name and a rented car to pay for. Luckily, I was with John and family, but I was still terrified. John had paid for the flights and everything else while we were there, but I wanted to pay for the car.

The next day I phoned home and Jill told me she'd made a big deposit into my account just two days prior. I told her what had happened and she said she still had more that she could deposit so at least I could pay for the rental car. By the time we arrived in Toronto, I had another call from her waiting for me. Fred's two daughters and their husbands, she told me, had gone to my place with a video camera and removed all Fred's personal belongings and the family car. Then she hit me with the big one. Fred, she said, wanted a divorce. I was in shock. Not for a second did I think this was Fred's doing, for he was too sick to be up to something like this. Or was he, I wondered. His family thought he was dying and were looking to kick me out of his insurance. Next, I phoned his lawyer who said Fred wanted a divorce and me out of the house that he claimed was his. I informed her that the house was mine as well. Only the land had belonged to his family, and his brother had legally sold it to both of us for a dollar.

When John heard about this, he only had one thing to say.

"Gail, you can't go home alone to this. They'll eat you alive, and take everything away from you. I'm coming back with you."

"What about your life?" I argued. "You've put it on hold long enough."

"Well, I can't let you go into the lion's den. I'm coming with you, and that's that," he said, hugging and kissing me as I started to cry.

Later that day, my sister Marilyn took me to the bank and again we discovered all my money was gone. Marilyn knew a lot about the law and made me feel more at ease as she explained things to me. Fred couldn't just kick me out, she said, it wasn't that easy.

After a last evening of fun, going to a bar to drink and listen to music, it was time for us to fly back to PEI. Jill's husband Kane picked us up at the airport in Charlottetown and filled us in on all the happenings. Fred had cut off the phone and electricity, so that meant there was no heat in the house. Here it was, the second week in February, and I was stranded with a freezing cold house and no car. I had Cory's car, but it was put up on blocks for the winter, plus the nearest grocery store was thirty-five miles away. Plus I had no money in the bank. Once we arrived back at the house, we would be virtually stranded. By the time they dropped us off and I'd paid Jill for minding the store, I'd also learned that the customers had stopped coming, having heard wild stories about how there wasn't a thing left in the place. If I wanted to make a phone call, I had to go outside and plug the cell phone into the car.

Not surprisingly, my first call was to the phone and electric companies, both of which wanted a deposit because nothing had been in my name prior to this. My only hope for money was a five-thousand-dollar line of credit I had in my name for the store, the one thing Fred hadn't gotten his hands on. Nor did I owe anything on it.

Soon the customers started to trickle back in, either out of curiosity or compassion, I wasn't sure which. No matter the reason, I was grateful to see some money coming in again. Then John took Cory's car off the blocks and I drove to the hospital to see Fred for the first time since I'd gotten back. His sister was there, as the family members were all taking turns guarding him like was King Tut. I don't know what they thought I was, some kind of deranged fool? Maybe they thought I was going to kill him or something. His sister just sat there while Fred started to yell and scream at me. Feeling myself beginning to cry, I asked what the hell he was trying to do, drive me crazy. After telling Fred to calm down, his sister left, probably because she could see I wasn't a wild woman after all. On the contrary, Fred was the one doing all the yelling.

"I want you out of the house!" he screamed at me. "What is that bastard doing back?"

"John wasn't going to come back, but he heard what had happened. He didn't want to see me left alone with nowhere to go," I told him. "At least someone has some compassion for me. Have you forgotten I just lost my son? I can't believe you're doing this to me after you told me to go to Florida."

"You didn't even phone once while you were in Florida to see how I was," Fred insisted. It seemed incredible that someone so abusive could still feel sorry for himself.

"Oh yes I did," I assured him. "You were downstairs having a smoke. I phoned twice and the nurses said you were fine. I had even bought gifts for you and your grandchildren, but I returned them after I found out what you had done. Have you forgotten how I stuck by you all those years? Not your family, Fred, it was me. And this is the gratitude I get for wasting all my young life."

By now, I knew that Fred had told his lawyer he'd left me back in September, before Cory died.

"What were you thinking?" I exclaimed. "You know I visited you in the hospital all those months. Why didn't you tell me you had left me for good? Didn't you have the guts? Or did you just want to watch me suffer as I walked past the room where Cory died every day? Were you wishing I would crack up and end up in a rubber room for the rest of my life?" By now, I could feel myself really letting go.

"I've got news for you," I continued. "I'll pull through this and anything else that comes my way. It will take a better man than you to break my spirit. I'll fight for what is mine, make no mistake, because I'm not walking away empty-handed. All I can say is good luck to you. Your family is here now, but the excitement will wear off and you'll be alone, as sure as the sun sets. The money you took out of the bank wasn't yours, it was Cory's, and was left to me. I want it back. How could you lie to a priest and say I left you with no money? Fred, I had no intention of leaving you, but if that's what you want, good luck."

As I left the hospital for the last time, I was crying in fear of what was going to happen to me. What turn in the road was my life going to take? I had no education, no house, and no job. The only thing I was sure of was that John was with me, but I wondered how long he would put up with me and my heartache. He certainly didn't need this mess. I knew we had a connection, but I didn't know how deep it was, or if it would last. Perhaps it was just pity for me, and I sure didn't want that.

On the way home I stopped in to see my lawyer, who didn't have any answers I wanted to hear. I asked, wasn't I entitled to some compensation for all the years I had nursed him? She said it wouldn't be much, and we would probably have to sell the house. At the moment, bankruptcy was the better option, since we owed more than it was worth. In the end, I left her office feeling even worse than before. I couldn't believe my son was gone, and I was about to have what little was left taken away as well. The one bonus was that I no longer had to run back and forth to the hospital, or deal with Fred's abuse. But I would soon have to run back and forth to the lawyer's office, and somehow find the money to fight for the roof over my head. If there was ever a time to sit and feel sorry for myself, this was it. Then the memories of selling flowers on the street in the dead of winter came rushing back, and I knew I never wanted to feel that way again, or live with the poverty of my adolescence. For the first time, I realized what desperation my mother must have felt when she was left with four children and no education or skills to fall back on. Here I was, feeling rejected and cast away like yesterday's news. Then I remembered Cory's last words to me.

"Mom," he had said, "please live your life as long and as good as you can. Don't let your life die with me. All I want for you is a happy life. Never give up." Now I knew the true meaning of those words.

When I finally got home, John was there waiting for me, the light and strength that I needed.

"Don't worry," he said as we sat and talked together. "I'm here, and I'll help you."

The days slowly passed and it was coming on to spring. Brenda was leaving for Vancouver and it was like another death for me. I loved her like a daughter. By now, I was sleeping a lot in the day, although I didn't realize it. I found it hard sleeping at night, even after a drink or two. The doctor would probably have given me something to help, but I didn't want that.

Although he was aware of what was happening, John let me go on like this for a while. Then one day he was glancing through the newspaper when he saw an ad for a computer course in Charlottetown. It was government funded program which guaranteed you six weeks training and your own computer to take home afterwards. When John first suggested I take it, I thought up all sorts of excuses—the distance, weather, whatever. He didn't buy it, arguing that it would be good because I could computerize my store when I was done. Gaining some knowledge of computers, he insisted, could only benefit me. Eventually he talked me into it, and probably saved me from falling into a deep depression without even knowing it was happening. All I could think was that I was getting some much-needed rest.

In the end, that computer course was a Godsend, taking me out of my slump and getting me focused on something new. Every morning I was up bright and early for the long drive, with plenty of time along the way to face reality and accept what I had to do. I knew now I had to take charge of my life, because if I didn't, who would? John could lead me out the door, but in the end, it had to be me who did the driving.

The whole time I was in school, John was home running the store. In between work, he found an antique desk and was stripping it down to keep busy. So now we both had less time to worry about what was going to happen if I found myself forced to leave the house and out on the street penniless. Looking back at my life, I realized what lengths I had gone to feel needed and loved, right to the point of abuse for myself. Confusing need and love, I realized now they weren't the same thing. Being needed was one thing, and being loved was another. Until now, no one had ever shown me the difference. A person can need you without also loving you. And someone who loves you doesn't need you in the same way, because they love you for whom you are, not what they can take from you. John showed me how to add and stop subtracting in my life. We can only subtract for so long before we end up with nothing.

CHAPTER FIFTEEN
The Strength of a Woman

The six weeks were now over and I was coming home with my computer. Getting me out the door to take the course had been the best thing John could have done for me, as I now felt like I had accomplished something concrete, and was taking control of my life. John even had the desk all stripped and refinished for me, ready to use as my workspace.

Although I hadn't paid much attention to the daily management of the store while I was taking my course, I now discovered that big-hearted John had let half the community set themselves up with a charge account. That was something I'd never permitted from day one. I even had a sign posted in the store stating the fact in a humourous sort of way. I already knew that the previous community store had closed because it went bust from customers charging too much. As John didn't know how to say no to anyone, people had been coming in droves once the word was out that we accepted charge accounts. After explaining to him how risky the situation was, I finally got things back on track by putting a limit to what customers could charge.

That summer of 1996, John's parents were coming for a two-week visit. I was pretty excited at the thought, for I really loved his mom and dad. All the excitement ended, however, when Fred suddenly dropped his latest bombshell, a letter from his lawyer asking me to start paying five hundred dollars a month support and five hundred dollars rent. Since Fred felt the house was now his, and didn't want to pay the mortgage while John was living there with me, he was now demanding rent. In his eyes, the store was making a fortune, so he also felt entitled to support. Apparently, the deal was that if John left the premises, Fred would pay the mortgage. Seeing as how he'd never paid it so far, why would he start now, I thought. The whole issue was just his way of manipulating and keeping control over me. He also asked for things he'd left behind, most of them stupid things with little value. I couldn't believe his lawyer and mine were now playing this little game of possessions at the cost of two hundred dollars a letter. But then, why not? They probably figured they had two fools who knew nothing about the law. Instead, I decided to go and do some research on the laws of divorce at the library.

Realizing we were getting nowhere with this, I was glad when we were able to have a preliminary hearing with Judge Joe Ghiz, the former Premier of PEI. Having been brought up living upstairs over the family grocery store in Charlottetown, he knew firsthand how hard it was to survive on such an income. The judge told Fred that instead of receiving support, he would have to pay some to me for all the years of care I had given him, adding that a store was not a great source of income and a very hard way to make a living. He also informed us to come to a happy decision, because the only two who were going to benefit from this were the lawyers. Our liabilities, he said, outweighed our assets, so I would most likely be given the home, and the mere thought of Fred looking to get support or rent was ridiculous. The look on Fred's face when he heard this was worth the trip alone.

Leaving the court, I felt like a tremendous weight had been lifted from me. After that, I was really able to enjoy the rest of John's parents' visit. He was so happy to see his mom and dad having such a great time. Only Cory's death put a cloud over the visit. It took John's dad a week before he could walk into Cory's room, although his mom went in the first day. She knew what it was like to lose children, having lost six back in Portugal. Alive and well for the first few years, they had eventually died of different ailments as there were no antibiotics available to poor people at that time. Cory's death opened up old wounds for her, and she understood my grief. We didn't say anything, but it was a meeting of our hearts. This was all that remained of the one grandchild she had not been able to watch growing up. It was a huge mistake John and I had made, something we could never change. I could only be glad that they had met Cory before he died.

At the end of September, John and I were invited to the wedding of two of Cory's best friends. We had a great time, and that night would chart us on a course that would change our lives forever. We had no idea at the time, but would find out soon enough.

Fall had always been a season I truly enjoyed, but now it had a cold and empty place in my heart, for October 27 would be the first anniversary of Cory's death. Then afterwards would come his birthday and Christmas, times which continually reminded me of what had been lost. Falling into a bit of a depression, I found myself starting to sleep again during the day. As it turned out, there was another cause for all my tiredness, something that had nothing to do with depression.

On October 27, I went to the drugstore to get a home pregnancy test. Never in my wildest dreams had I thought it possible that I would be pregnant, but I decided to check just in case. While John paced outside the bathroom door waiting for the results, I did the test. Moments later, I knew I was expecting a child.

"Are you pregnant?" John asked when I opened the door.

"Yes!" I exclaimed, throwing myself in his arms and bursting into tears.

I just couldn't believe it. Exactly a year to the day since Cory had died, I'd discovered I was pregnant with another child.

"Gail," John said, "this isn't what we wanted. I just wanted you and me to travel and have fun together."

"I know," I told him. "I'm too old for this. I'm thirty-eight years old."

"I thought you couldn't get pregnant," John added.

"I honestly thought I couldn't after Cory."

All I could think was that I didn't want to bring another child into this world if it was going to get sick like Cory. By now I was so confused, wondering if I should have an abortion or not.

A couple of days later, as my head began to clear; I started to think about it. Who was I, I wondered, to even think of an abortion. There had to be a reason for this child to have been conceived. It was a gift from God and Cory, I was sure. Otherwise, why would I have found out about it on that day of all days?

I decided to go and see the oncologist for advice. Could this child have

the same cancer as Cory, I asked. No, he assured me. Cory's cancer was
environmental, not genetic. Next, I paid a visit to my family doctor to see
if I was too old to carry a baby. He assured me lots of women did it at my
age. The only problem he could see was an increased risk of Down syndrome and Spina Bifida, but there were tests that could be done early in
the pregnancy. Two down and one to go, I thought. Only John remained.
He wasn't enthusiastic about starting a family again after his last marriage.
Here he was, estranged from his two other children, and having missed out
on raising Cory. He certainly didn't want to go down that road again. Plus,
to some extent, I still had my reservations, to the point that I actually made
an appointment for an abortion. Weeks went by and still I worried, mostly
about Down syndrome. John's brother and wife had a child with it, which
only worried me more. Always at the back of mind, however, I wondered
how I could take the life of this child after trying for two years to save
Cory's. What if this was a healthy, beautiful child, sent here for a purpose?
I would never know if I had an abortion. Finally I made a decision.

"I can't do this," I told John. "We have to keep the baby. It's not right
to end its life."

"I know," he agreed. "I've thought about that as well."

"It's a gift," I added. "A gift from Cory and God."

Canceling the abortion, we started to think of the baby as a joyous
event. Encouraged by John, I ate as healthily as possible. Deep down inside,
I felt it was going to be a boy, although in many ways I longed for girl so it
wouldn't have to walk in Cory's shadow. As time went by, I began asking
myself why, after all these years, I was being given a second chance at moth-
erhood. Why was one child taken and another being returned? No matter
how much I wondered and longed for the answer, it would only come later
once the child was born. Suddenly I had a great diversion from the pain and
loss of losing Cory, as being a mother had always been the ultimate joy for
me. It gave me focus in life and new goals to strive for, as well as keeping me
young at heart. John's and my lives and love were coming full circle and we
were being given a second chance to do something right this time.

By now I was getting bigger and the baby was starting to kick. It was
one of the most wonderful feelings I ever remember feeling, just the thought
of a life growing inside of me. It was a feeling of completeness. As the time
for the baby to be born approached, John and I went shopping for things

to put in the baby's room. It was such a different experience this time, with John there to help pick out the crib and everything. This was the way I had longed for it to be the first time around. While we were in the store, John turned to me.

"I can't believe I'm doing this at my age. I never would have believed I'd be experiencing this again, and definitely not with you, Gail."

"We never know the future," I replied, "and thank God we don't. Most of life seems like a journey we do blindfolded, with certain paths and people we meet and walk with along the way. It's all a mystery that only gets solved along the journey when we look back and learn life's lessons. Only when we are able to love and teach and guide each other do we truly understand our purpose in life. You and I have been given a second chance to do it right, something most people never get to accomplish, so I feel we've been blessed."

"I guess you're right," he agreed. "I've been feeling something along those lines also."

By May 22, 1997, I was nearing the end of my pregnancy and due for a doctor's appointment. By now my stomach was so large I couldn't fit behind the steering wheel of our small Ford Ranger, so I had to borrow a friend's 4x4. After hearing from the doctor that I still had another five weeks to go, I wondered how I was ever going to make it, the baby was weighing so heavily on me. Stopping at the mall, I did some grocery shopping, and then went back outside to the parking lot where I found that someone had parked behind me and I couldn't get out. Back inside I went to have the person paged, but no one responded so I called the police. Just as the police arrived, so did the woman whose car it was.

"You can't park three deep," I informed her. "You're very inconsiderate. What if I was in labour?"

"Well, everyone else is parked like that," she remarked.

"If everyone else was jumping off the roof, would you follow?" I asked.

The officer turned to the woman. "Do you always do what other people do, even if it's illegal?"

By now, the woman was starting to look uncomfortable, so I got in my truck, thanked the officer, and left for home. On the way, I noticed I was leaking, which my friend Jonnie, who was a nurse, told me meant my water had broken.

"You better go to the hospital right away," she said when I called her.

"But I don't have any pain."

"That doesn't matter," she insisted.

John closed the store and drove me to the hospital, the same hospital where a year and a half ago I had watched my only child take his last breath. By now I was having contractions, but nothing serious. At three o'clock in the morning, John and I decided he'd better go home, as there were milk deliveries coming to the store, and it didn't look like I was going to have this baby soon. Kissing me goodbye, he said he'd come back the minute the hospital called. As soon as he left, the tears started to flow like a river. Then my mind started wandering back to a time not so long ago, just a year and a half or so. Here I was, ready to bring a new soul into the world, while Cory had died on the floor just above me. I still felt like somehow I had betrayed Cory. As his mother, I should have been able to save his life. Being so young when I had him, I'd just adored Cory. It was almost like we had grown up together, we'd been so close.

By five o'clock the next afternoon, the doctor decided to induce me. Stopping in to check on me, the nurse said not to be surprised if the baby came out blue and not breathing. She told me that was what babies tended to do when they were born early. The hospital then called John to come back. I was so happy to see him. This time he would be with me for the birth. As the baby started to come, I looked over at John as he leaned over to kiss me. Here I was with the man I loved to the very depths of my being, a man I had not seen in eighteen years. And now, twenty-one years later, we had created a new life. All I could think was, when do I wake up? Everything seemed too good to be true, and all because of Cory's wish to meet his father through the Children's Wish Foundation. If only he could have been here to feel the love and happiness his wish had given us, to see how we had come full circle into a complete and loving family.

"Just another push, Babe," John encouraged me. "You can do it." One more push and there was the baby, a perfect little boy. The doctor looked surprised, saying the baby didn't look early, as he was very alert. He was just beautiful, with jet black hair and big almond eyes, just like his dad. Then I had a glimmer from the past as I saw how much he looked like Cory, with even the same little tail of hair down the back of his head. The only difference was how alert and aware he was, looking all around in quite a nosy fashion as if he was thinking, where am I? We decided to name him for Cory's initials, J.C., only we would spell it Jaycee. Looking at the baby, I knew in my heart that this was Cory's gift. As much as I was enjoying this birth, my emotions were in turmoil, as I was also grieving for Cory.

My last night in the hospital, the weather was so bad that John phoned and asked if he could skip the evening visit. We talked for a while, and then I took the baby for a stroll to the TV room where I sat rocking him in the rocking chair by the window. Looking at my little boy, I felt overwhelmed by it all and started to slowly weep, trying to contain myself. I felt I was holding my past and future in my arms. Finally getting myself together, I noticed Jaycee was attentively listening to the wind howling and the rain pounding on the window. He was looking in the direction of the sounds, aware like anyone else would be. Most newborn babies, I thought, would not be that tuned-in so young to what was going on around them.

The next day, just before it was time for me to go home, the doctor came to check the baby. Looking Jaycee over, he asked me to keep a check on the baby's eyes. Why, I asked, but didn't get a reasonable answer. He just told me to ask my family doctor to check on them.

Six weeks flew by, with John and me enjoying our new son, until it was time to visit the doctor for a checkup. Looking Jaycee all over, the doctor shone a light in the baby's eyes, then turned and looked at me.

"This baby is blind," he said.

I felt like I was going to get sick. The look of horror on his face scared me to death. Putting the light back in Jaycee's eyes, he didn't get any reaction.

"I'd say this baby was stone cold blind," he went on. "I can't see in the back of his eyes when I put the light there."

By now my mind was going off in a hundred different directions. I didn't know what to think, for he was the doctor and supposed to know what he was talking about.

"Then why does he look at his mobile?" I asked.

"Does it play music?" inquired the doctor. I said yes. "He's not watching it, he's listening to it. He's blind, or he might just be seeing shadows."

The doctor said he would make an appointment with a pediatrician as soon as possible, and then we would see an optometrist.

As I left the doctor's office, I didn't even feel fit to drive home. Do I phone John and tell him, or do I wait until I get home, I wondered. Maybe waiting was better, as I couldn't imagine telling him this over the telephone. I was so confused. Back at the car, I started to cry as I looked at my beautiful baby. God, I thought, I don't have the strength for this one, it's just one too many. Driving home through the tears and shock of it, I had a sudden thought to end it all. Just drive as fast as I could and ram into a light pole, killing both of us. Then something came over me and I knew I couldn't do this to John. He would never know what or why it had happened. The least I could do was go home and tell him, as it wasn't just up to me to decide what to do. Besides, what if by some slim chance the doctor was wrong? I had never contemplated suicide before, having already seen enough of my mother trying it ever since I could remember. And people do live blind. Finally talking myself out of it, I drove all the way home. It felt like the longest drive of my life. As I walked into the house, John could immediately see I was a mess. Waiting until the one customer in the store had left, I could hardly get the words out.

"What's wrong, Gail?" John said. Spitting the words out, I could see the same shock beginning to register on his face.

"Do you think the doctor is right?" he finally managed to ask. I didn't know what to say. After all, doctors were supposed to know what they were talking about.

For the next week, while we waited for the day of the appointment with the pediatrician, John and I were out of minds, dangling things in front of the baby. It seemed to us like he could see, but then maybe it was just wishful thinking on our part. I began going to the library to find books on how to raise a blind child.

Finally the week of hell was over and we went to see the pediatrician. The doctor checked Jaycee over and said he didn't think the baby was blind, but if we wanted another opinion, he would send us to an eye doctor. At first he said it would be a year before we could get an appointment, but I got so upset he managed to schedule one in two weeks, still assuring us he didn't think the baby was blind and not to worry. If we weren't confused enough already, this sure didn't help. How could one doctor say the baby was stone cold blind while another insisted he wasn't?

The two weeks came and went, but it felt like an eternity. Going to the appointment with a friend, I watched as the eye doctor put a spray of solution in the baby's eyes and waited twenty minutes to check. Taking one look, he said everything was fine, the baby could definitely see. He explained that it's impossible to see behind the back of the eye without spraying a solution first. He didn't know why my doctor would say something like this, but assured me our baby was not blind. Rushing to the phone, I called John to tell him the good news. We were both so happy. I still thank God to this day for my better judgment on that lonely and confused ride home from the doctor's office, or I would have taken a beautiful new life along with my own. And all because I had put my blind faith in a doctor. So if I had lost my faith in doctors before, this sure didn't do a thing to restore it.

Looking back over my life, I realized that as God closes a door, he opens a tiny little crack in the window, and it's up to us to find it, and open it so wide that we are never totally locked inside. No matter what the outcome is to any situation, I now know each of us has the power to transcend it and not be defeated. After that, it's up to us to decide what we will do with that knowledge and experience, and how we will live our lives.

A Mother's Dream

If I had a dream it would be only one
To awake in morn and hold my son.
Someday I will as sure as life is new
I'll go on to heaven and be with you.
Life's road hasn't been very kind
To take what I thought was only mine.
When life's journey comes to an end
I'll reflect back and say,
Could I do it all again?